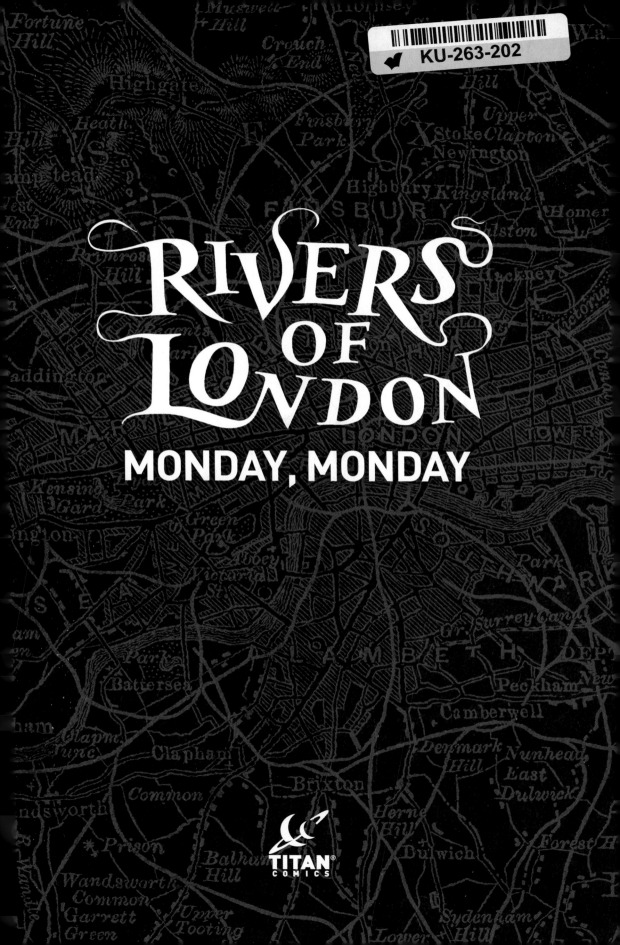

KU-263-202

RIVERS OF LONDON
MONDAY, MONDAY

Titan
COMICS

RIVERS OF LONDON GRAPHIC NOVELS
BODY WORK
NIGHT WITCH
BLACK MOULD
DETECTIVE STORIES
CRY FOX
WATER WEED
ACTION AT A DISTANCE
THE FEY AND THE FURIOUS
BODY WORK WRITERS' EDITION

RIVERS OF LONDON: MONDAY, MONDAY
ISBN: 9781787736269

TITAN COMICS

EDITOR: DAVID LEACH

MANAGING EDITOR Martin Eden
SENIOR CREATIVE EDITOR David Leach
SENIOR EDITOR Jake Devine
EDITOR Phoebe Hedges
PRODUCTION CONTROLLERS Caterina Falqui
and Kelly Fenlon
PRODUCTION MANAGER Jackie Flook
SENIOR DESIGNER Andrew Leung
ART DIRECTOR Oz Browne

SALES AND CIRCULATION MANAGER Steve Tothill
MARKETING COORDINATOR Lauren Noding
PUBLICIST Phoebe Trillo
DIGITAL AND MARKETING MANAGER Jo Teather
HEAD OF RIGHTS Jenny Boyce
ACQUISITIONS EDITOR Duncan Baizley
PUBLISHING DIRECTORS Ricky Claydon
and John Dziewiatkowski
OPERATIONS DIRECTOR Leigh Baulch
PUBLISHERS Vivian Cheung and Nick Landau

Published by Titan Comics, a division of Titan Publishing Group, Ltd.,
144 Southwark Street, London SE1 0UP

Rivers of London is trademark™ and copyright © 2021 Ben Aaronovitch. All rights reserved.

Rivers of London logo designed by Patrick Knowles.
Cover illustration by Veronica Fish.

Titan Comics is a registered trademark of Titan Publishing Group, Ltd. All rights reserved.

No part of this publication may be reproduced, stored in a retrieval system, or transmitted, in any
form or by any means, without the prior written permission of the publisher. Names, characters,
places and incidents featured in this publication are either the product of the author's
imagination or used fictitiously. Any resemblance to actual persons, living or dead
(except for satirical purposes), is entirely coincidental.

A CIP catalogue record for this title is available from the British Library.

First edition: November 2021

10 9 8 7 6 5 4 3 2

Printed in SPAIN.

For rights information contact jenny.boyce@titanemail.com

WWW.TITAN-COMICS.COM

Become a fan on Facebook.com/comicstitan

Follow us on Twitter @ComicsTitan

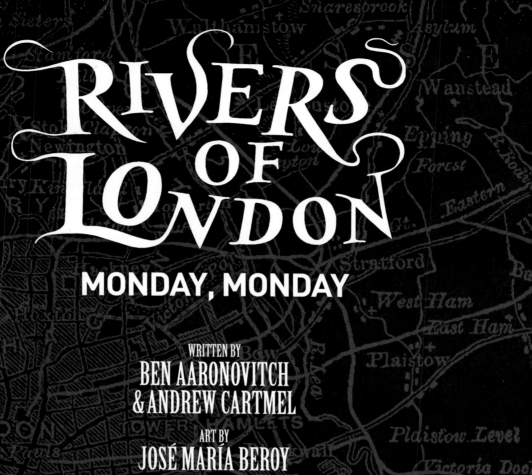

RIVERS OF LONDON

MONDAY, MONDAY

WRITTEN BY
**BEN AARONOVITCH
& ANDREW CARTMEL**

ART BY
JOSÉ MARÍA BEROY

INKS (ISSUE 3 & 4) BY
SANDRA MARÍA PEREA

COLOURS BY
JORDI ESCUIN LLORACH

LETTERING BY
ROB STEEN

Titan
COMICS

RIVERS OF LONDON

READER'S GUIDE

The *Rivers of London* comics and graphic novels are an essential part of the saga. Though they each stand alone, together they add a fascinating depth to the wider world of Peter Grant, Thomas Nightingale, and Miria Stephanopoulos as they investigate crimes of a supernatural nature...

BEN AARONOVITCH CARTMEL • WILLIAMSON • RENNE
RIVERS OF LONDON
ACTION AT A DISTANCE

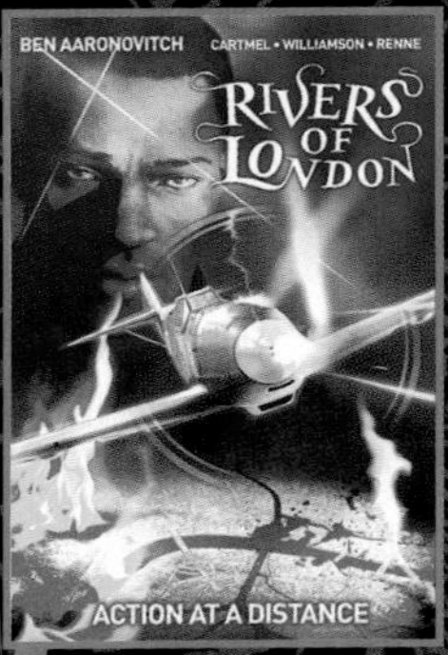

ACTION AT A DISTANCE
Graphic Novel 7

BEN AARONOVITCH
MOON OVER SOHO

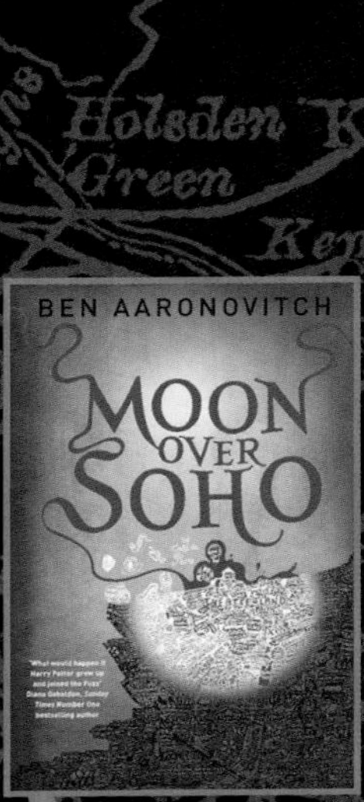

MOON OVER SOHO
Novel 2

BEN AARONOVITCH
The Sunday Times Bestselling Peter Grant series
BROKEN HOMES
Stuff gets serious South of the River...

BROKEN HOMES
Novel 4

"PICK THIS BOOK UP. YOU WON'T REGRET IT!" – NERDLY
RIVERS OF LONDON
NIGHT WITCH
BEN AARONOVITCH CARTMEL • SULLIVAN • GUERRERO

NIGHT WITCH
Graphic Novel 2

BEN AARONOVITCH
The Sunday Times bestselling Peter Grant series
FOXGLOVE SUMMER
Two missing children. One lost copper.

FOXGLOVE SUMMER
Novel 5

A Bestselling Rivers of London Novel
BEN AARONOVITCH
RIVERS OF LONDON

RIVERS OF LONDON
Novel 1

BEN AARONOVITCH
The Sunday Times bestselling series
WHISPERS UNDER GROUND
If you've been on the Underground you know what horrors await...

WHISPERS UNDER GROUND
Novel 3

"A PERFECT BLEND OF CSI AND HARRY POTTER." – io9
RIVERS OF LONDON
BODY WORK

BODY WORK
Graphic Novel 1

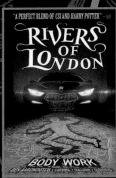

BLACK MOULD

Graphic Novel 3

THE HANGING TREE

Novel 6

CRY FOX

Graphic Novel 5

FEY AND FURIOUS

Graphic Novel Novel 8

THE FURTHEST STATION

Novella 1

DETECTIVE STORIES

Graphic Novel 4

LIES SLEEPING

Novel 7

YOU ARE HERE

WHAT ABIGAIL DID THAT SUMMER

Novella 3

WATERWEED

Graphic Novel 6

THE OCTOBER MAN

Novella 2

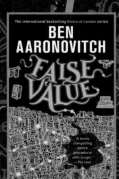

FALSE VALUE

Novel 8

THE STORY SO FAR

Monday, Monday follows on from *The Fey and The Furious* and takes place after the events of *Lies Sleeping*, the seventh novel in the *Rivers of London* series.

Trainee wizard and full-time cop Peter Grant has been assigned to the Metropolitan Police Force Department's Special Assessment Unit known as *The Folly*. There, under the guidance and tutorage of England's last officially registered wizard, Thomas Nightingale, they investigate crimes involving the supernatural.

Peter quickly found himself becoming deeply entangled in the magical world, known as the demi-monde. He was promoted to the rank of Detective Constable thanks to his work investigating Falcon crimes ranging from possessed killer-cars, to drug-dealers dabbling in magically enhanced drugs, to the criminal activities of the Fairy Queen, and most significantly in the apprehension of The Faceless Man.

In what was, at the time, Peter's biggest case, he tracked down and arrested Martin Chorley: The Faceless Man - a powerful practitioner of magic who used his power to hide his face, thus allowing him get away with countless criminal activities, including multiple counts of murder. He had been a thorn in the Folly's side for years, and most recently had tried to destroy London by luring out one of the city's oldest and most deranged gods.

Following a suspension for using unorthodox methods in arresting Chorley, Peter returned to the force undercover to infiltrate an illegal street racing racket organised by criminal mastermind Emmanuel Cross, who was using the race as a front to smuggle unicorn horns. Peter ended up trapped in the magical realm of Fairy Land and forced to take on the Fairy Queen in a race to the death to escape back home...

CHARACTER PROFILES

PETER GRANT

Wizarding cop for the Special Assesment Unit. Returning from suspension. First officially sanctioned practicioner of magic since 1945. First time dad to twins. Curious and quick-thinking with a dry wit and a habit of landing himself in trouble.

THOMAS NIGHTINGALE

Peter's boss and mentor. Age unknown. An extremely powerful wizard, private man, and technophobe. Served in World War II and has been head of the Folly since his return to Britain.

MIRIAM STEPHANOPOULOS

A DI who typically works homicides but has been brought onto Operation Willow to get results. Hard-working, no-nonsense. Just because she knows about magic, doesn't mean she has to like it.

ABIGAIL KAMARA

"Junior apprentice" to the Folly, learning under Nightingale. An eager student, though she prefers adventure and action to book learning. Peter's cousin. Fox-whisperer.

BEVERLY BROOK

Envrionmental Science scholar, River Goddess and new mother to twins. Has a knack for saving her boyfriend Peter from trouble and keeping his feet firmly on the ground.

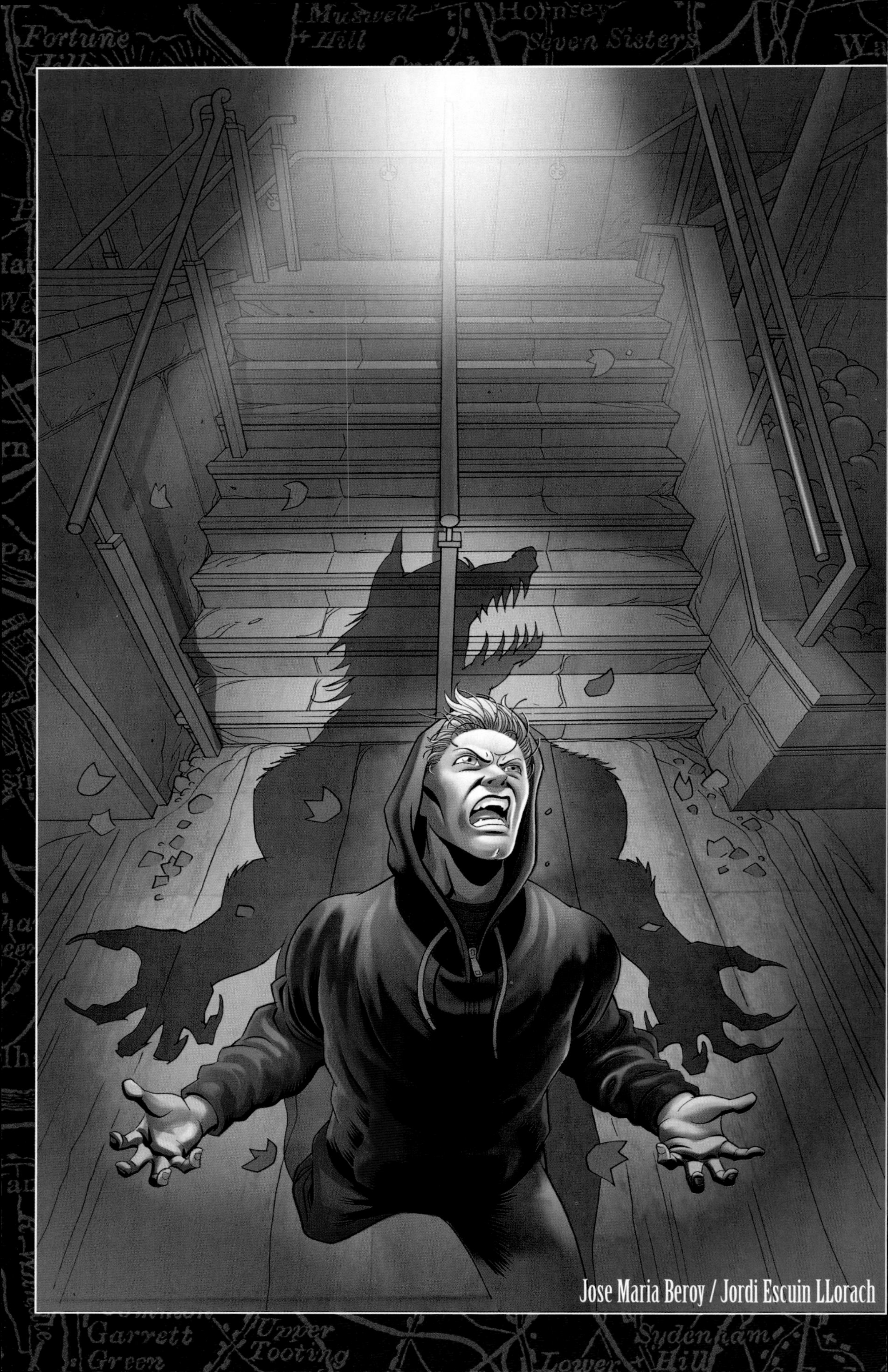
Fortune
Muswell
Hill
Hornsey
Seven Sisters
Garrett
Green
Upper
Tooting
Sydenham
Hill
Lower
Jose Maria Beroy / Jordi Escuin LLorach

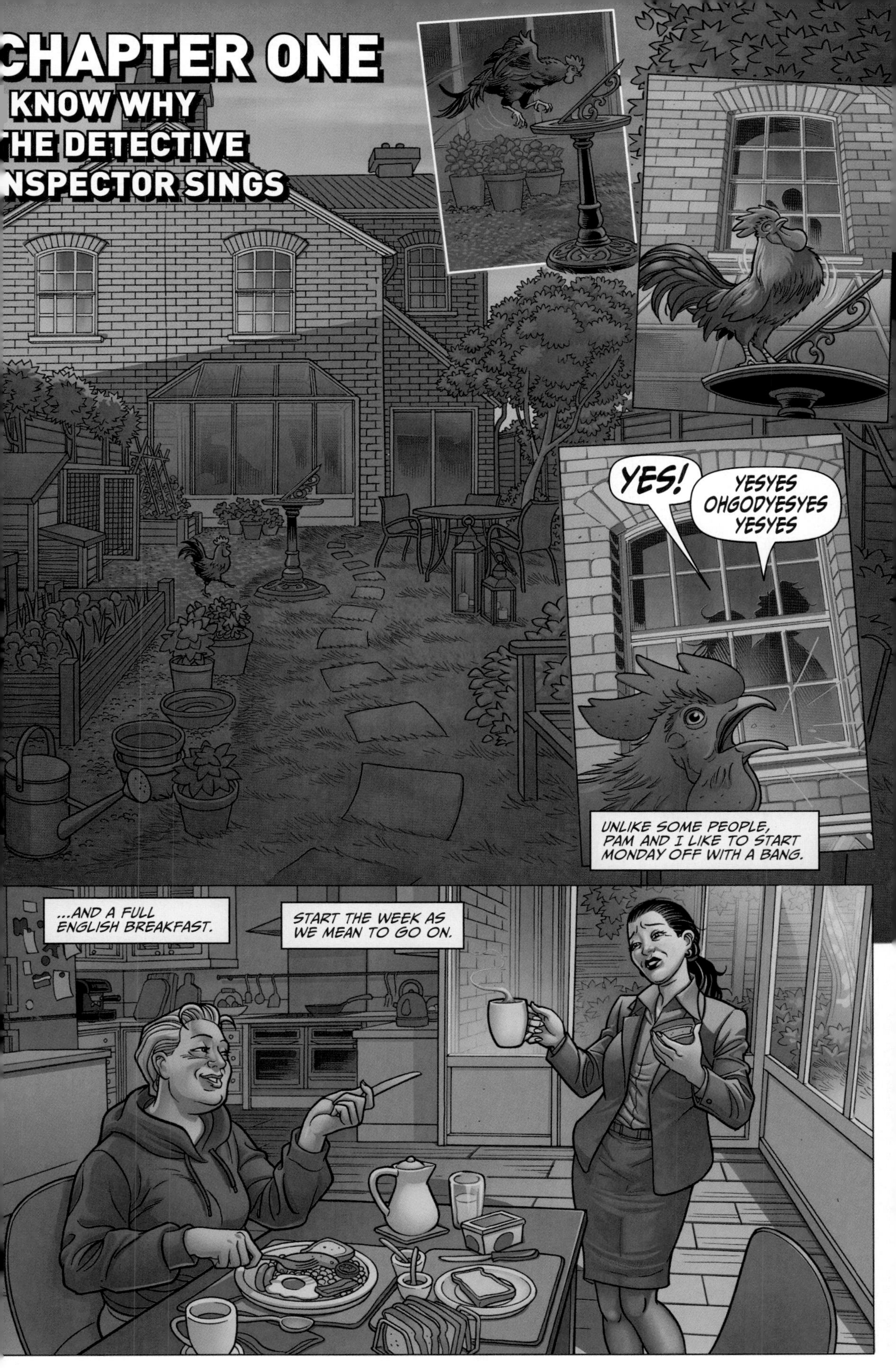

CHAPTER ONE
KNOW WHY
HE DETECTIVE
NSPECTOR SINGS
YES!
YESYES OHGODYESYES YESYES
UNLIKE SOME PEOPLE, PAM AND I LIKE TO START MONDAY OFF WITH A BANG.
...AND A FULL ENGLISH BREAKFAST.
START THE WEEK AS WE MEAN TO GO ON.

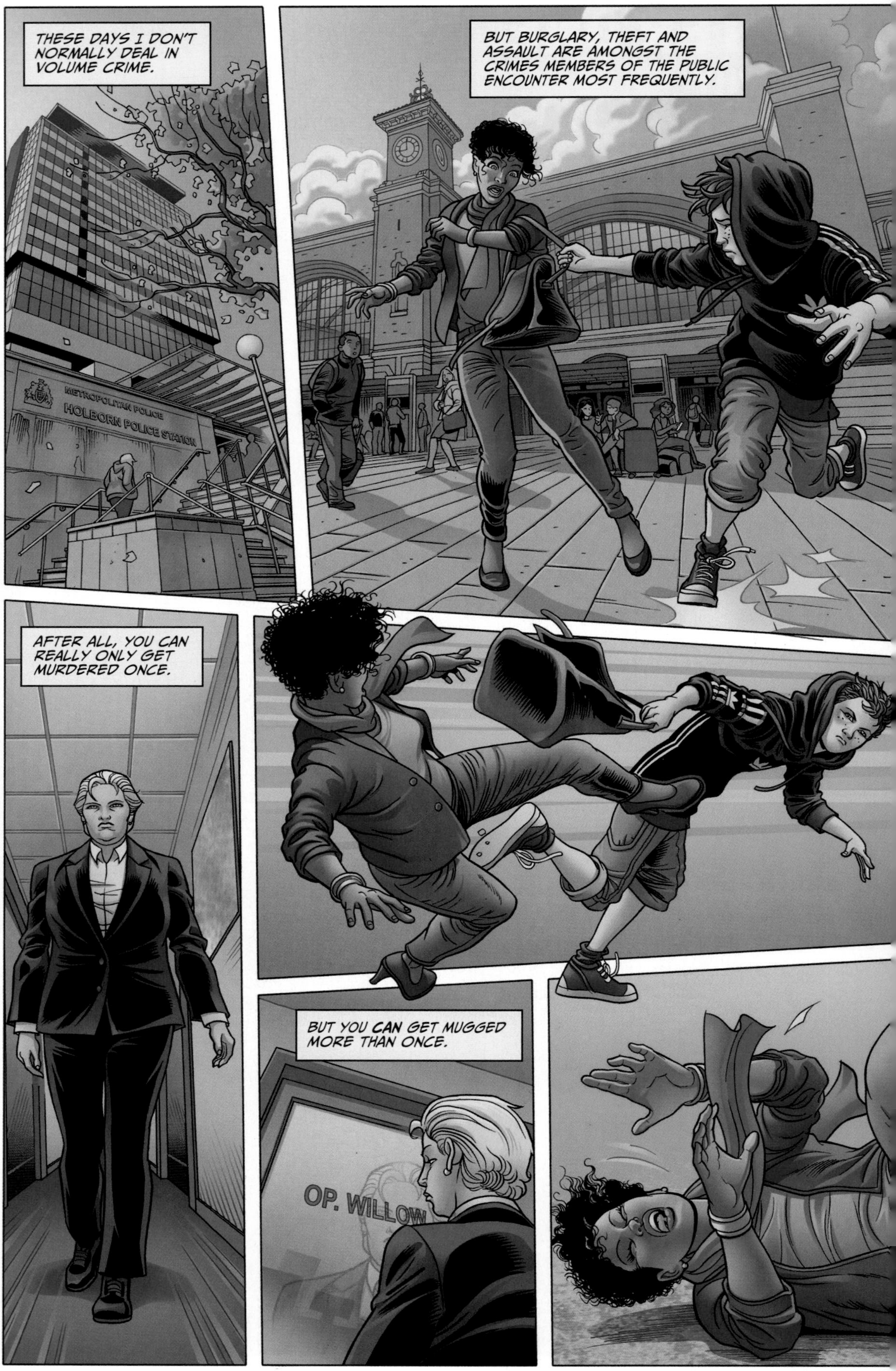

THESE DAYS I DON'T NORMALLY DEAL IN VOLUME CRIME.
METROPOLITAN POLICE
HOLBORN POLICE STATION
BUT BURGLARY, THEFT AND ASSAULT ARE AMONGST THE CRIMES MEMBERS OF THE PUBLIC ENCOUNTER MOST FREQUENTLY.
AFTER ALL, YOU CAN REALLY ONLY GET MURDERED ONCE.
BUT YOU CAN GET MUGGED MORE THAN ONCE.
OP. WILLOW

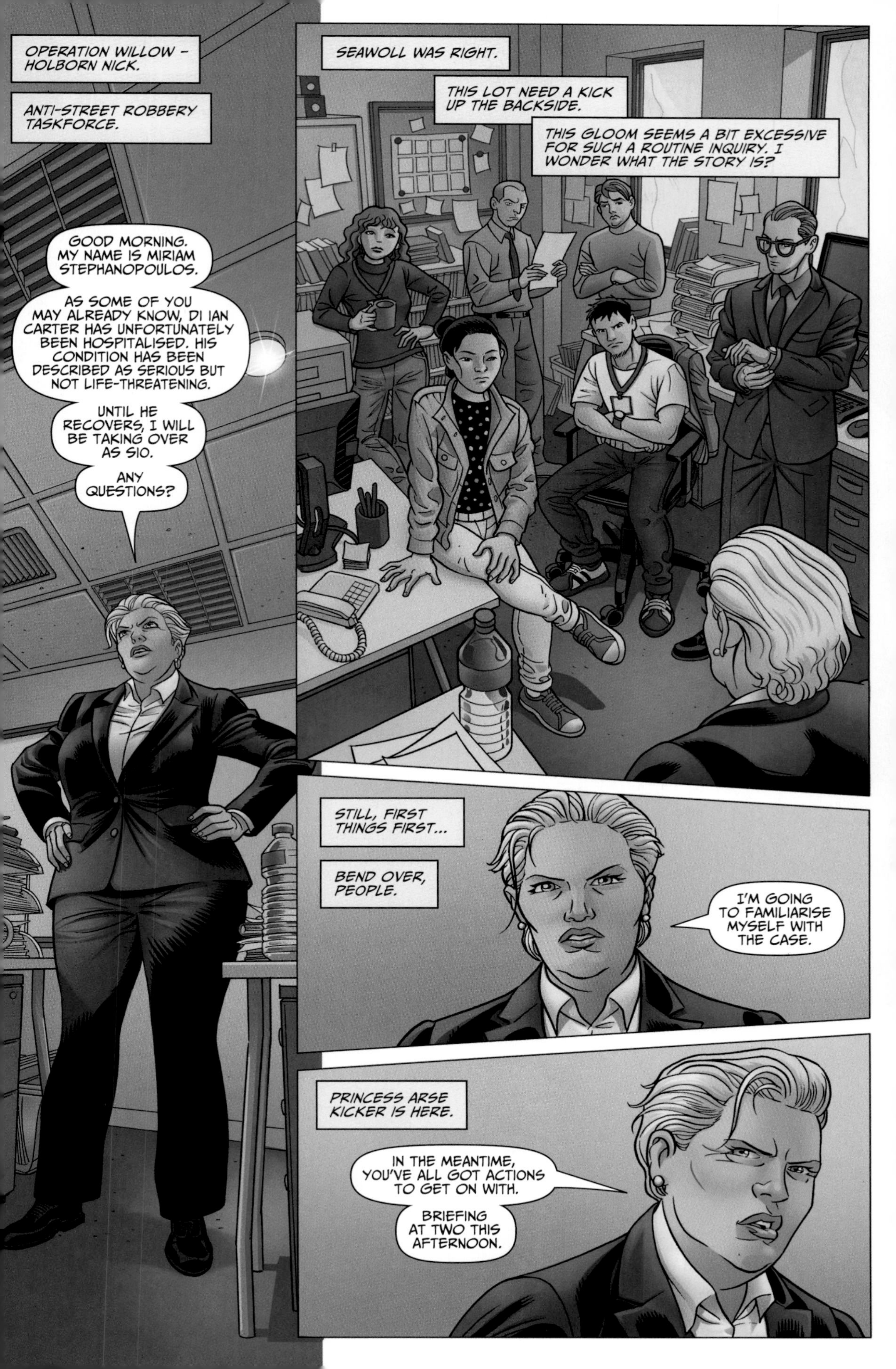
OPERATION WILLOW – HOLBORN NICK.
ANTI-STREET ROBBERY TASKFORCE.
GOOD MORNING. MY NAME IS MIRIAM STEPHANOPOULOS.
AS SOME OF YOU MAY ALREADY KNOW, DI IAN CARTER HAS UNFORTUNATELY BEEN HOSPITALISED. HIS CONDITION HAS BEEN DESCRIBED AS SERIOUS BUT NOT LIFE-THREATENING.
UNTIL HE RECOVERS, I WILL BE TAKING OVER AS SIO.
ANY QUESTIONS?
SEAWOLL WAS RIGHT.
THIS LOT NEED A KICK UP THE BACKSIDE.
THIS GLOOM SEEMS A BIT EXCESSIVE FOR SUCH A ROUTINE INQUIRY. I WONDER WHAT THE STORY IS?
STILL, FIRST THINGS FIRST...
BEND OVER, PEOPLE.
I'M GOING TO FAMILIARISE MYSELF WITH THE CASE.
PRINCESS ARSE KICKER IS HERE.
IN THE MEANTIME, YOU'VE ALL GOT ACTIONS TO GET ON WITH.
BRIEFING AT TWO THIS AFTERNOON.

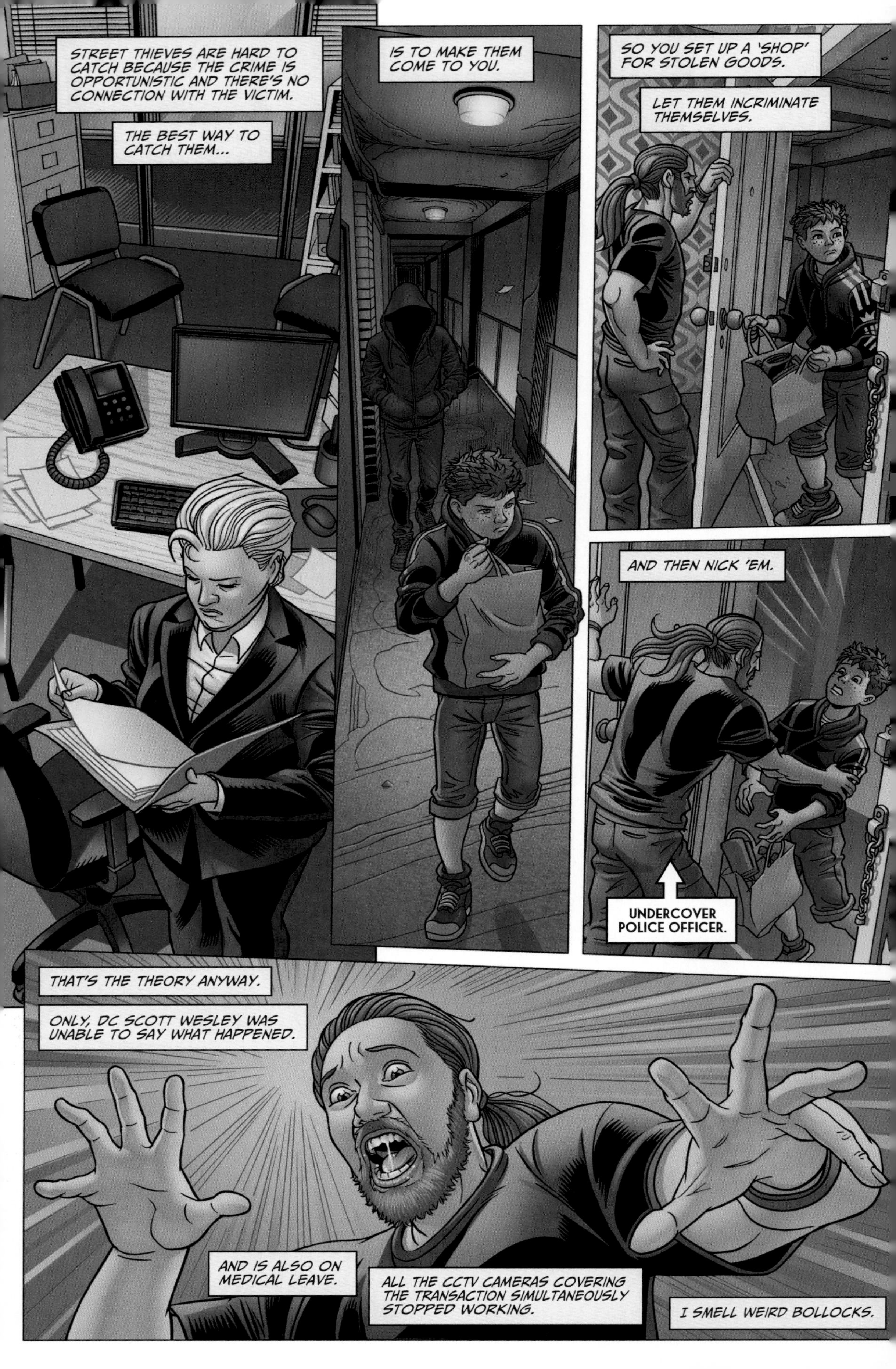
STREET THIEVES ARE HARD TO CATCH BECAUSE THE CRIME IS OPPORTUNISTIC AND THERE'S NO CONNECTION WITH THE VICTIM.
THE BEST WAY TO CATCH THEM...
IS TO MAKE THEM COME TO YOU.
SO YOU SET UP A 'SHOP' FOR STOLEN GOODS.
LET THEM INCRIMINATE THEMSELVES.
AND THEN NICK 'EM.
UNDERCOVER POLICE OFFICER.
THAT'S THE THEORY ANYWAY.
ONLY, DC SCOTT WESLEY WAS UNABLE TO SAY WHAT HAPPENED.
AND IS ALSO ON MEDICAL LEAVE.
ALL THE CCTV CAMERAS COVERING THE TRANSACTION SIMULTANEOUSLY STOPPED WORKING.
I SMELL WEIRD BOLLOCKS.

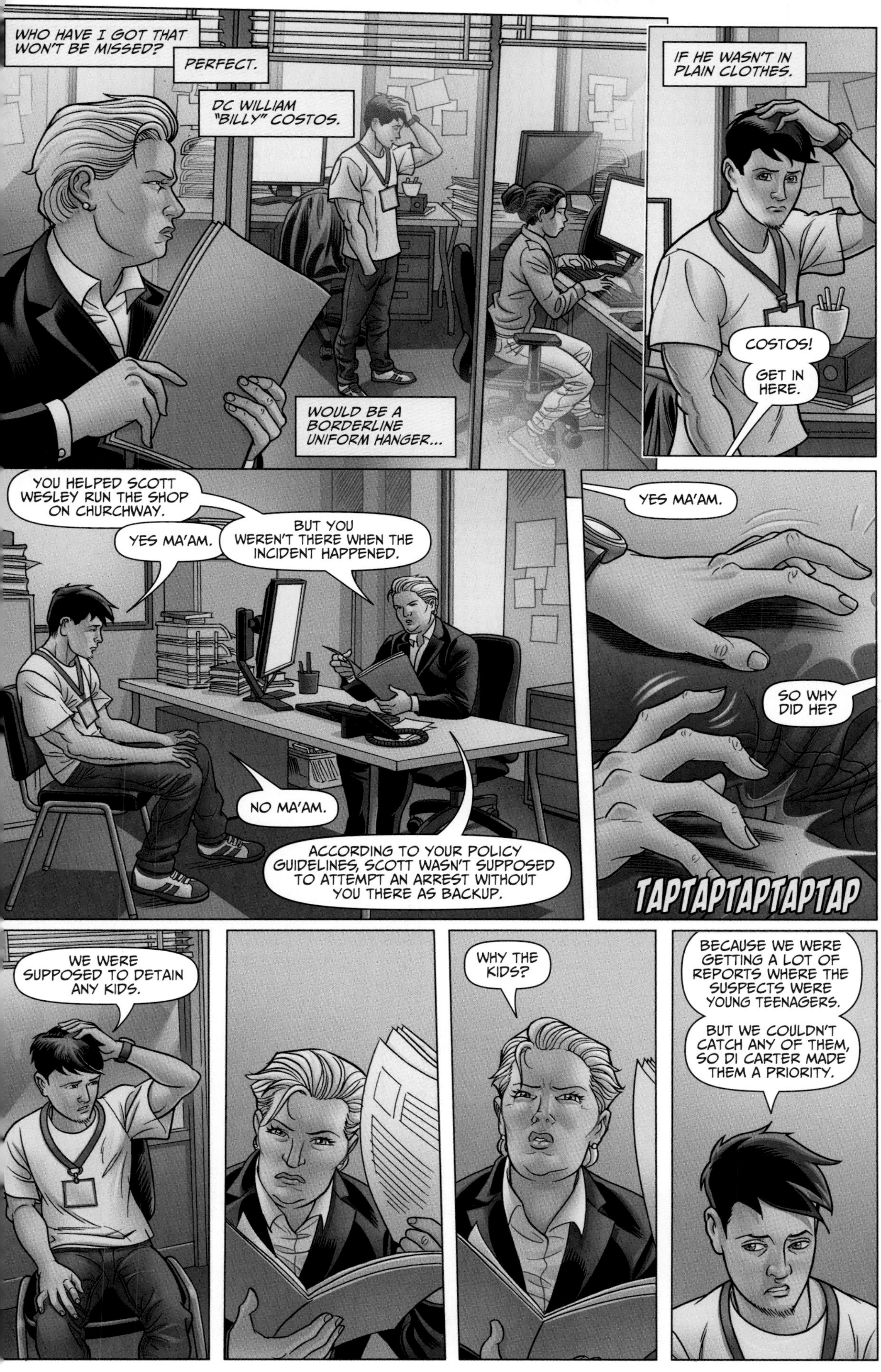
WHO HAVE I GOT THAT WON'T BE MISSED?
PERFECT.
DC WILLIAM "BILLY" COSTOS.
WOULD BE A BORDERLINE UNIFORM HANGER...
IF HE WASN'T IN PLAIN CLOTHES.
COSTOS!
GET IN HERE.
YOU HELPED SCOTT WESLEY RUN THE SHOP ON CHURCHWAY.
YES MA'AM.
BUT YOU WEREN'T THERE WHEN THE INCIDENT HAPPENED.
NO MA'AM.
ACCORDING TO YOUR POLICY GUIDELINES, SCOTT WASN'T SUPPOSED TO ATTEMPT AN ARREST WITHOUT YOU THERE AS BACKUP.
YES MA'AM.
SO WHY DID HE?
TAPTAPTAPTAPTAP
WE WERE SUPPOSED TO DETAIN ANY KIDS.
WHY THE KIDS?
BECAUSE WE WERE GETTING A LOT OF REPORTS WHERE THE SUSPECTS WERE YOUNG TEENAGERS.
BUT WE COULDN'T CATCH ANY OF THEM, SO DI CARTER MADE THEM A PRIORITY.

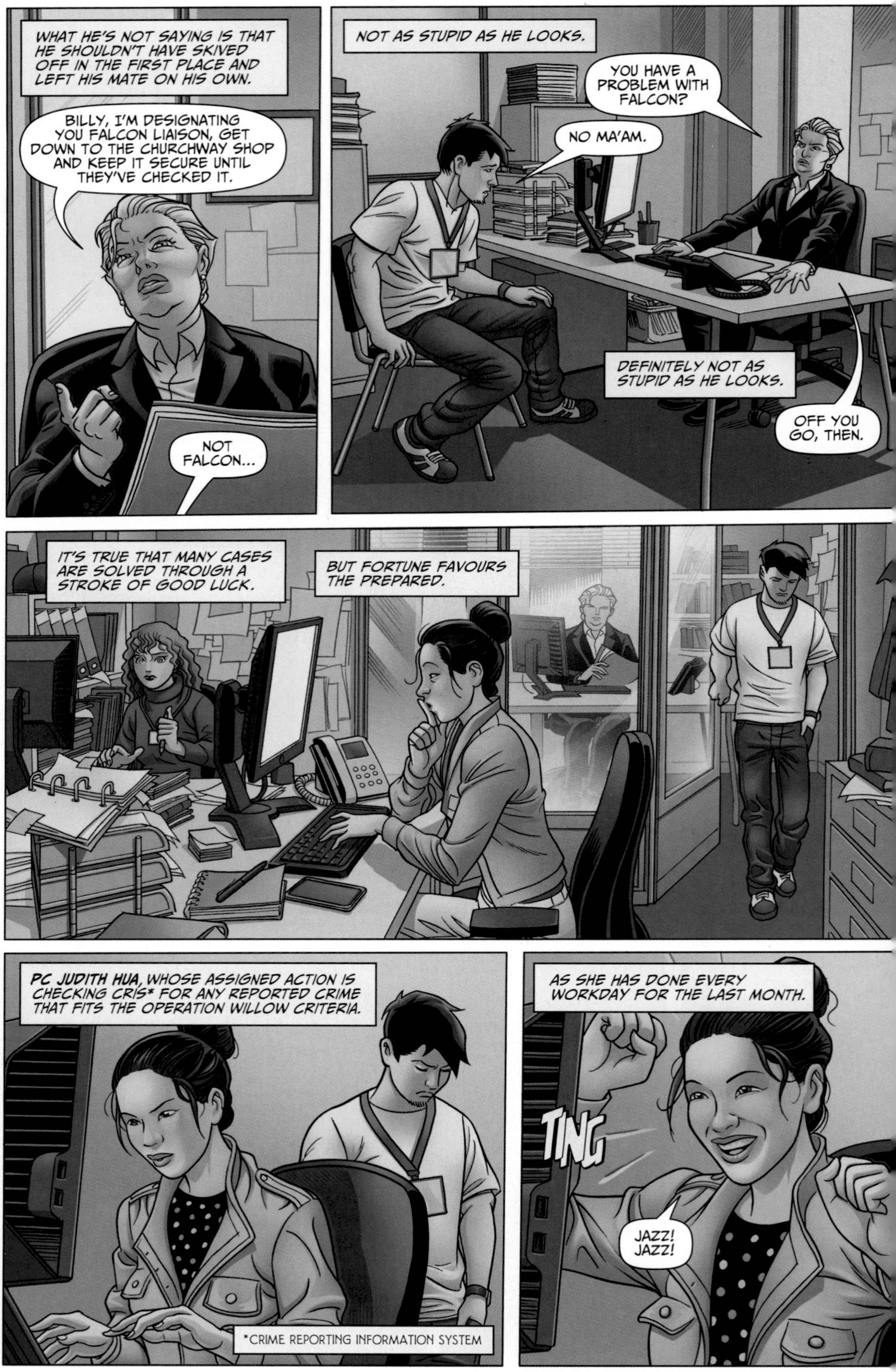
WHAT HE'S NOT SAYING IS THAT HE SHOULDN'T HAVE SKIVED OFF IN THE FIRST PLACE AND LEFT HIS MATE ON HIS OWN.
BILLY, I'M DESIGNATING YOU FALCON LIAISON, GET DOWN TO THE CHURCHWAY SHOP AND KEEP IT SECURE UNTIL THEY'VE CHECKED IT.
NOT FALCON...
NOT AS STUPID AS HE LOOKS.
YOU HAVE A PROBLEM WITH FALCON?
NO MA'AM.
DEFINITELY NOT AS STUPID AS HE LOOKS.
OFF YOU GO, THEN.
IT'S TRUE THAT MANY CASES ARE SOLVED THROUGH A STROKE OF GOOD LUCK.
BUT FORTUNE FAVOURS THE PREPARED.
PC JUDITH HUA, WHOSE ASSIGNED ACTION IS CHECKING CRIS* FOR ANY REPORTED CRIME THAT FITS THE OPERATION WILLOW CRITERIA.
*CRIME REPORTING INFORMATION SYSTEM
AS SHE HAS DONE EVERY WORKDAY FOR THE LAST MONTH.
TING
JAZZ! JAZZ!

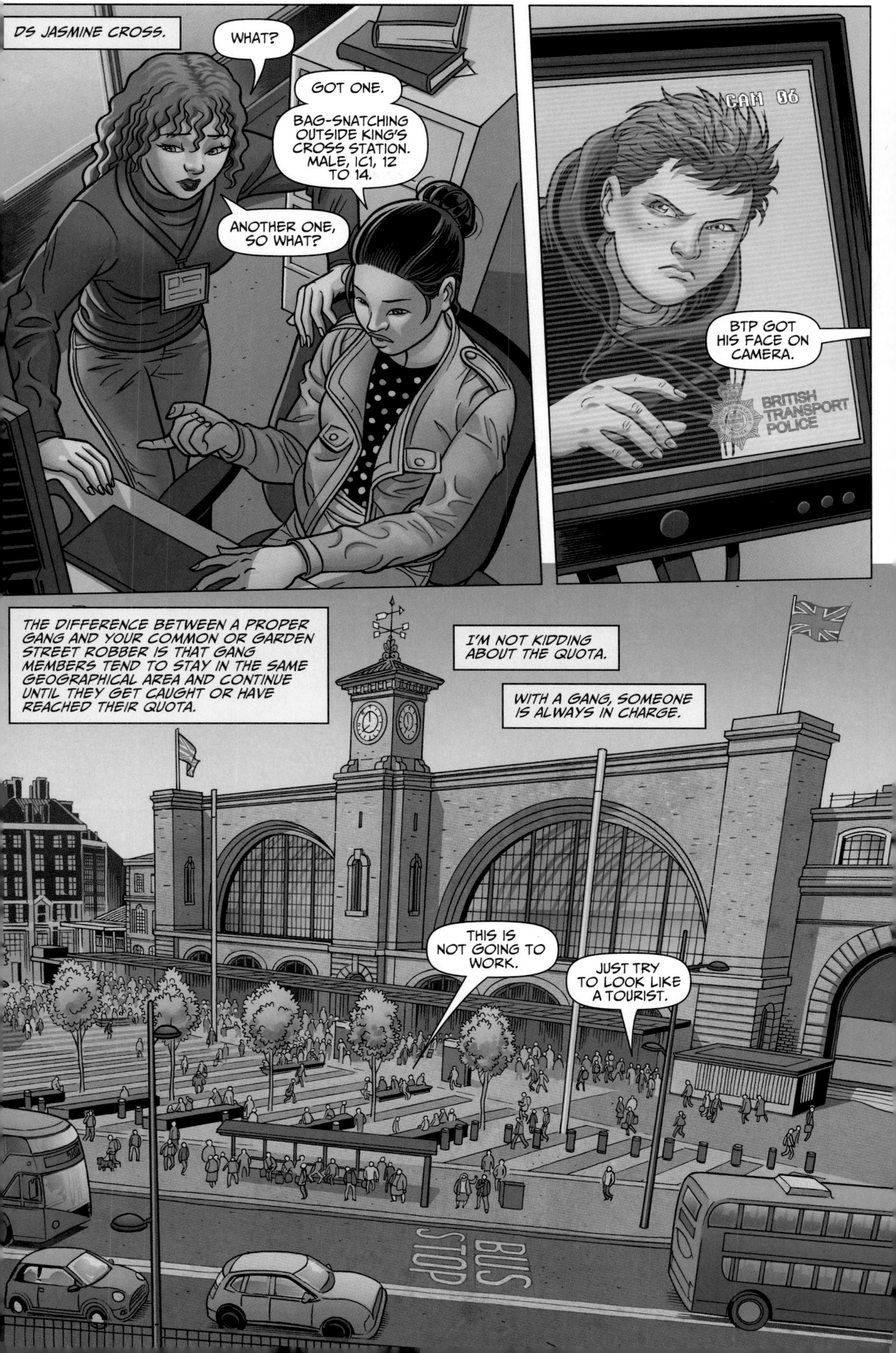
DS JASMINE CROSS.
WHAT?
GOT ONE.
BAG-SNATCHING OUTSIDE KING'S CROSS STATION. MALE, IC1, 12 TO 14.
ANOTHER ONE, SO WHAT?
CAM 06
BTP GOT HIS FACE ON CAMERA.
BRITISH TRANSPORT POLICE
THE DIFFERENCE BETWEEN A PROPER GANG AND YOUR COMMON OR GARDEN STREET ROBBER IS THAT GANG MEMBERS TEND TO STAY IN THE SAME GEOGRAPHICAL AREA AND CONTINUE UNTIL THEY GET CAUGHT OR HAVE REACHED THEIR QUOTA.
I'M NOT KIDDING ABOUT THE QUOTA.
WITH A GANG, SOMEONE IS ALWAYS IN CHARGE.
THIS IS NOT GOING TO WORK.
JUST TRY TO LOOK LIKE A TOURIST.
BUS STOP

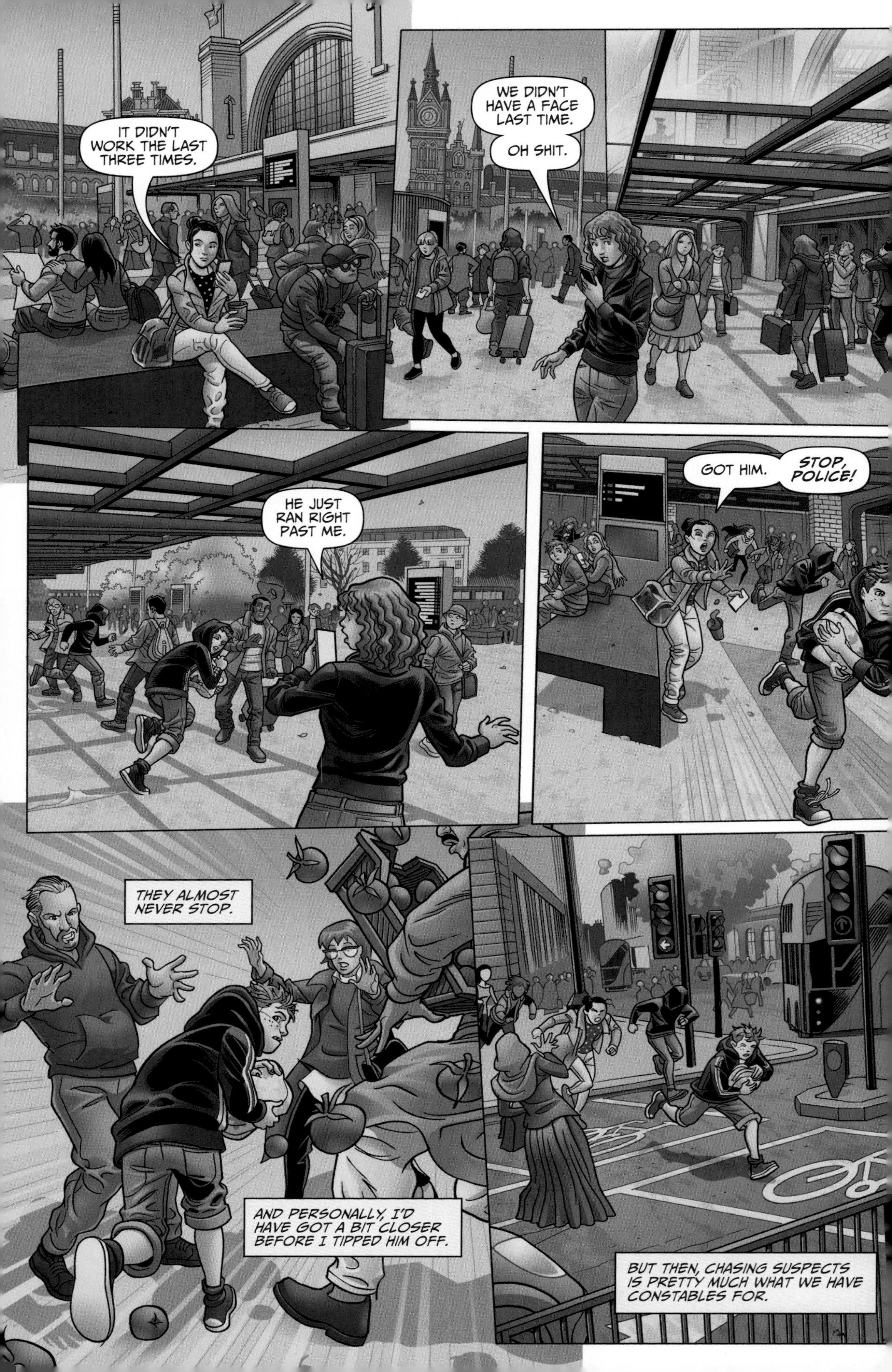

IT DIDN'T WORK THE LAST THREE TIMES.
WE DIDN'T HAVE A FACE LAST TIME.
OH SHIT.
HE JUST RAN RIGHT PAST ME.
GOT HIM.
STOP, POLICE!
THEY ALMOST NEVER STOP.
AND PERSONALLY, I'D HAVE GOT A BIT CLOSER BEFORE I TIPPED HIM OFF.
BUT THEN, CHASING SUSPECTS IS PRETTY MUCH WHAT WE HAVE CONSTABLES FOR.

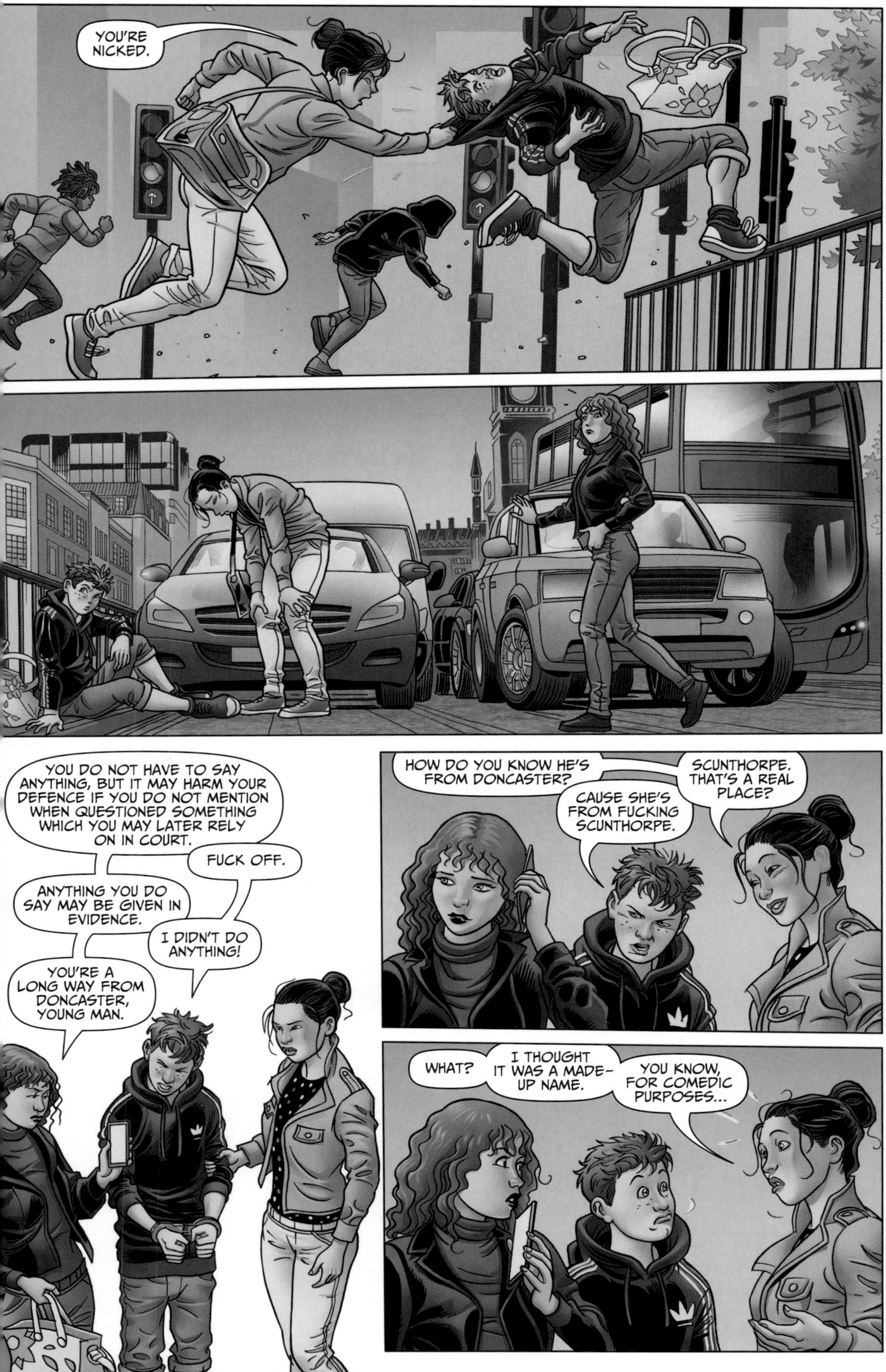
YOU'RE NICKED.
YOU DO NOT HAVE TO SAY ANYTHING, BUT IT MAY HARM YOUR DEFENCE IF YOU DO NOT MENTION WHEN QUESTIONED SOMETHING WHICH YOU MAY LATER RELY ON IN COURT.
FUCK OFF.
ANYTHING YOU DO SAY MAY BE GIVEN IN EVIDENCE.
I DIDN'T DO ANYTHING!
YOU'RE A LONG WAY FROM DONCASTER, YOUNG MAN.
HOW DO YOU KNOW HE'S FROM DONCASTER?
CAUSE SHE'S FROM FUCKING SCUNTHORPE.
SCUNTHORPE. THAT'S A REAL PLACE?
WHAT?
I THOUGHT IT WAS A MADE-UP NAME.
YOU KNOW, FOR COMEDIC PURPOSES...

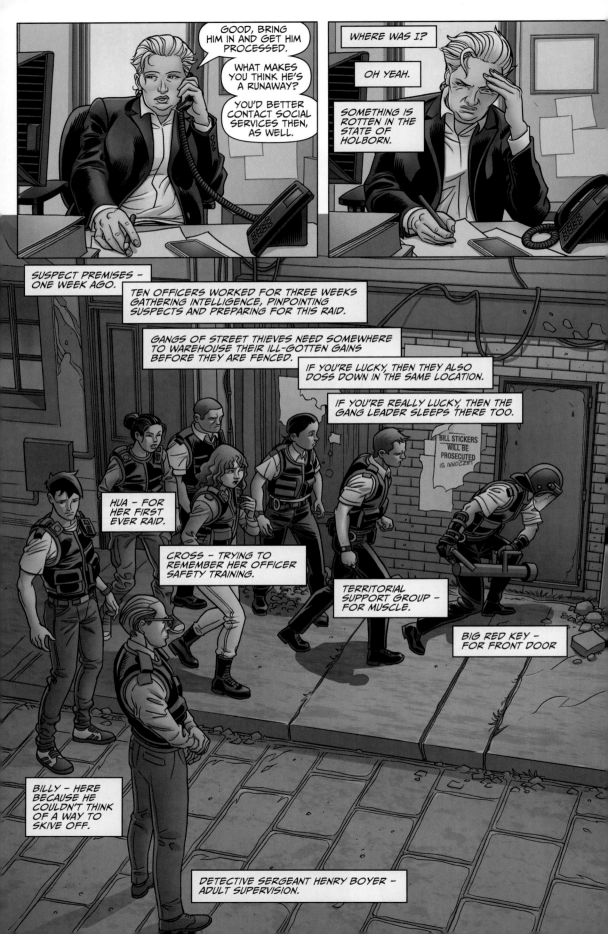

GOOD, BRING HIM IN AND GET HIM PROCESSED.

WHAT MAKES YOU THINK HE'S A RUNAWAY?

YOU'D BETTER CONTACT SOCIAL SERVICES THEN, AS WELL.

WHERE WAS I?

OH YEAH.

SOMETHING IS ROTTEN IN THE STATE OF HOLBORN.

SUSPECT PREMISES – ONE WEEK AGO.

TEN OFFICERS WORKED FOR THREE WEEKS GATHERING INTELLIGENCE, PINPOINTING SUSPECTS AND PREPARING FOR THIS RAID.

GANGS OF STREET THIEVES NEED SOMEWHERE TO WAREHOUSE THEIR ILL-GOTTEN GAINS BEFORE THEY ARE FENCED.

IF YOU'RE LUCKY, THEN THEY ALSO DOSS DOWN IN THE SAME LOCATION.

IF YOU'RE REALLY LUCKY, THEN THE GANG LEADER SLEEPS THERE TOO.

BILL STICKERS WILL BE PROSECUTED IS INNOZER?

HUA – FOR HER FIRST EVER RAID.

CROSS – TRYING TO REMEMBER HER OFFICER SAFETY TRAINING.

TERRITORIAL SUPPORT GROUP – FOR MUSCLE.

BIG RED KEY – FOR FRONT DOOR

BILLY – HERE BECAUSE HE COULDN'T THINK OF A WAY TO SKIVE OFF.

DETECTIVE SERGEANT HENRY BOYER – ADULT SUPERVISION.

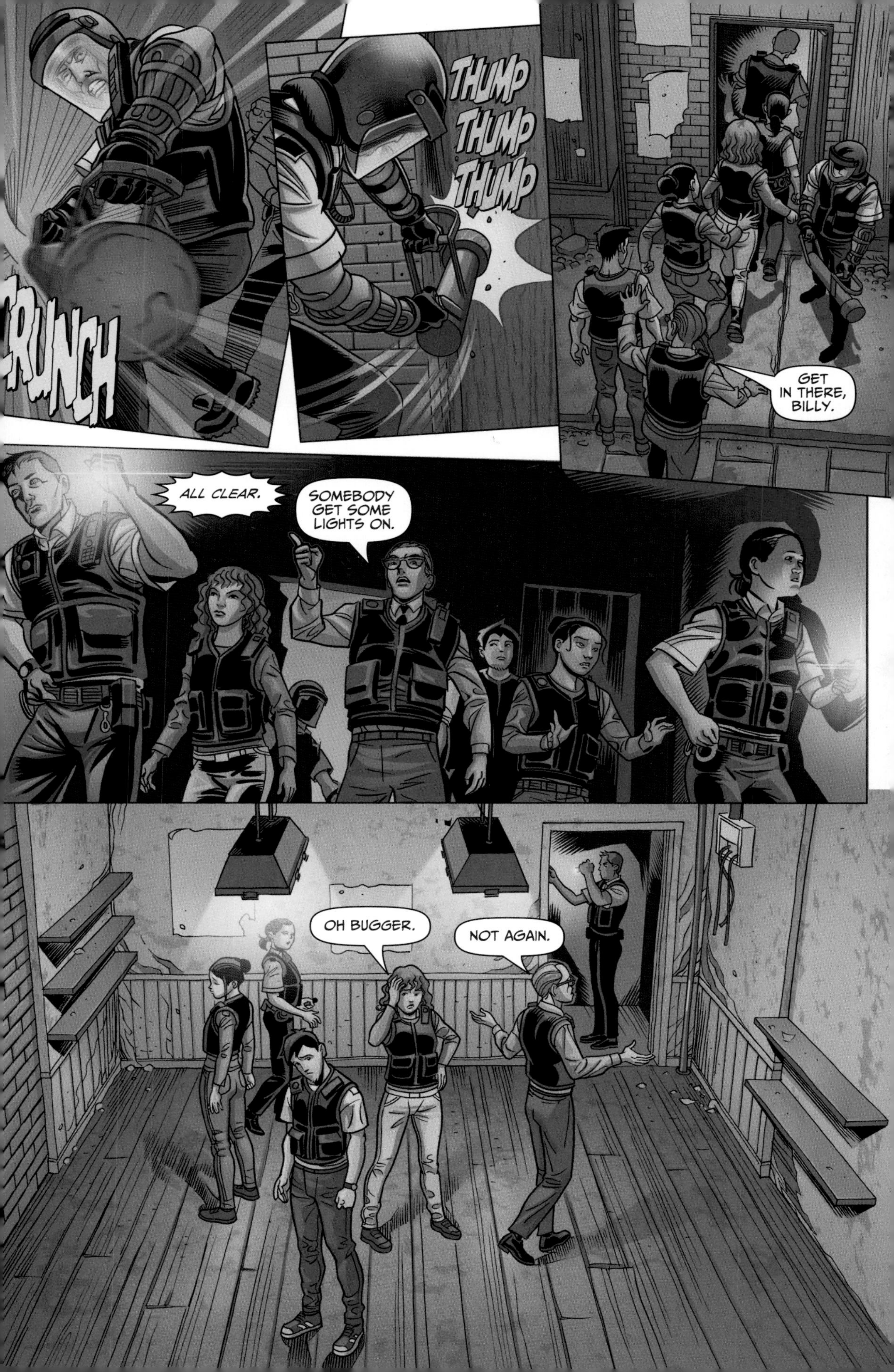
CRUNCH
THUMP THUMP THUMP
GET IN THERE, BILLY.
ALL CLEAR.
SOMEBODY GET SOME LIGHTS ON.
OH BUGGER.
NOT AGAIN.

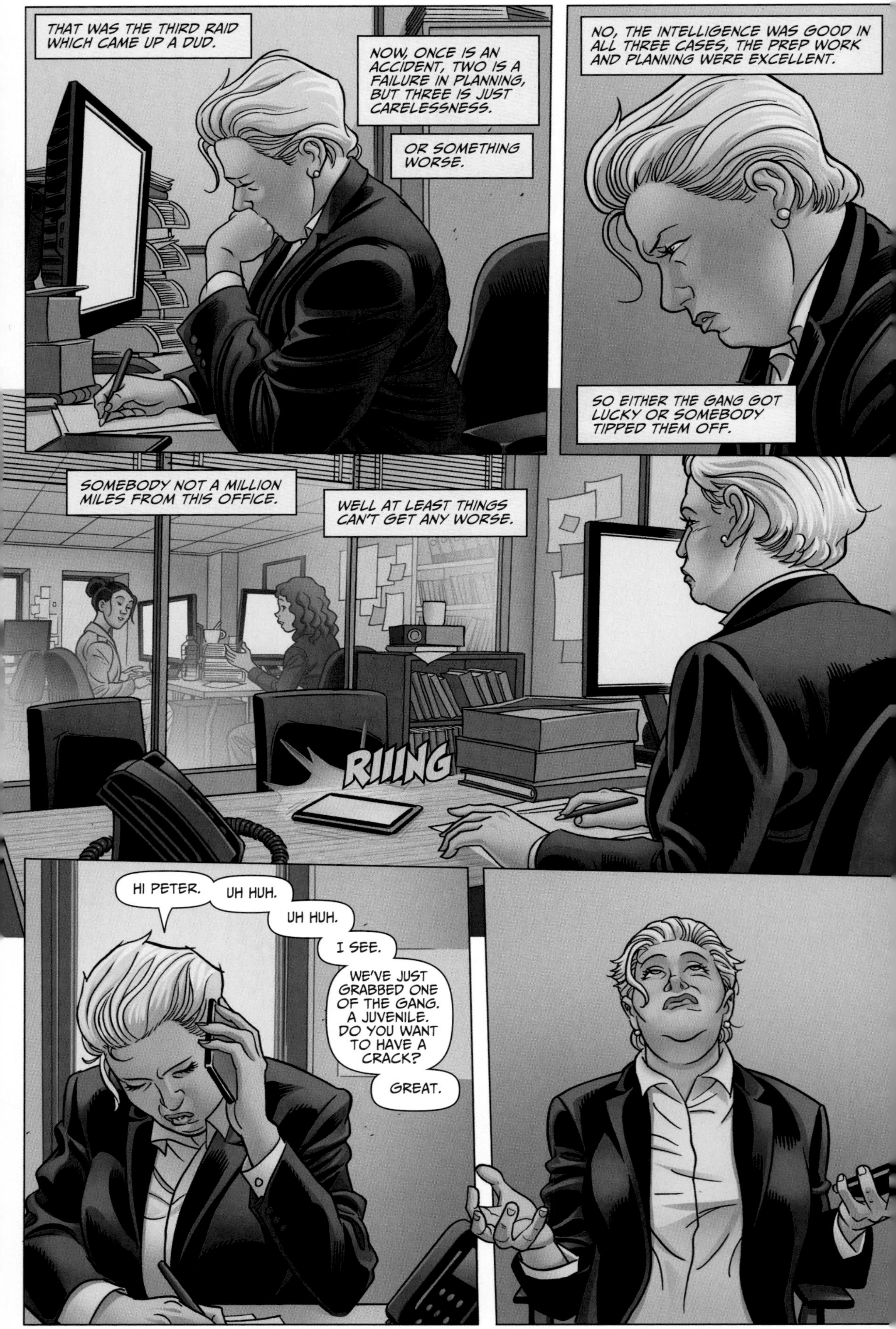
THAT WAS THE THIRD RAID WHICH CAME UP A DUD.
NOW, ONCE IS AN ACCIDENT, TWO IS A FAILURE IN PLANNING, BUT THREE IS JUST CARELESSNESS.
OR SOMETHING WORSE.
NO, THE INTELLIGENCE WAS GOOD IN ALL THREE CASES, THE PREP WORK AND PLANNING WERE EXCELLENT.
SO EITHER THE GANG GOT LUCKY OR SOMEBODY TIPPED THEM OFF.
SOMEBODY NOT A MILLION MILES FROM THIS OFFICE.
WELL AT LEAST THINGS CAN'T GET ANY WORSE.
RIIING
HI PETER.
UH HUH.
UH HUH.
I SEE.
WE'VE JUST GRABBED ONE OF THE GANG. A JUVENILE. DO YOU WANT TO HAVE A CRACK?
GREAT.

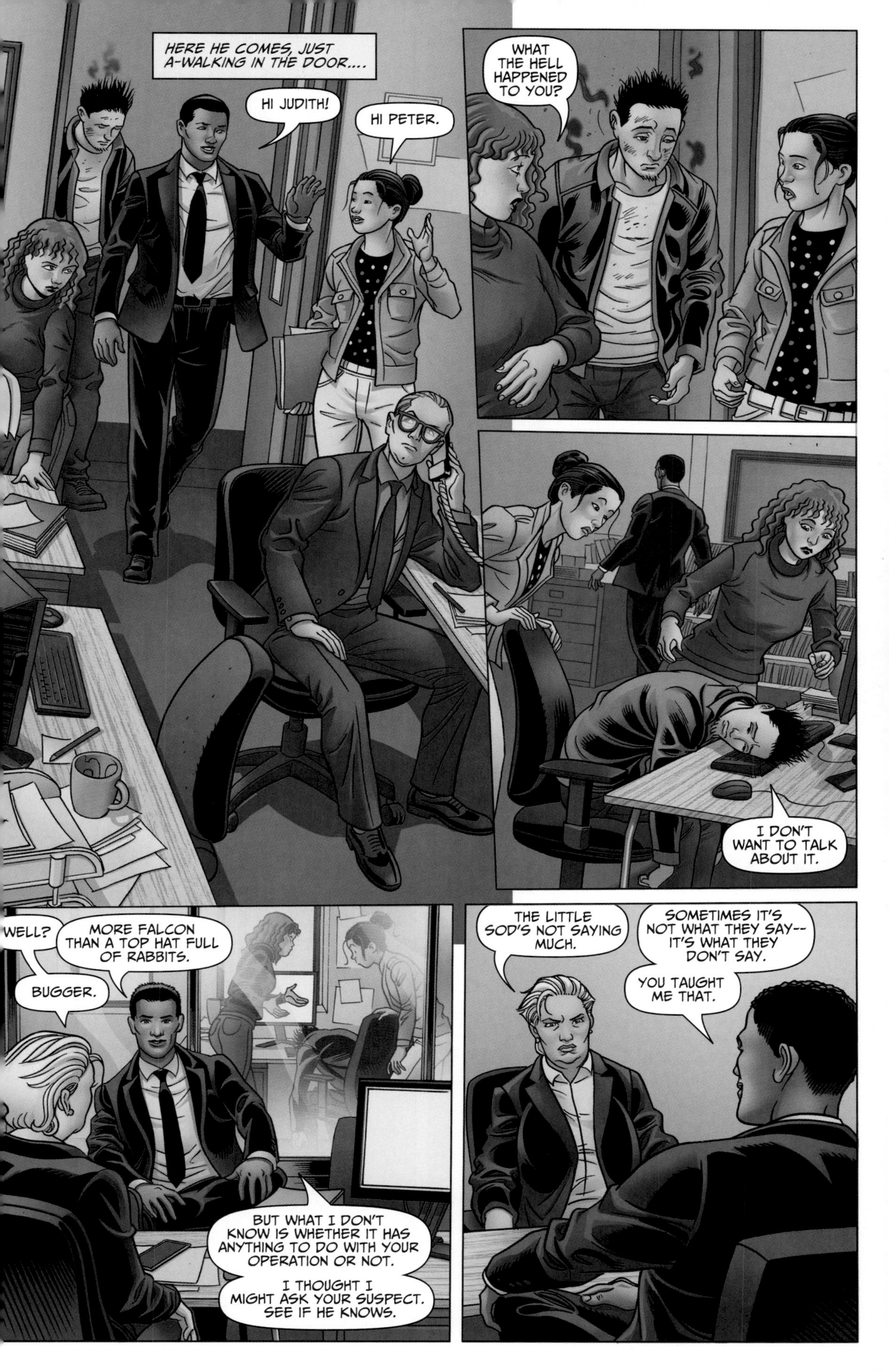
HERE HE COMES, JUST A-WALKING IN THE DOOR....
HI JUDITH!
HI PETER.
WHAT THE HELL HAPPENED TO YOU?
I DON'T WANT TO TALK ABOUT IT.
WELL?
MORE FALCON THAN A TOP HAT FULL OF RABBITS.
BUGGER.
BUT WHAT I DON'T KNOW IS WHETHER IT HAS ANYTHING TO DO WITH YOUR OPERATION OR NOT.
I THOUGHT I MIGHT ASK YOUR SUSPECT. SEE IF HE KNOWS.
THE LITTLE SOD'S NOT SAYING MUCH.
SOMETIMES IT'S NOT WHAT THEY SAY-- IT'S WHAT THEY DON'T SAY.
YOU TAUGHT ME THAT.

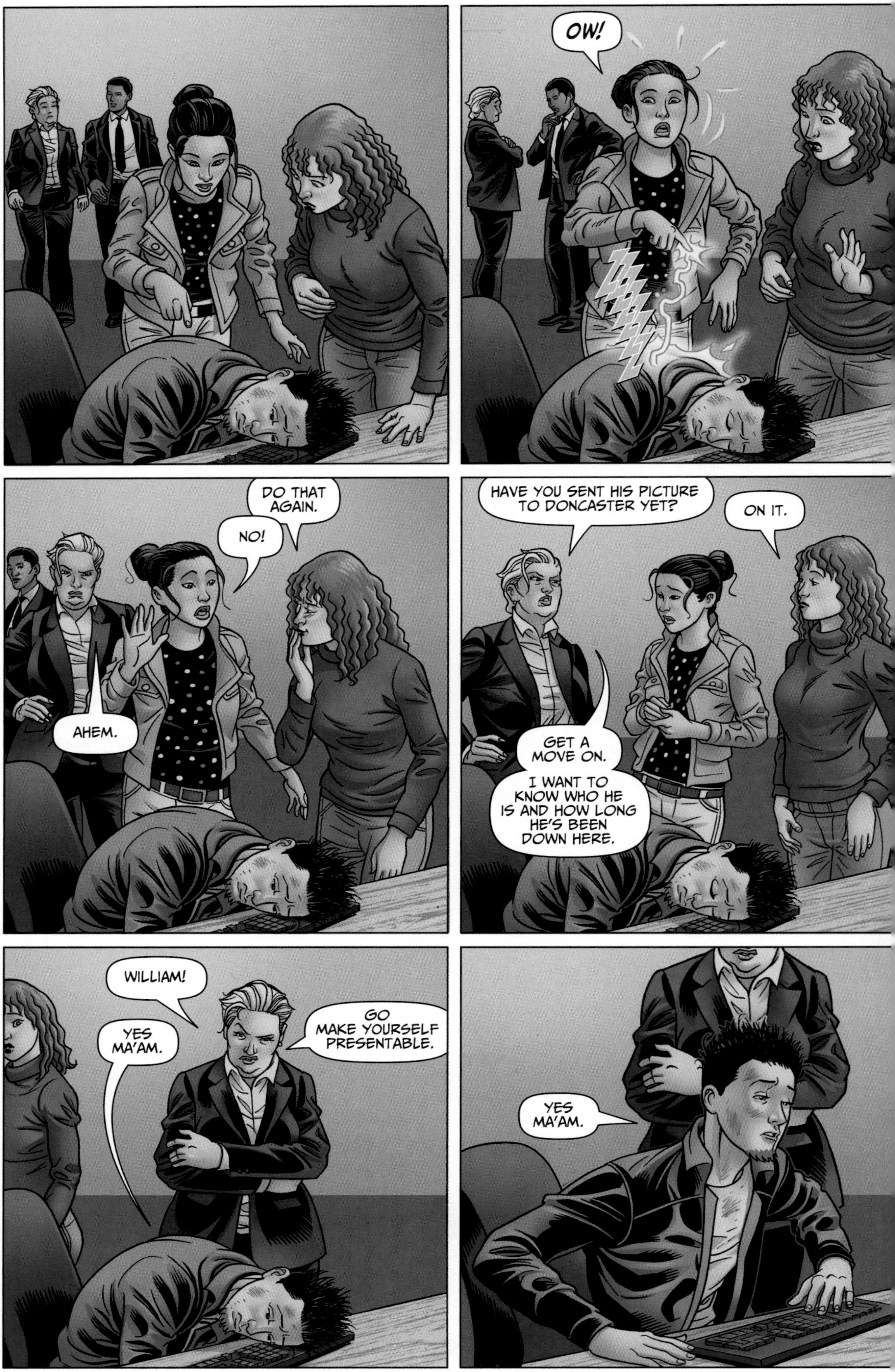
OW!
DO THAT AGAIN.
NO!
AHEM.
HAVE YOU SENT HIS PICTURE TO DONCASTER YET?
ON IT.
GET A MOVE ON.
I WANT TO KNOW WHO HE IS AND HOW LONG HE'S BEEN DOWN HERE.
WILLIAM!
GO MAKE YOURSELF PRESENTABLE.
YES MA'AM.
YES MA'AM.

AFTERNOON BRIEFING OR IDENTIFICATION PARADE?

YOU DECIDE.

DC KENNEDY AND DC MICHELMORE.

THESE TWO DIDN'T JOIN THE OPERATION UNTIL AFTER THE SECOND RAID.

PETER VOUCHES FOR HER, BUT PETER'S BEEN WRONG BEFORE.

WE HAVE A SUSPECT IN CUSTODY, WHITE MALE, 12-14, POSSIBLY A RUNAWAY FROM DONCASTER.

GOOD WORK BY JUDITH AND JASMINE.

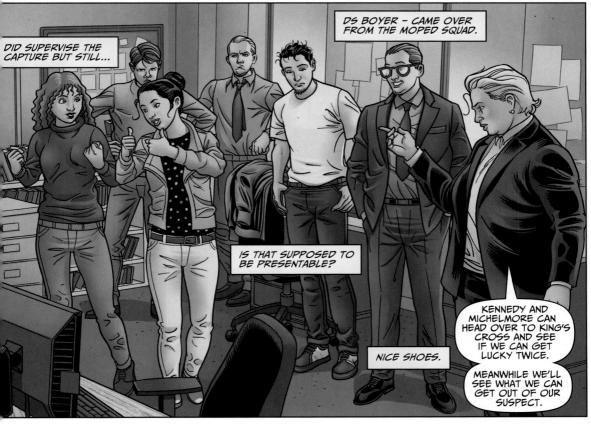

DS BOYER – CAME OVER FROM THE MOPED SQUAD.

DID SUPERVISE THE CAPTURE BUT STILL...

IS THAT SUPPOSED TO BE PRESENTABLE?

NICE SHOES.

KENNEDY AND MICHELMORE CAN HEAD OVER TO KING'S CROSS AND SEE IF WE CAN GET LUCKY TWICE.

MEANWHILE WE'LL SEE WHAT WE CAN GET OUT OF OUR SUSPECT.

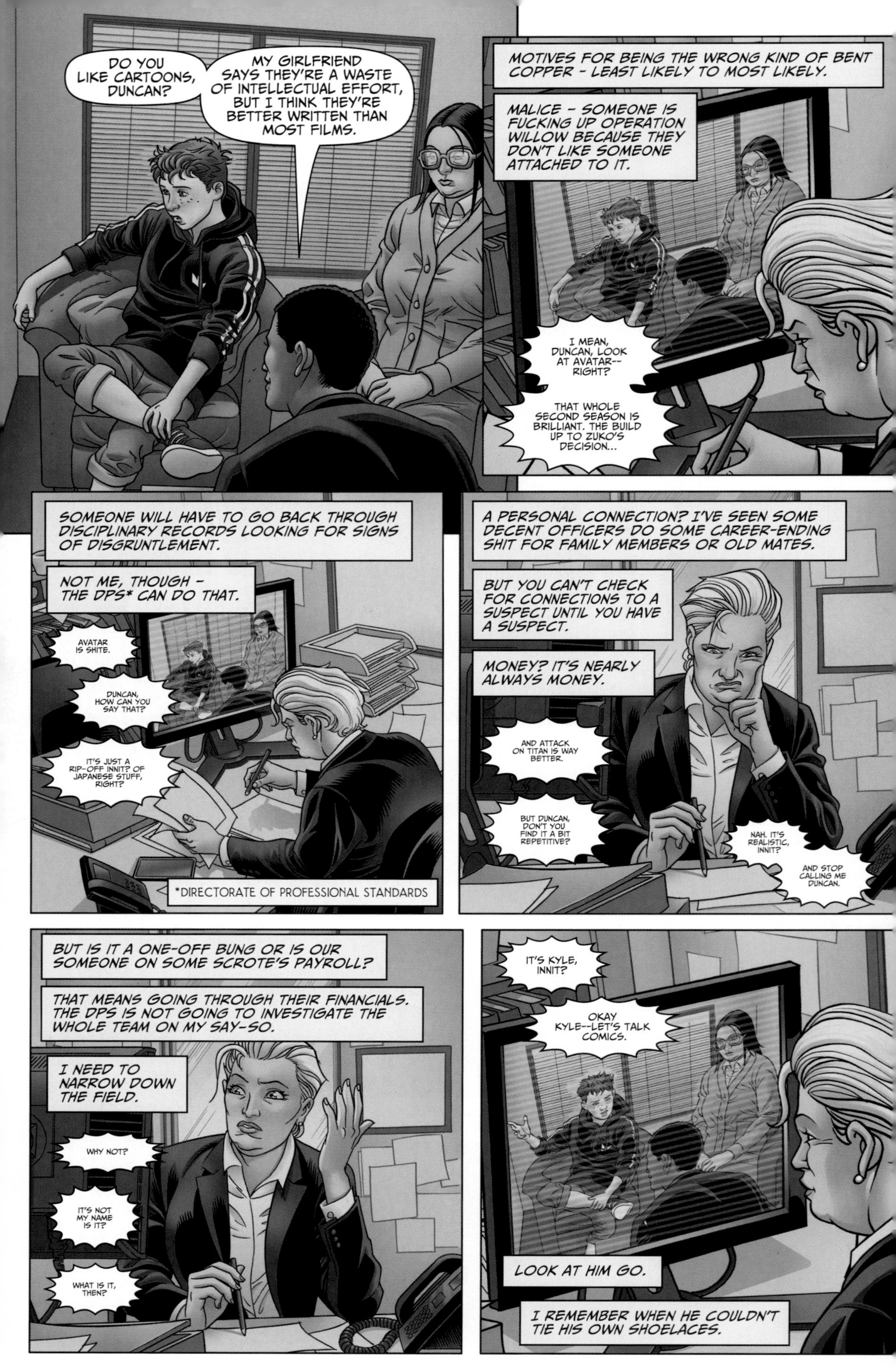
DO YOU LIKE CARTOONS, DUNCAN?
MY GIRLFRIEND SAYS THEY'RE A WASTE OF INTELLECTUAL EFFORT, BUT I THINK THEY'RE BETTER WRITTEN THAN MOST FILMS.
MOTIVES FOR BEING THE WRONG KIND OF BENT COPPER - LEAST LIKELY TO MOST LIKELY.
MALICE - SOMEONE IS FUCKING UP OPERATION WILLOW BECAUSE THEY DON'T LIKE SOMEONE ATTACHED TO IT.
I MEAN, DUNCAN, LOOK AT AVATAR--RIGHT?
THAT WHOLE SECOND SEASON IS BRILLIANT. THE BUILD UP TO ZUKO'S DECISION...
SOMEONE WILL HAVE TO GO BACK THROUGH DISCIPLINARY RECORDS LOOKING FOR SIGNS OF DISGRUNTLEMENT.
NOT ME, THOUGH - THE DPS* CAN DO THAT.
AVATAR IS SHITE.
DUNCAN, HOW CAN YOU SAY THAT?
IT'S JUST A RIP-OFF INNIT? OF JAPANESE STUFF, RIGHT?
*DIRECTORATE OF PROFESSIONAL STANDARDS
A PERSONAL CONNECTION? I'VE SEEN SOME DECENT OFFICERS DO SOME CAREER-ENDING SHIT FOR FAMILY MEMBERS OR OLD MATES.
BUT YOU CAN'T CHECK FOR CONNECTIONS TO A SUSPECT UNTIL YOU HAVE A SUSPECT.
MONEY? IT'S NEARLY ALWAYS MONEY.
AND ATTACK ON TITAN IS WAY BETTER.
BUT DUNCAN, DON'T YOU FIND IT A BIT REPETITIVE?
NAH. IT'S REALISTIC, INNIT?
AND STOP CALLING ME DUNCAN.
BUT IS IT A ONE-OFF BUNG OR IS OUR SOMEONE ON SOME SCROTE'S PAYROLL?
THAT MEANS GOING THROUGH THEIR FINANCIALS. THE DPS IS NOT GOING TO INVESTIGATE THE WHOLE TEAM ON MY SAY-SO.
I NEED TO NARROW DOWN THE FIELD.
WHY NOT?
IT'S NOT MY NAME IS IT?
WHAT IS IT, THEN?
IT'S KYLE, INNIT?
OKAY KYLE--LET'S TALK COMICS.
LOOK AT HIM GO.
I REMEMBER WHEN HE COULDN'T TIE HIS OWN SHOELACES.

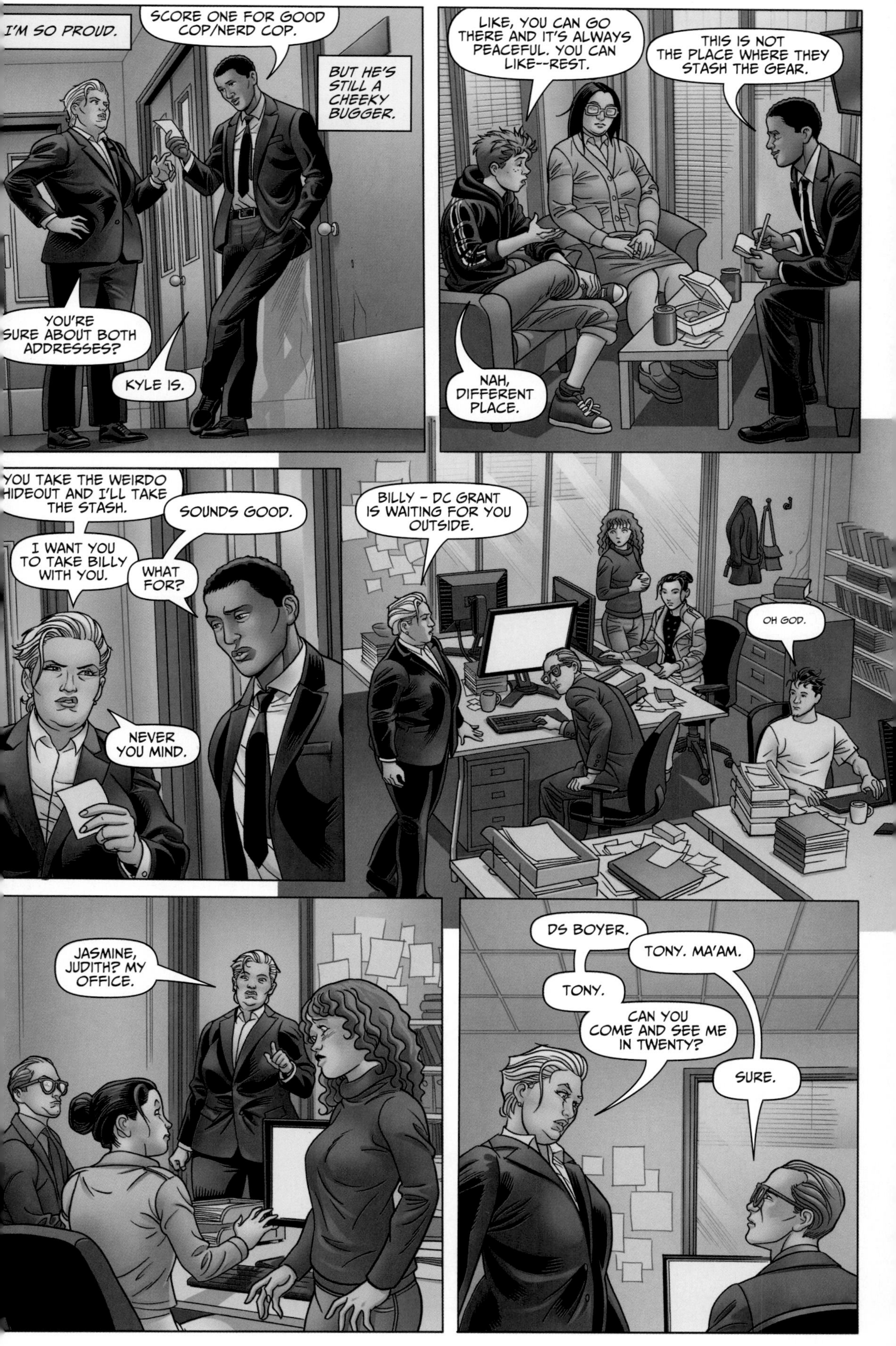
I'M SO PROUD.
SCORE ONE FOR GOOD COP/NERD COP.
BUT HE'S STILL A CHEEKY BUGGER.
YOU'RE SURE ABOUT BOTH ADDRESSES?
KYLE IS.
LIKE, YOU CAN GO THERE AND IT'S ALWAYS PEACEFUL. YOU CAN LIKE--REST.
THIS IS NOT THE PLACE WHERE THEY STASH THE GEAR.
NAH, DIFFERENT PLACE.
YOU TAKE THE WEIRDO HIDEOUT AND I'LL TAKE THE STASH.
SOUNDS GOOD.
I WANT YOU TO TAKE BILLY WITH YOU.
WHAT FOR?
NEVER YOU MIND.
BILLY – DC GRANT IS WAITING FOR YOU OUTSIDE.
OH GOD.
JASMINE, JUDITH? MY OFFICE.
DS BOYER.
TONY. MA'AM.
TONY.
CAN YOU COME AND SEE ME IN TWENTY?
SURE.

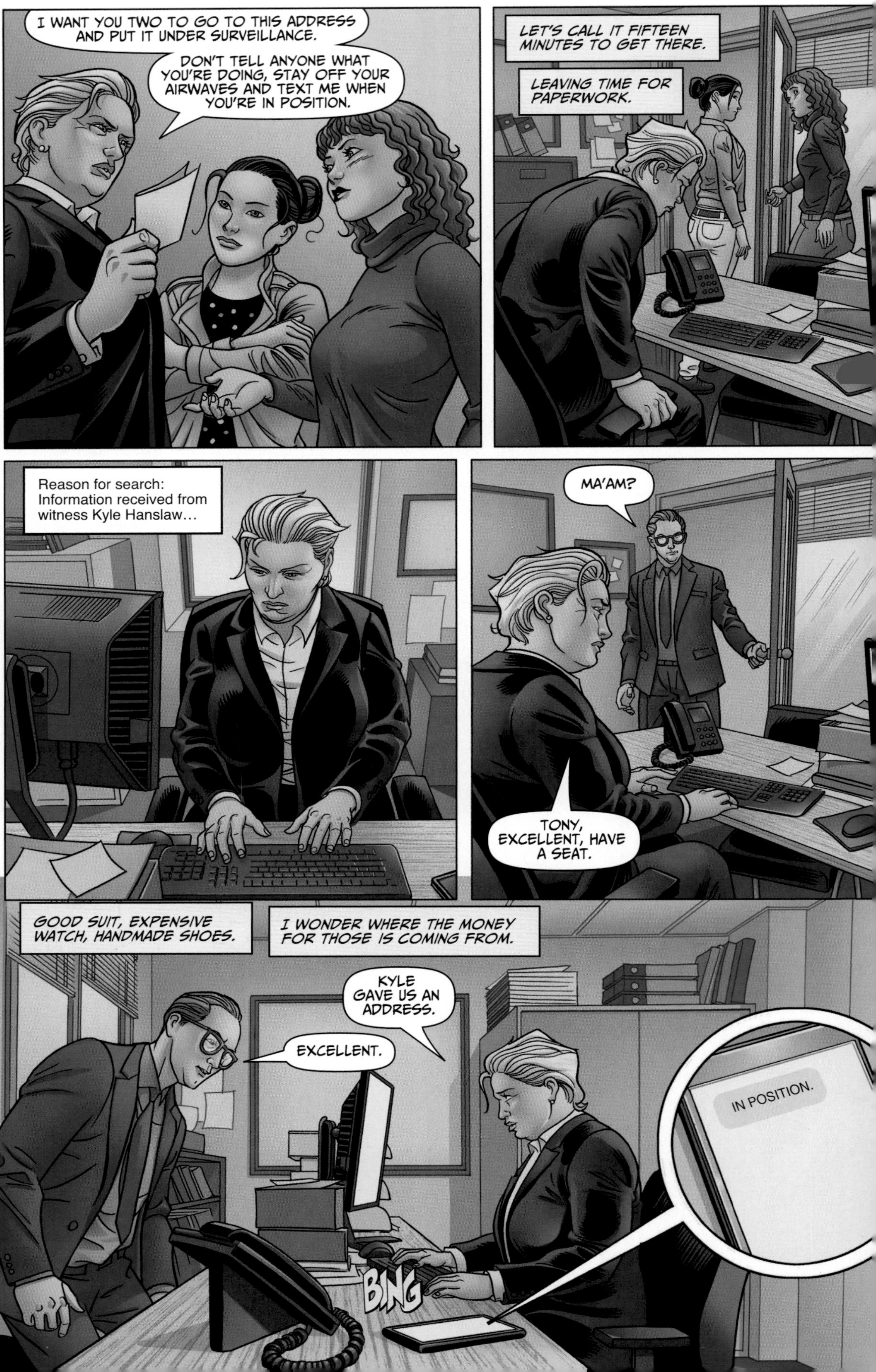
I WANT YOU TWO TO GO TO THIS ADDRESS AND PUT IT UNDER SURVEILLANCE.
DON'T TELL ANYONE WHAT YOU'RE DOING, STAY OFF YOUR AIRWAVES AND TEXT ME WHEN YOU'RE IN POSITION.
LET'S CALL IT FIFTEEN MINUTES TO GET THERE.
LEAVING TIME FOR PAPERWORK.
Reason for search: Information received from witness Kyle Hanslaw…
MA'AM?
TONY, EXCELLENT, HAVE A SEAT.
GOOD SUIT, EXPENSIVE WATCH, HANDMADE SHOES.
I WONDER WHERE THE MONEY FOR THOSE IS COMING FROM.
KYLE GAVE US AN ADDRESS.
EXCELLENT.
IN POSITION.
BING

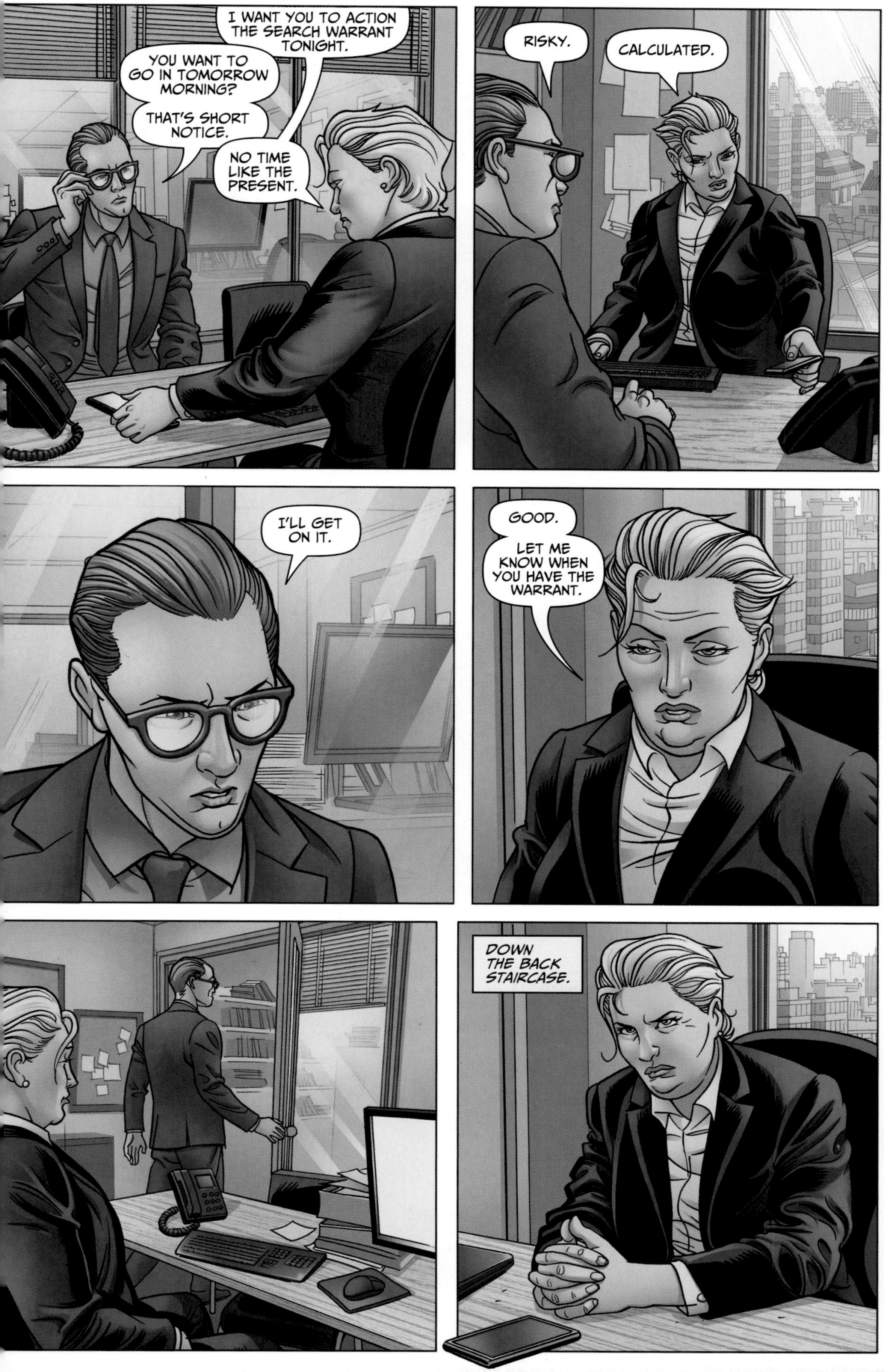
I WANT YOU TO ACTION THE SEARCH WARRANT TONIGHT.
YOU WANT TO GO IN TOMORROW MORNING?
THAT'S SHORT NOTICE.
NO TIME LIKE THE PRESENT.
RISKY.
CALCULATED.
I'LL GET ON IT.
GOOD.
LET ME KNOW WHEN YOU HAVE THE WARRANT.
DOWN THE BACK STAIRCASE.

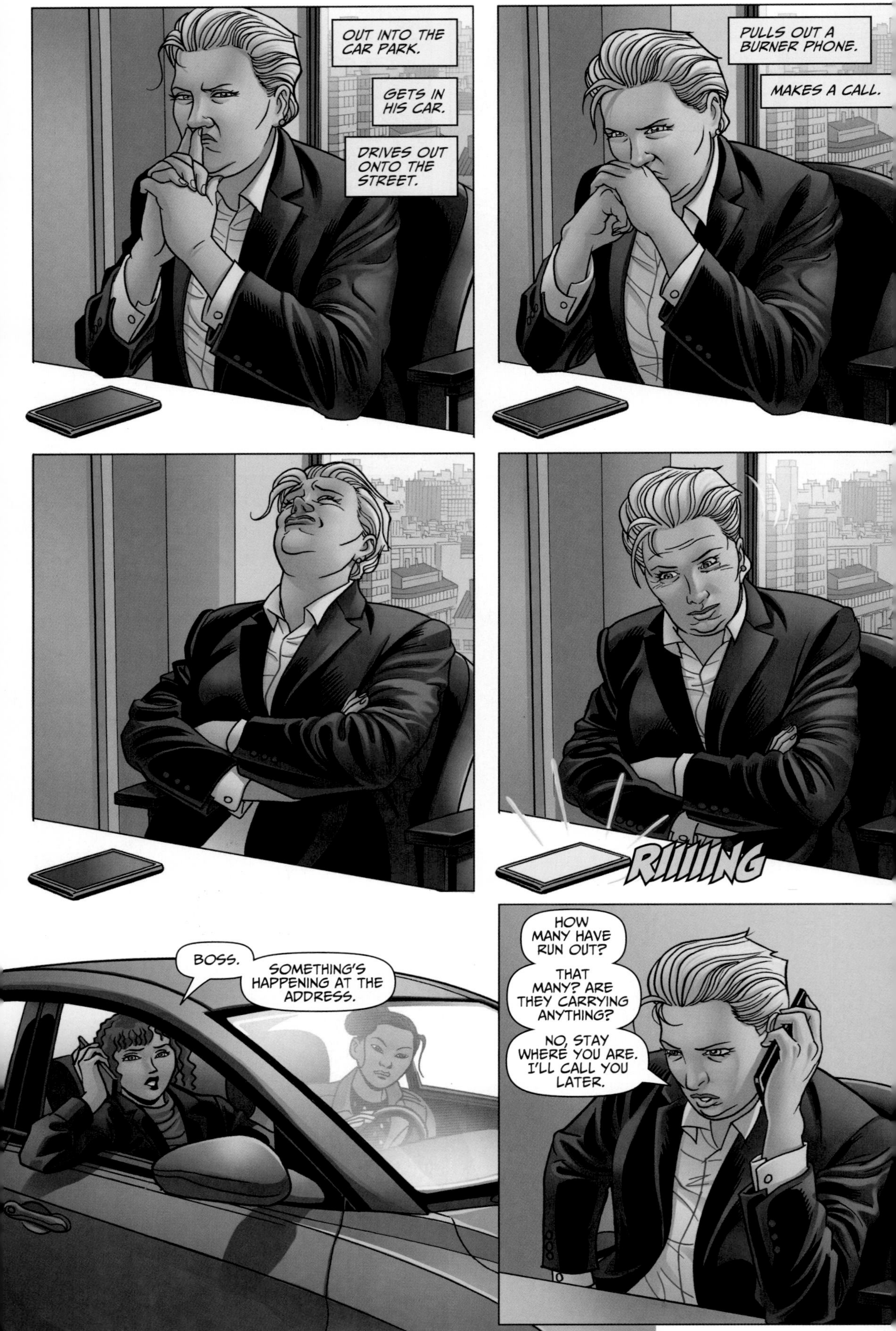
OUT INTO THE CAR PARK.
GETS IN HIS CAR.
DRIVES OUT ONTO THE STREET.
PULLS OUT A BURNER PHONE.
MAKES A CALL.
RIIIING
BOSS.
SOMETHING'S HAPPENING AT THE ADDRESS.
HOW MANY HAVE RUN OUT?
THAT MANY? ARE THEY CARRYING ANYTHING?
NO, STAY WHERE YOU ARE. I'LL CALL YOU LATER.

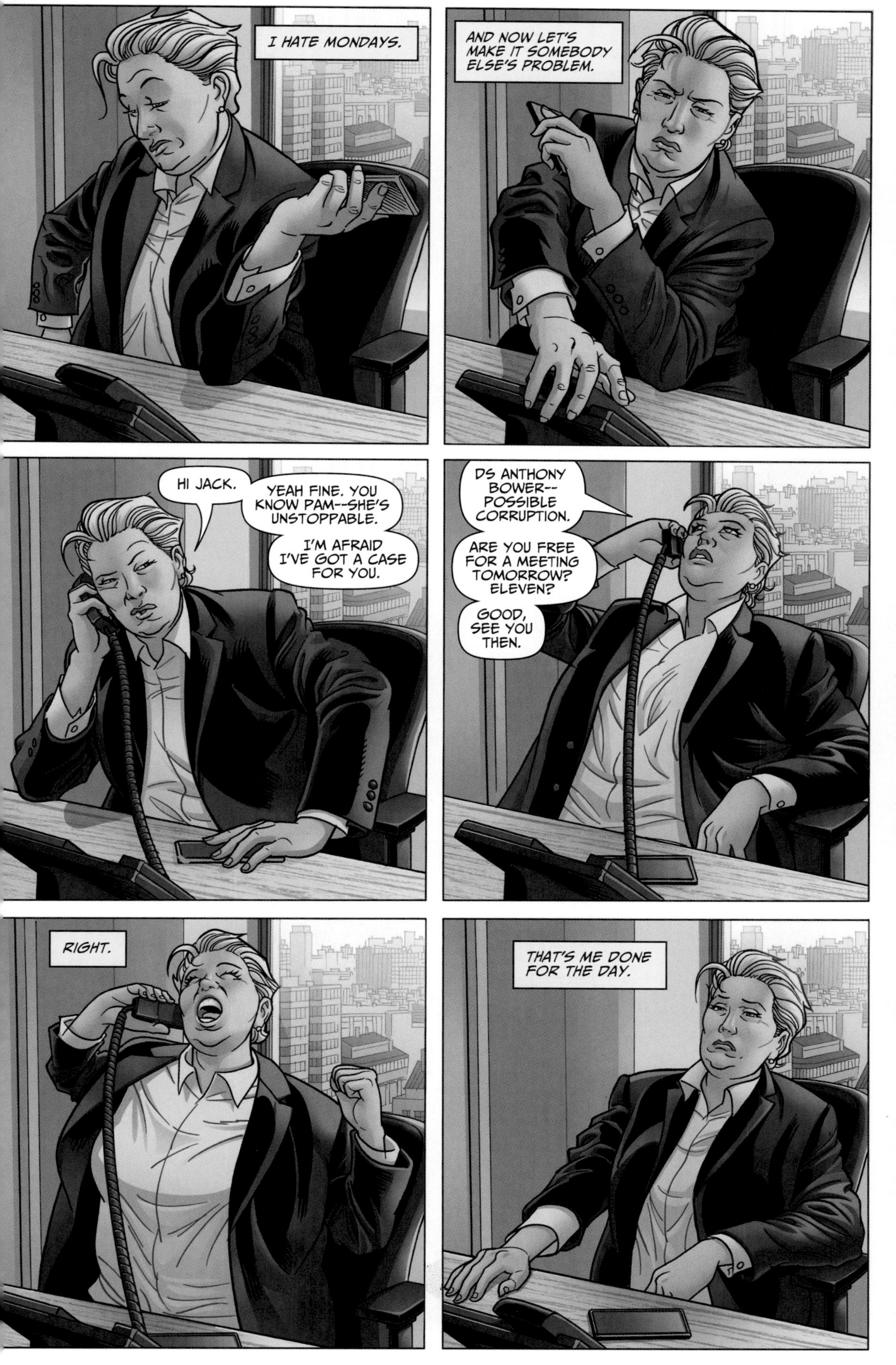
I HATE MONDAYS.
AND NOW LET'S MAKE IT SOMEBODY ELSE'S PROBLEM.
HI JACK.
YEAH FINE. YOU KNOW PAM--SHE'S UNSTOPPABLE.
I'M AFRAID I'VE GOT A CASE FOR YOU.
DS ANTHONY BOWER-- POSSIBLE CORRUPTION.
ARE YOU FREE FOR A MEETING TOMORROW? ELEVEN?
GOOD, SEE YOU THEN.
RIGHT.
THAT'S ME DONE FOR THE DAY.

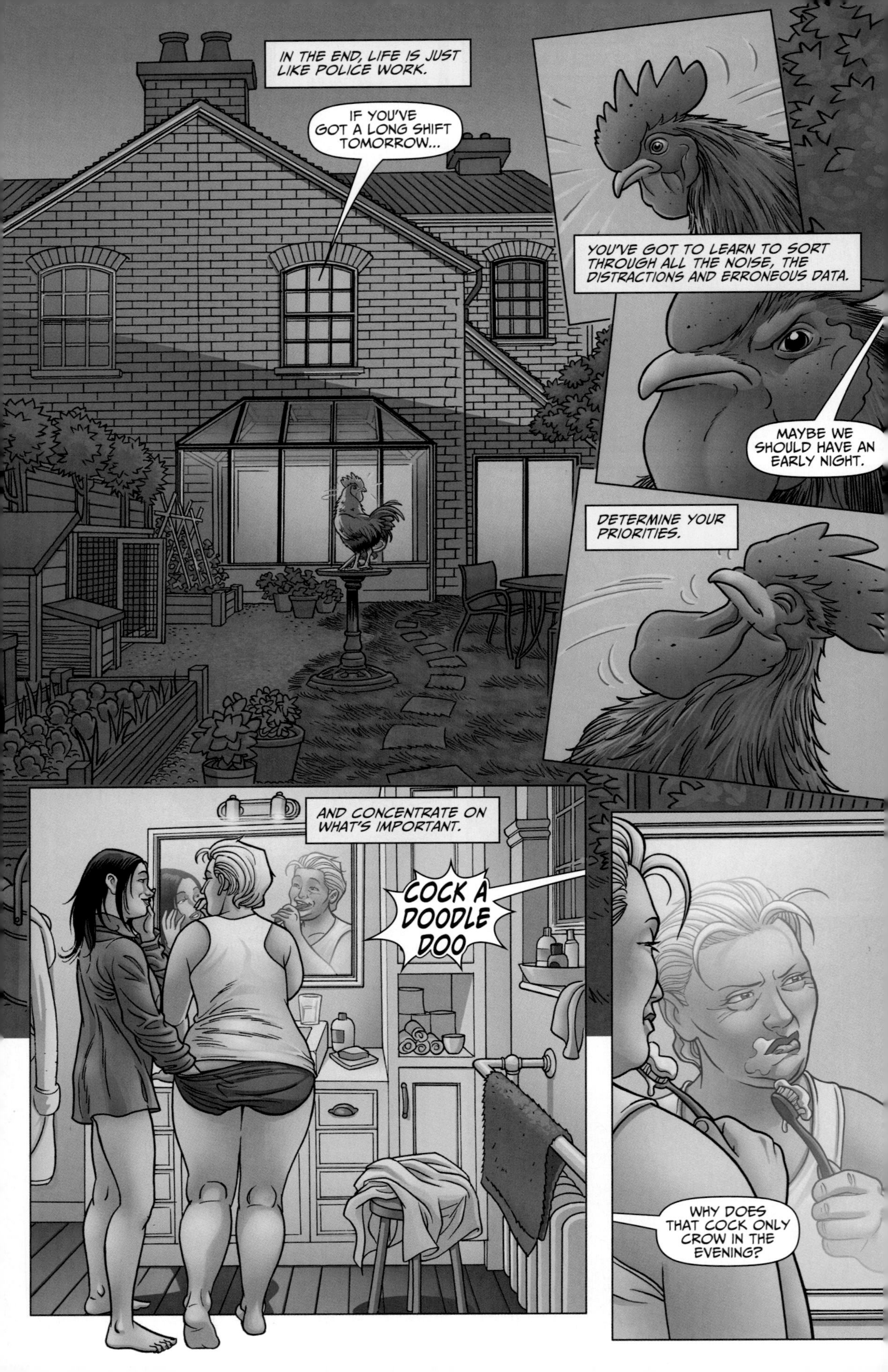
IN THE END, LIFE IS JUST LIKE POLICE WORK.
IF YOU'VE GOT A LONG SHIFT TOMORROW...
YOU'VE GOT TO LEARN TO SORT THROUGH ALL THE NOISE, THE DISTRACTIONS AND ERRONEOUS DATA.
MAYBE WE SHOULD HAVE AN EARLY NIGHT.
DETERMINE YOUR PRIORITIES.
AND CONCENTRATE ON WHAT'S IMPORTANT.
COCK A DOODLE DOO
WHY DOES THAT COCK ONLY CROW IN THE EVENING?

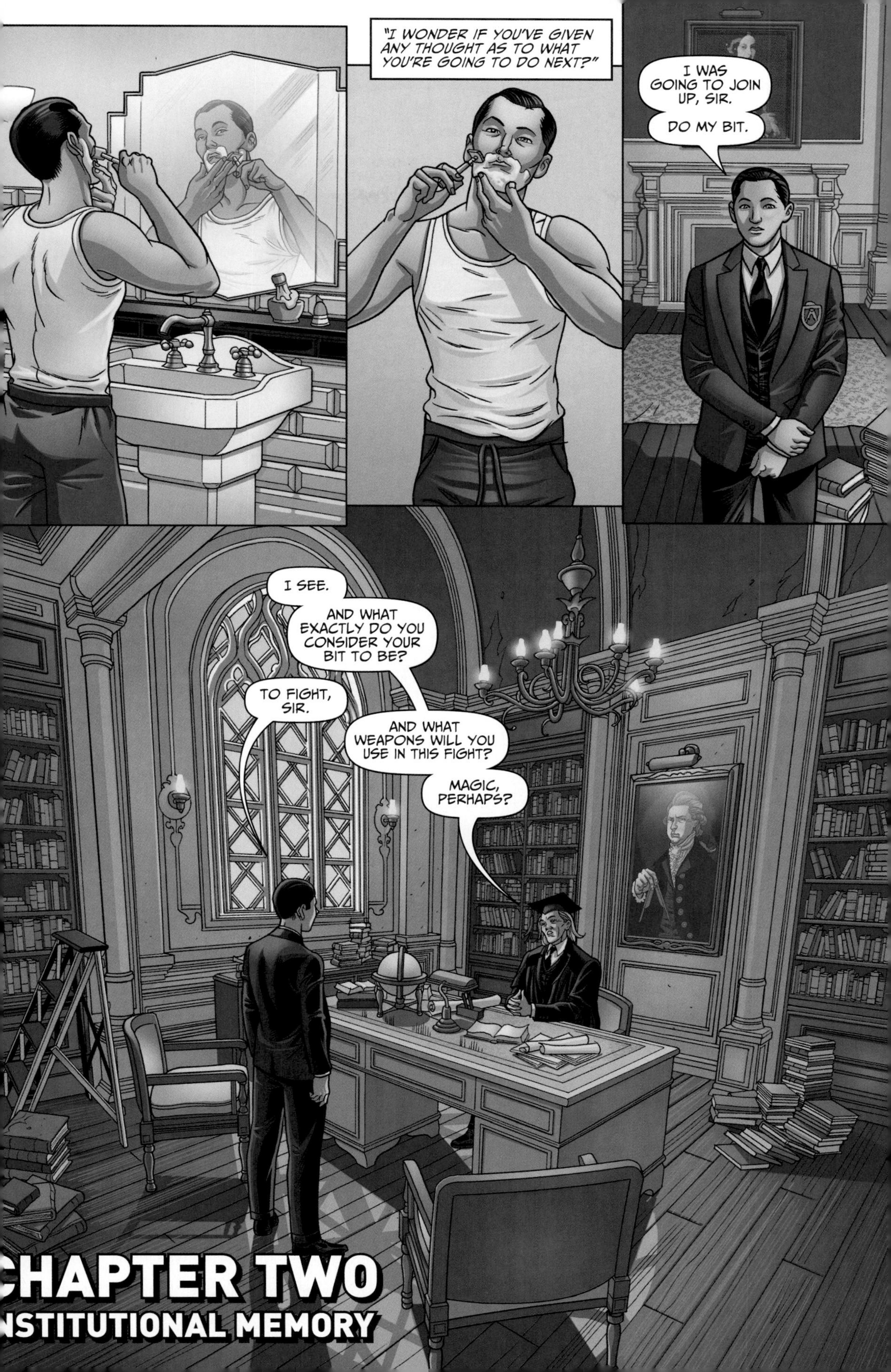
"I WONDER IF YOU'VE GIVEN ANY THOUGHT AS TO WHAT YOU'RE GOING TO DO NEXT?"
I WAS GOING TO JOIN UP, SIR.
DO MY BIT.
I SEE.
AND WHAT EXACTLY DO YOU CONSIDER YOUR BIT TO BE?
TO FIGHT, SIR.
AND WHAT WEAPONS WILL YOU USE IN THIS FIGHT?
MAGIC, PERHAPS?

CHAPTER TWO
INSTITUTIONAL MEMORY

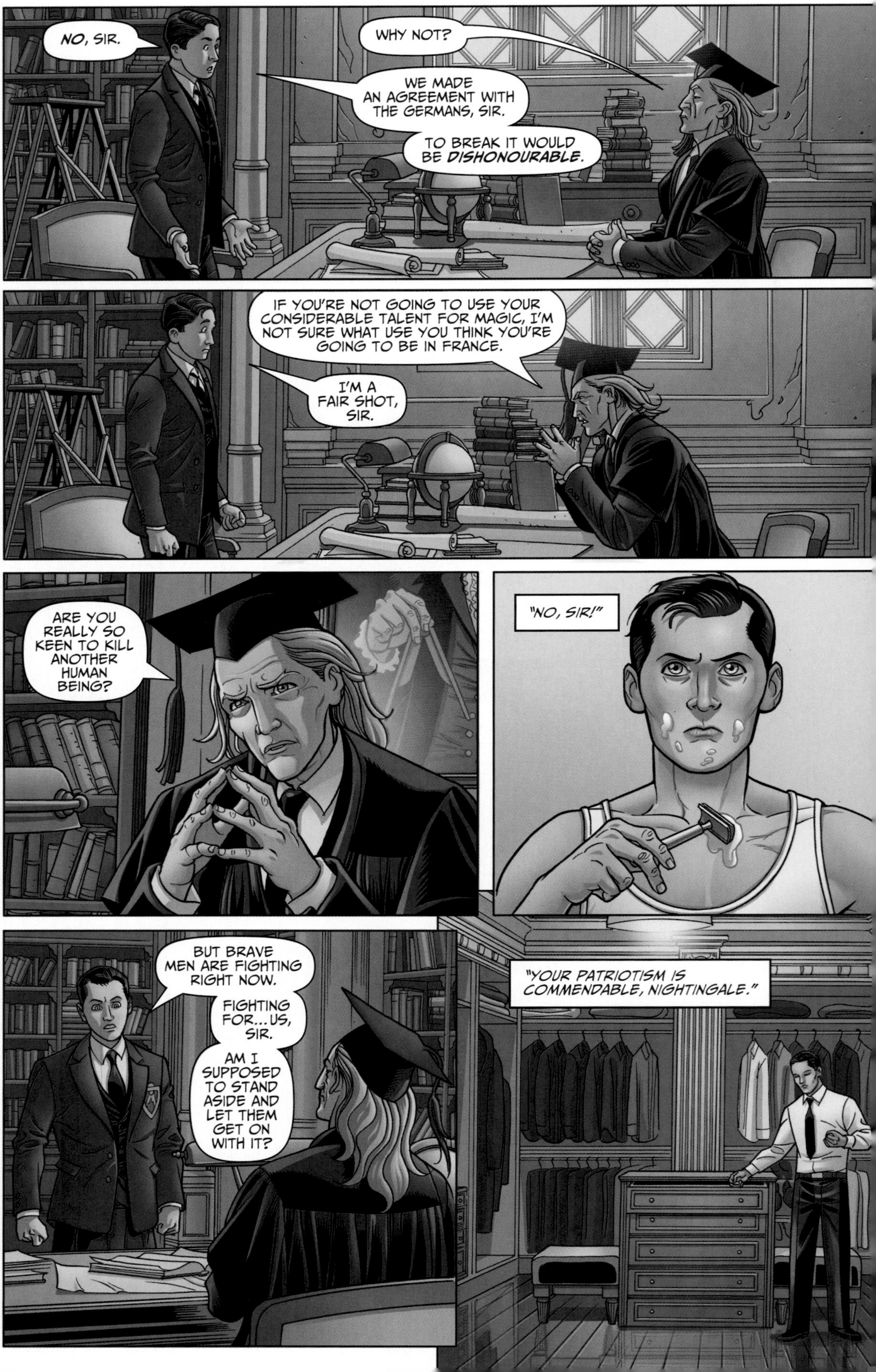

NO, SIR.
WHY NOT?
WE MADE AN AGREEMENT WITH THE GERMANS, SIR.
TO BREAK IT WOULD BE DISHONOURABLE.
IF YOU'RE NOT GOING TO USE YOUR CONSIDERABLE TALENT FOR MAGIC, I'M NOT SURE WHAT USE YOU THINK YOU'RE GOING TO BE IN FRANCE.
I'M A FAIR SHOT, SIR.
ARE YOU REALLY SO KEEN TO KILL ANOTHER HUMAN BEING?
"NO, SIR!"
BUT BRAVE MEN ARE FIGHTING RIGHT NOW.
FIGHTING FOR... US, SIR.
AM I SUPPOSED TO STAND ASIDE AND LET THEM GET ON WITH IT?
"YOUR PATRIOTISM IS COMMENDABLE, NIGHTINGALE."

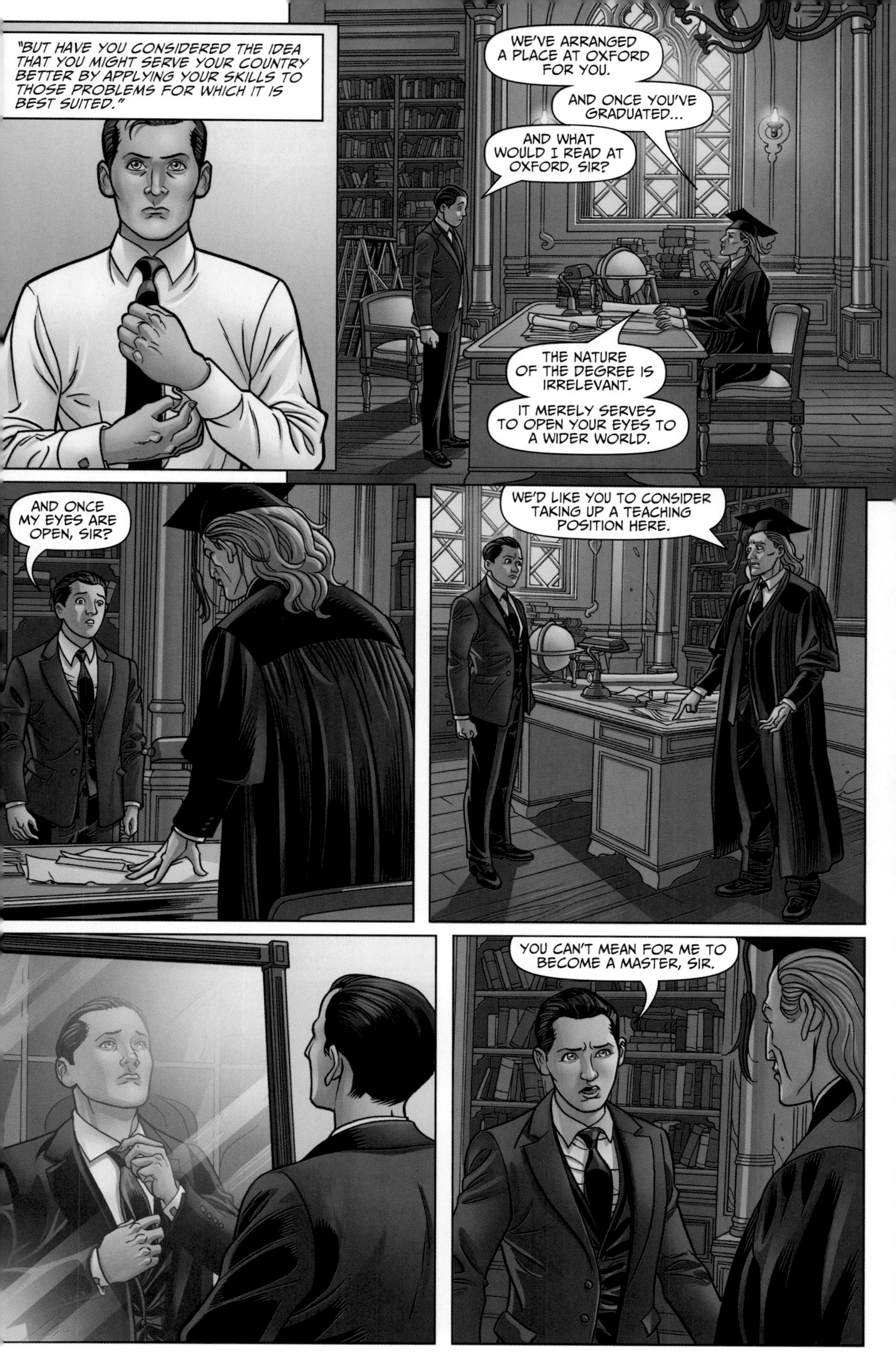
"BUT HAVE YOU CONSIDERED THE IDEA THAT YOU MIGHT SERVE YOUR COUNTRY BETTER BY APPLYING YOUR SKILLS TO THOSE PROBLEMS FOR WHICH IT IS BEST SUITED."
WE'VE ARRANGED A PLACE AT OXFORD FOR YOU.
AND ONCE YOU'VE GRADUATED...
AND WHAT WOULD I READ AT OXFORD, SIR?
THE NATURE OF THE DEGREE IS IRRELEVANT.
IT MERELY SERVES TO OPEN YOUR EYES TO A WIDER WORLD.
AND ONCE MY EYES ARE OPEN, SIR?
WE'D LIKE YOU TO CONSIDER TAKING UP A TEACHING POSITION HERE.
YOU CAN'T MEAN FOR ME TO BECOME A MASTER, SIR.

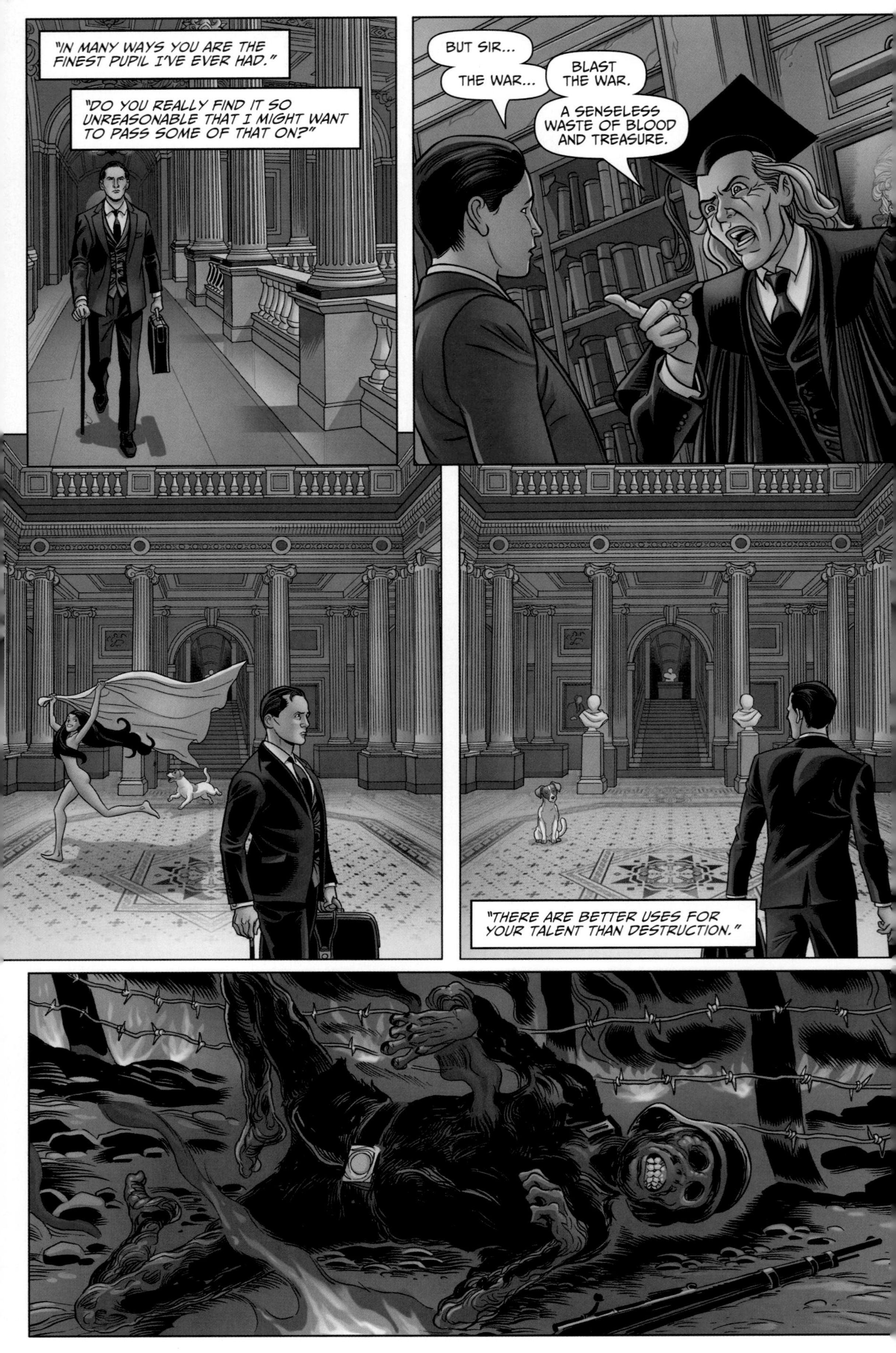
"IN MANY WAYS YOU ARE THE FINEST PUPIL I'VE EVER HAD."
"DO YOU REALLY FIND IT SO UNREASONABLE THAT I MIGHT WANT TO PASS SOME OF THAT ON?"
BUT SIR...
THE WAR...
BLAST THE WAR.
A SENSELESS WASTE OF BLOOD AND TREASURE.
"THERE ARE BETTER USES FOR YOUR TALENT THAN DESTRUCTION."

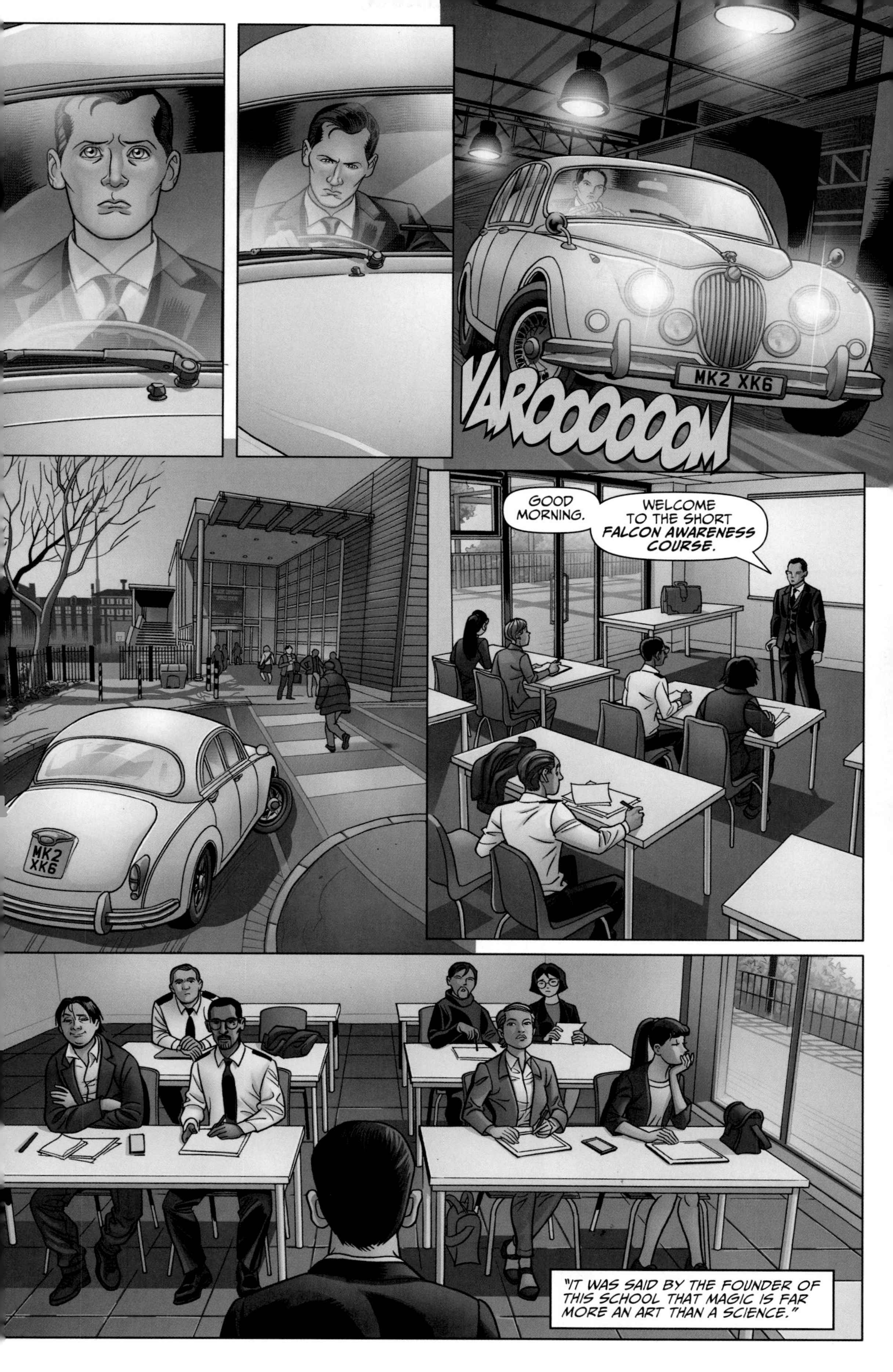
MK2 XK6
VAROOOOOOM
MK2 XK6
GOOD MORNING.
WELCOME TO THE SHORT *FALCON AWARENESS COURSE.*
"IT WAS SAID BY THE FOUNDER OF THIS SCHOOL THAT MAGIC IS FAR MORE AN ART THAN A SCIENCE."

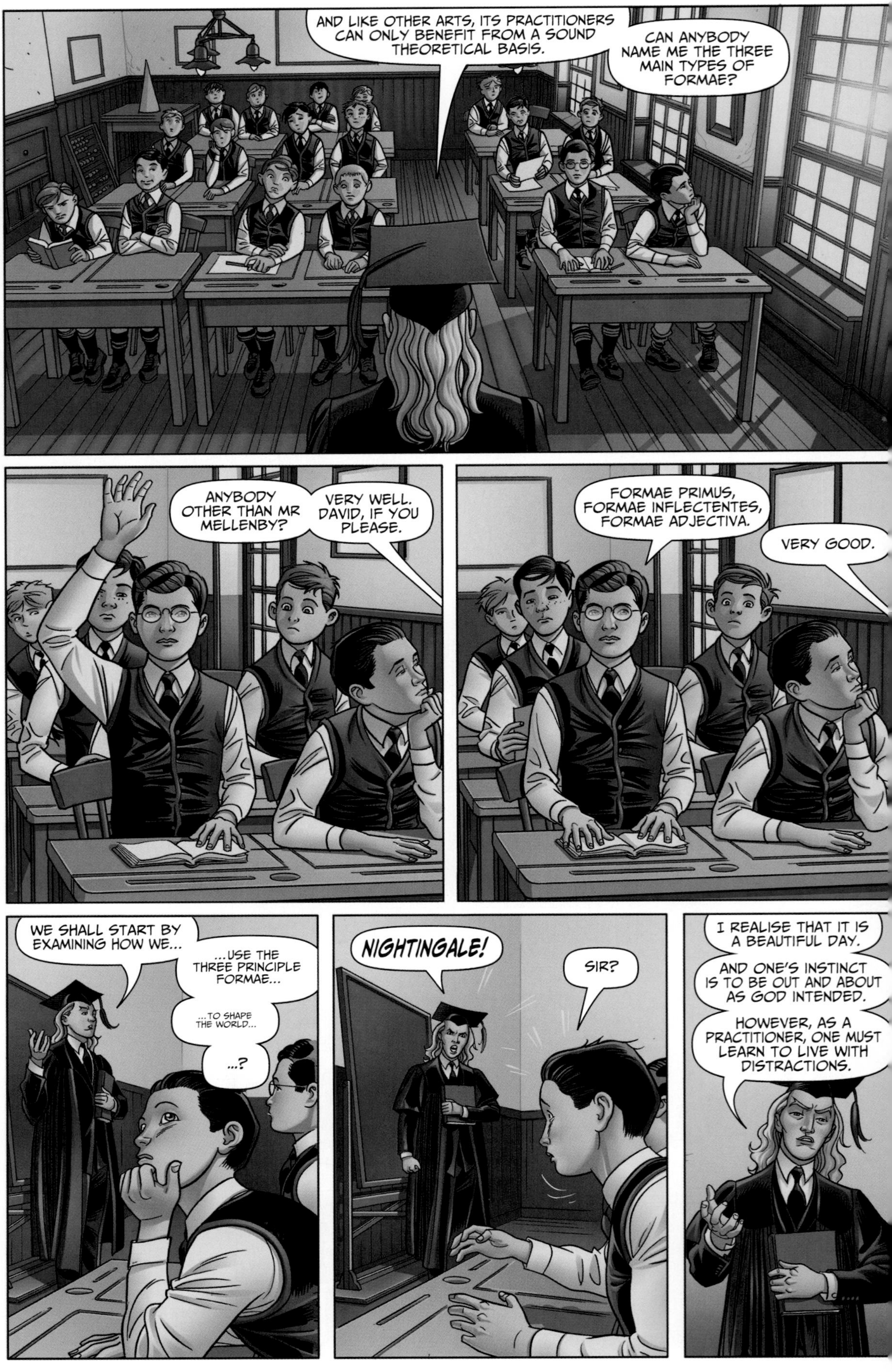
AND LIKE OTHER ARTS, ITS PRACTITIONERS CAN ONLY BENEFIT FROM A SOUND THEORETICAL BASIS.
CAN ANYBODY NAME ME THE THREE MAIN TYPES OF FORMAE?
ANYBODY OTHER THAN MR MELLENBY?
VERY WELL. DAVID, IF YOU PLEASE.
FORMAE PRIMUS, FORMAE INFLECTENTES, FORMAE ADJECTIVA.
VERY GOOD.
WE SHALL START BY EXAMINING HOW WE...
...USE THE THREE PRINCIPLE FORMAE...
...TO SHAPE THE WORLD...
...?
NIGHTINGALE!
SIR?
I REALISE THAT IT IS A BEAUTIFUL DAY.
AND ONE'S INSTINCT IS TO BE OUT AND ABOUT AS GOD INTENDED.
HOWEVER, AS A PRACTITIONER, ONE MUST LEARN TO LIVE WITH DISTRACTIONS.

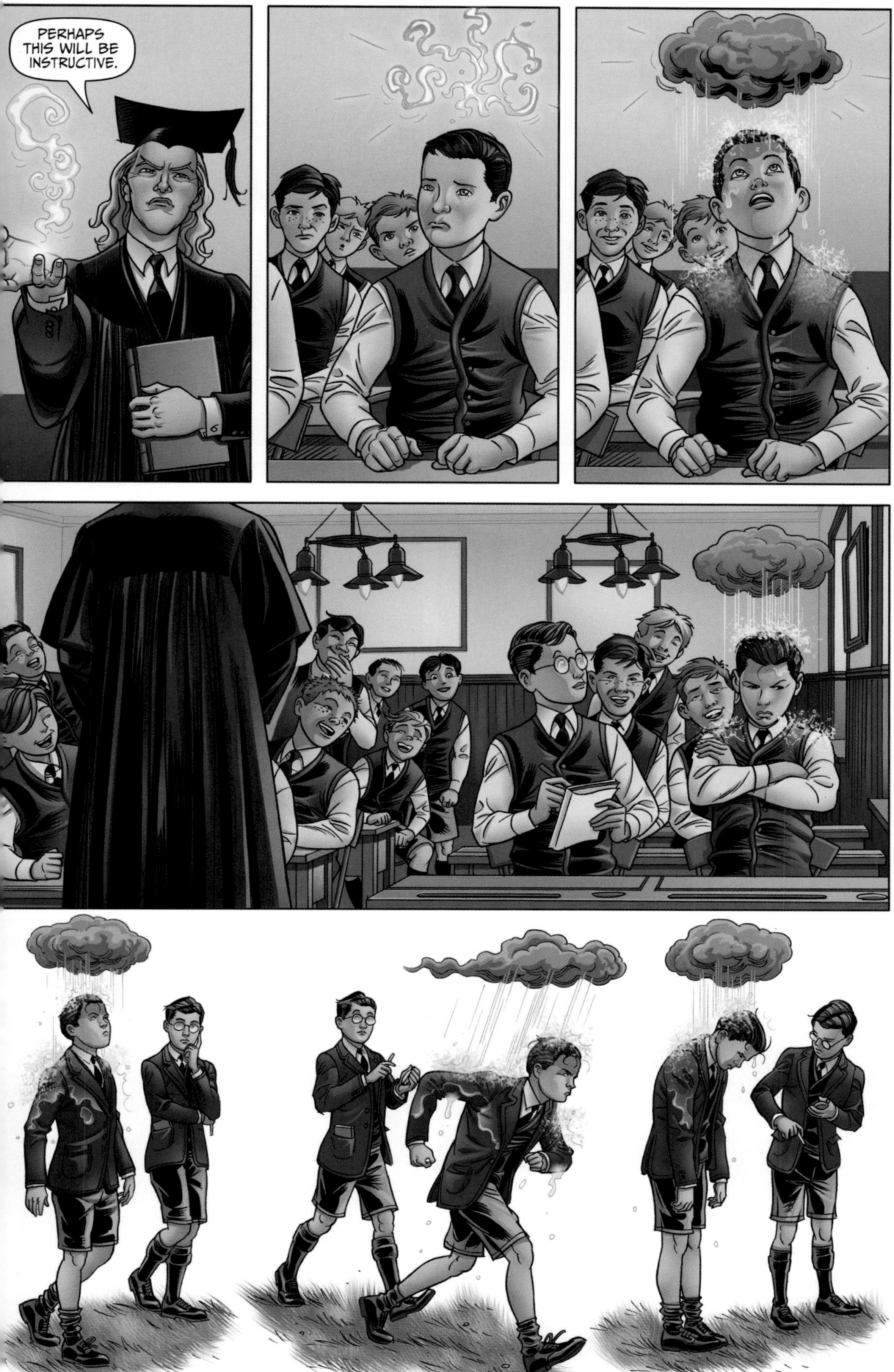
PERHAPS THIS WILL BE INSTRUCTIVE.

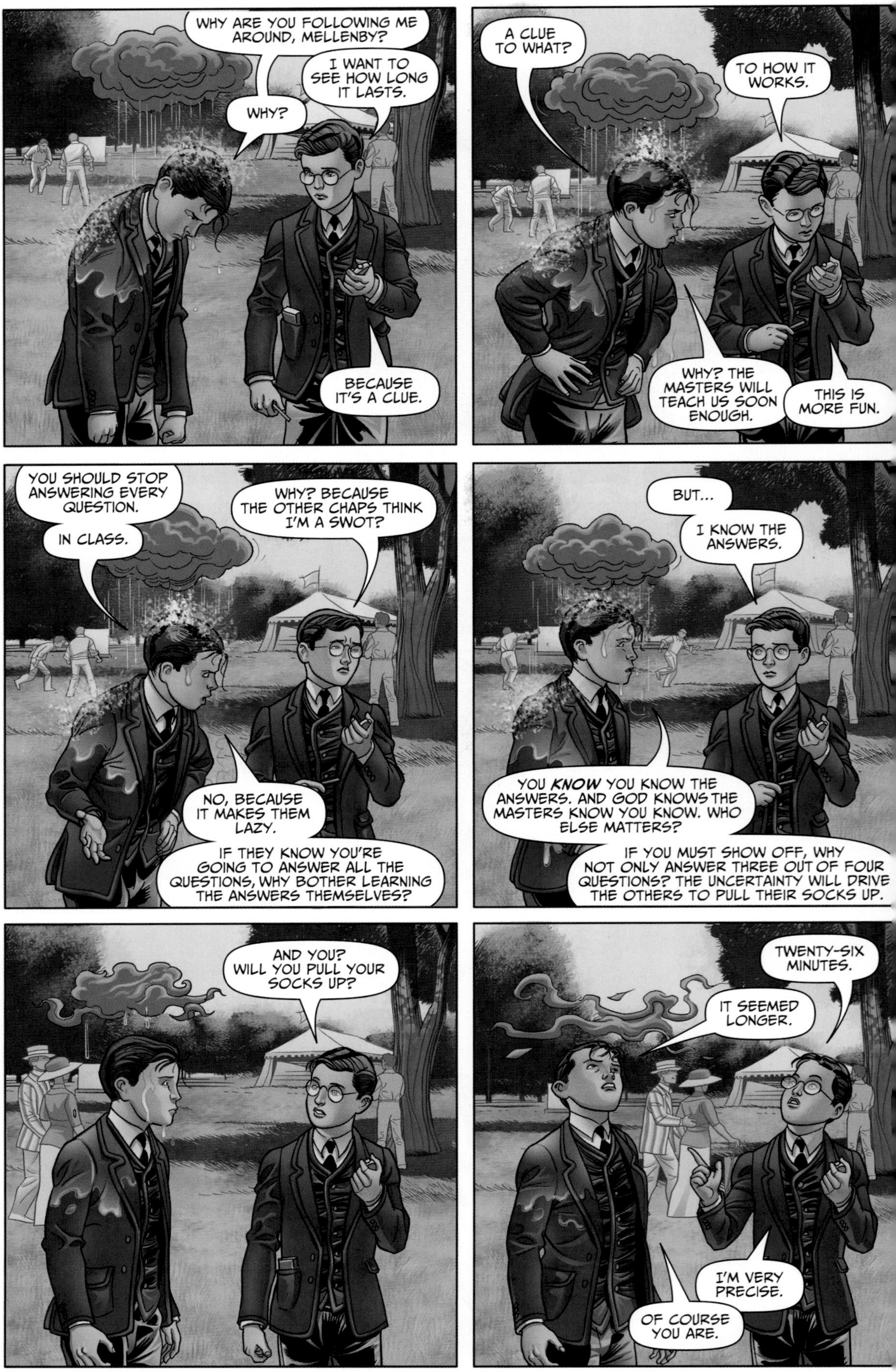
WHY ARE YOU FOLLOWING ME AROUND, MELLENBY?
I WANT TO SEE HOW LONG IT LASTS.
WHY?
BECAUSE IT'S A CLUE.
A CLUE TO WHAT?
TO HOW IT WORKS.
WHY? THE MASTERS WILL TEACH US SOON ENOUGH.
THIS IS MORE FUN.
YOU SHOULD STOP ANSWERING EVERY QUESTION.
IN CLASS.
WHY? BECAUSE THE OTHER CHAPS THINK I'M A SWOT?
NO, BECAUSE IT MAKES THEM LAZY.
IF THEY KNOW YOU'RE GOING TO ANSWER ALL THE QUESTIONS, WHY BOTHER LEARNING THE ANSWERS THEMSELVES?
BUT...
I KNOW THE ANSWERS.
YOU *KNOW* YOU KNOW THE ANSWERS. AND GOD KNOWS THE MASTERS KNOW YOU KNOW. WHO ELSE MATTERS?
IF YOU MUST SHOW OFF, WHY NOT ONLY ANSWER THREE OUT OF FOUR QUESTIONS? THE UNCERTAINTY WILL DRIVE THE OTHERS TO PULL THEIR SOCKS UP.
AND YOU? WILL YOU PULL YOUR SOCKS UP?
TWENTY-SIX MINUTES.
IT SEEMED LONGER.
I'M VERY PRECISE.
OF COURSE YOU ARE.

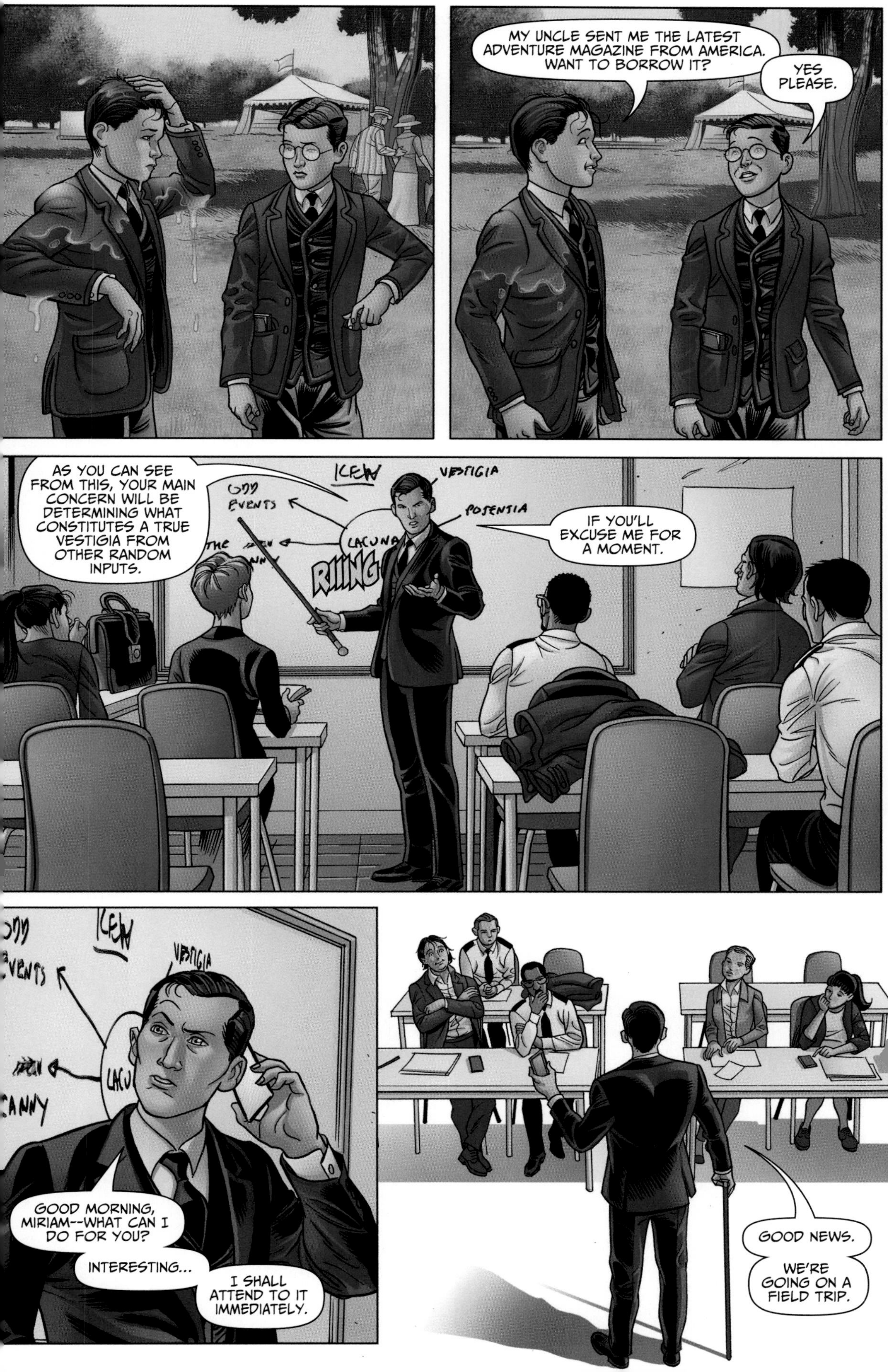
MY UNCLE SENT ME THE LATEST ADVENTURE MAGAZINE FROM AMERICA. WANT TO BORROW IT?
YES PLEASE.
AS YOU CAN SEE FROM THIS, YOUR MAIN CONCERN WILL BE DETERMINING WHAT CONSTITUTES A TRUE VESTIGIA FROM OTHER RANDOM INPUTS.
KEW
VESTIGIA
LACUNA
RIIING
IF YOU'LL EXCUSE ME FOR A MOMENT.
GOOD MORNING, MIRIAM--WHAT CAN I DO FOR YOU?
INTERESTING...
I SHALL ATTEND TO IT IMMEDIATELY.
GOOD NEWS.
WE'RE GOING ON A FIELD TRIP.

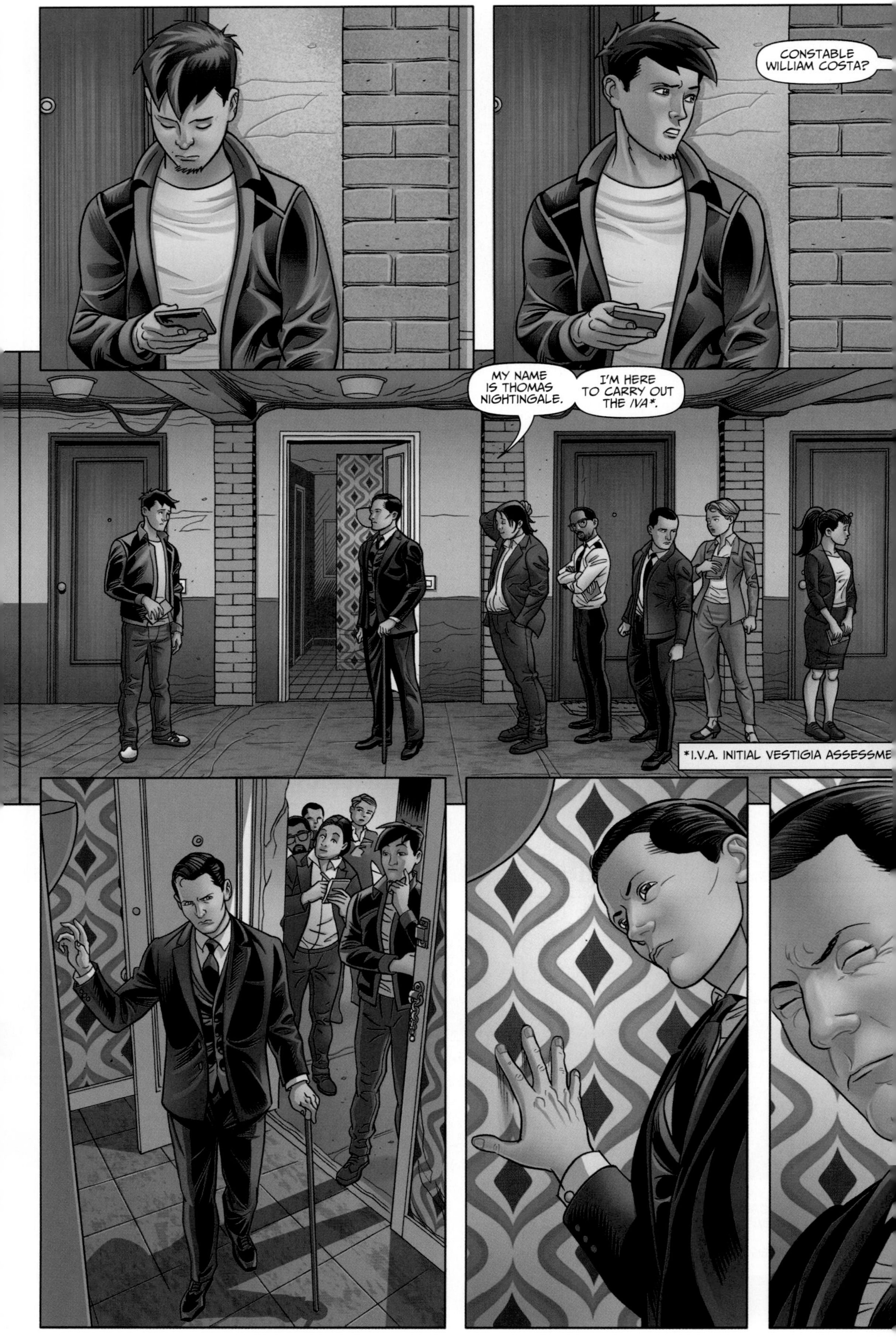
CONSTABLE WILLIAM COSTA?
MY NAME IS THOMAS NIGHTINGALE.
I'M HERE TO CARRY OUT THE IVA*.
*I.V.A. INITIAL VESTIGIA ASSESSME

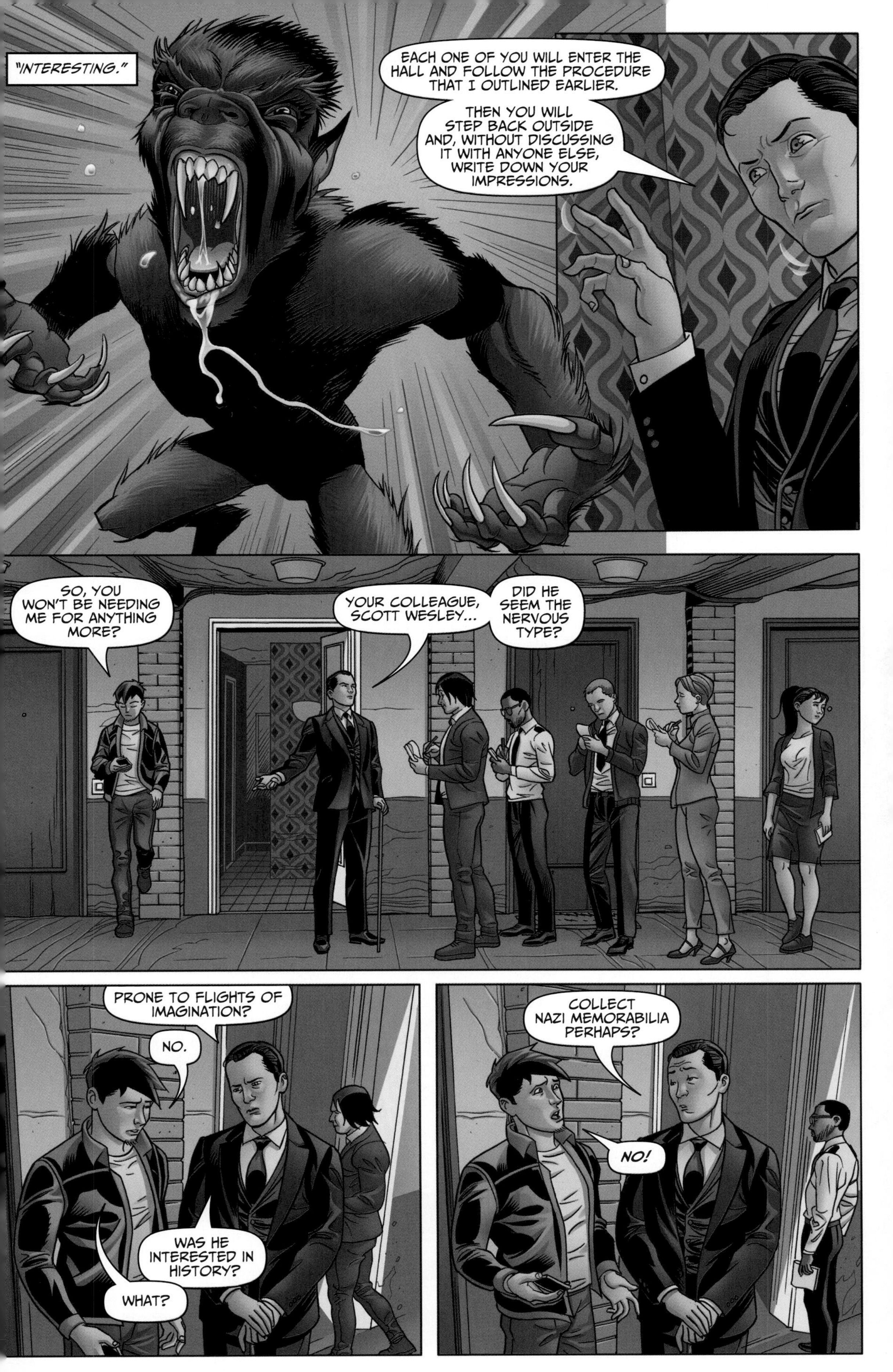
"INTERESTING."
EACH ONE OF YOU WILL ENTER THE HALL AND FOLLOW THE PROCEDURE THAT I OUTLINED EARLIER.
THEN YOU WILL STEP BACK OUTSIDE AND, WITHOUT DISCUSSING IT WITH ANYONE ELSE, WRITE DOWN YOUR IMPRESSIONS.
SO, YOU WON'T BE NEEDING ME FOR ANYTHING MORE?
YOUR COLLEAGUE, SCOTT WESLEY...
DID HE SEEM THE NERVOUS TYPE?
PRONE TO FLIGHTS OF IMAGINATION?
NO.
WAS HE INTERESTED IN HISTORY?
WHAT?
COLLECT NAZI MEMORABILIA PERHAPS?
NO!

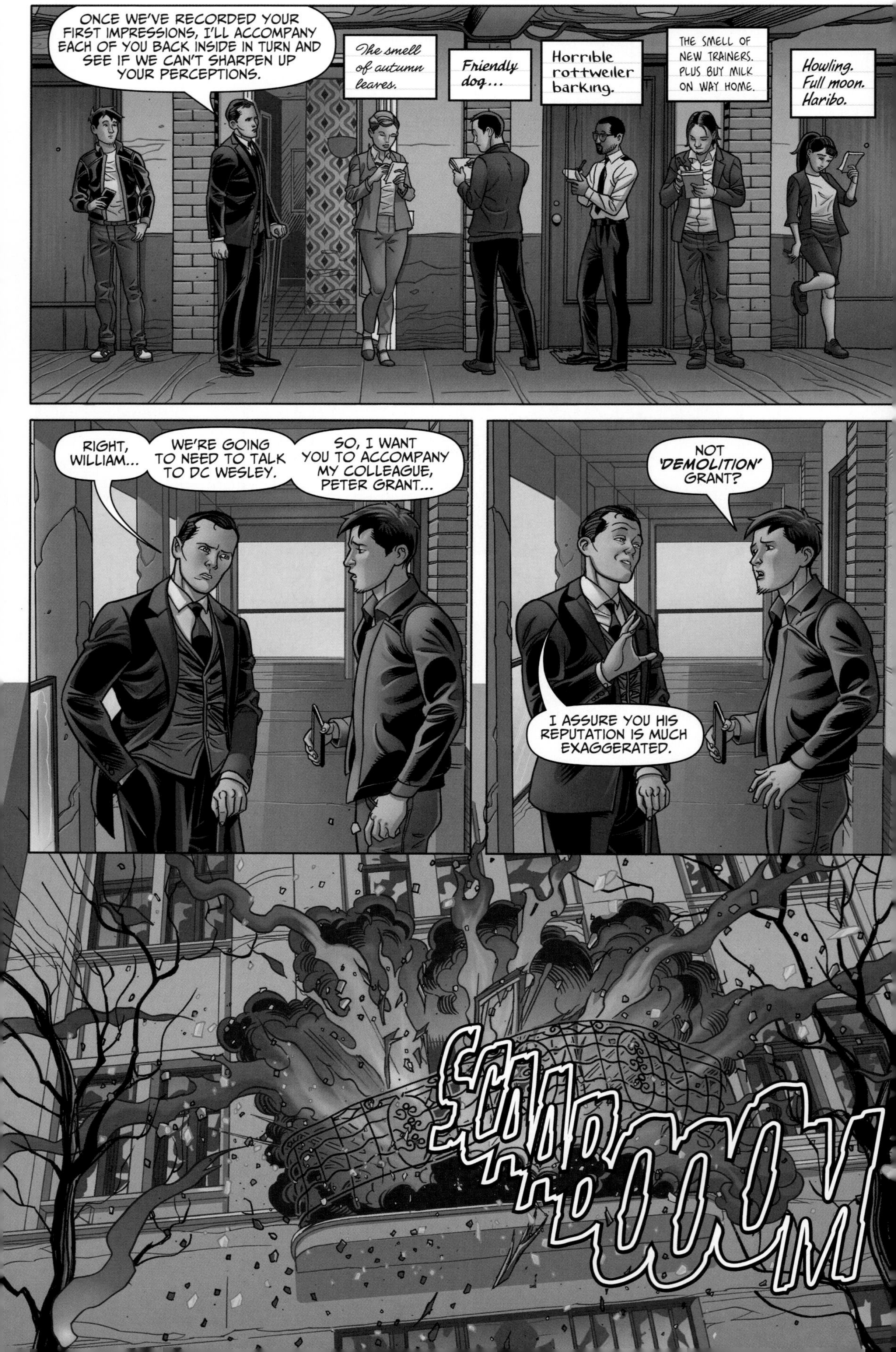

ONCE WE'VE RECORDED YOUR FIRST IMPRESSIONS, I'LL ACCOMPANY EACH OF YOU BACK INSIDE IN TURN AND SEE IF WE CAN'T SHARPEN UP YOUR PERCEPTIONS.
The smell of autumn leaves.
Friendly dog...
Horrible rottweiler barking.
THE SMELL OF NEW TRAINERS. PLUS BUY MILK ON WAY HOME.
Howling. Full moon. Haribo.
RIGHT, WILLIAM...
WE'RE GOING TO NEED TO TALK TO DC WESLEY.
SO, I WANT YOU TO ACCOMPANY MY COLLEAGUE, PETER GRANT...
NOT 'DEMOLITION' GRANT?
I ASSURE YOU HIS REPUTATION IS MUCH EXAGGERATED.
SCHHBOOOOM

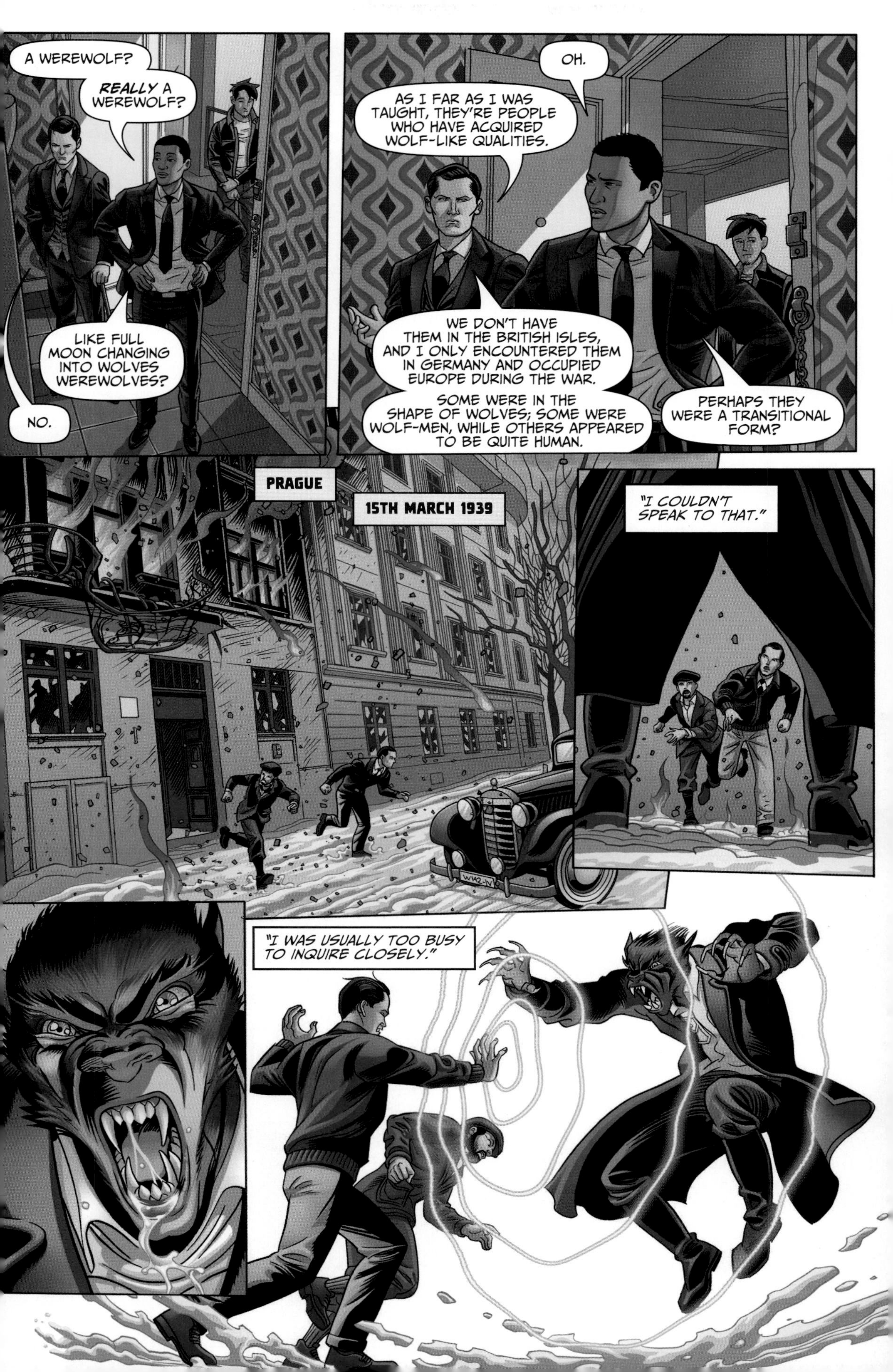
A WEREWOLF?
REALLY A WEREWOLF?
LIKE FULL MOON CHANGING INTO WOLVES WEREWOLVES?
NO.
OH.
AS I FAR AS I WAS TAUGHT, THEY'RE PEOPLE WHO HAVE ACQUIRED WOLF-LIKE QUALITIES.
WE DON'T HAVE THEM IN THE BRITISH ISLES, AND I ONLY ENCOUNTERED THEM IN GERMANY AND OCCUPIED EUROPE DURING THE WAR.
SOME WERE IN THE SHAPE OF WOLVES; SOME WERE WOLF-MEN, WHILE OTHERS APPEARED TO BE QUITE HUMAN.
PERHAPS THEY WERE A TRANSITIONAL FORM?
PRAGUE
15TH MARCH 1939
W142-IV
"I COULDN'T SPEAK TO THAT."
"I WAS USUALLY TOO BUSY TO INQUIRE CLOSELY."

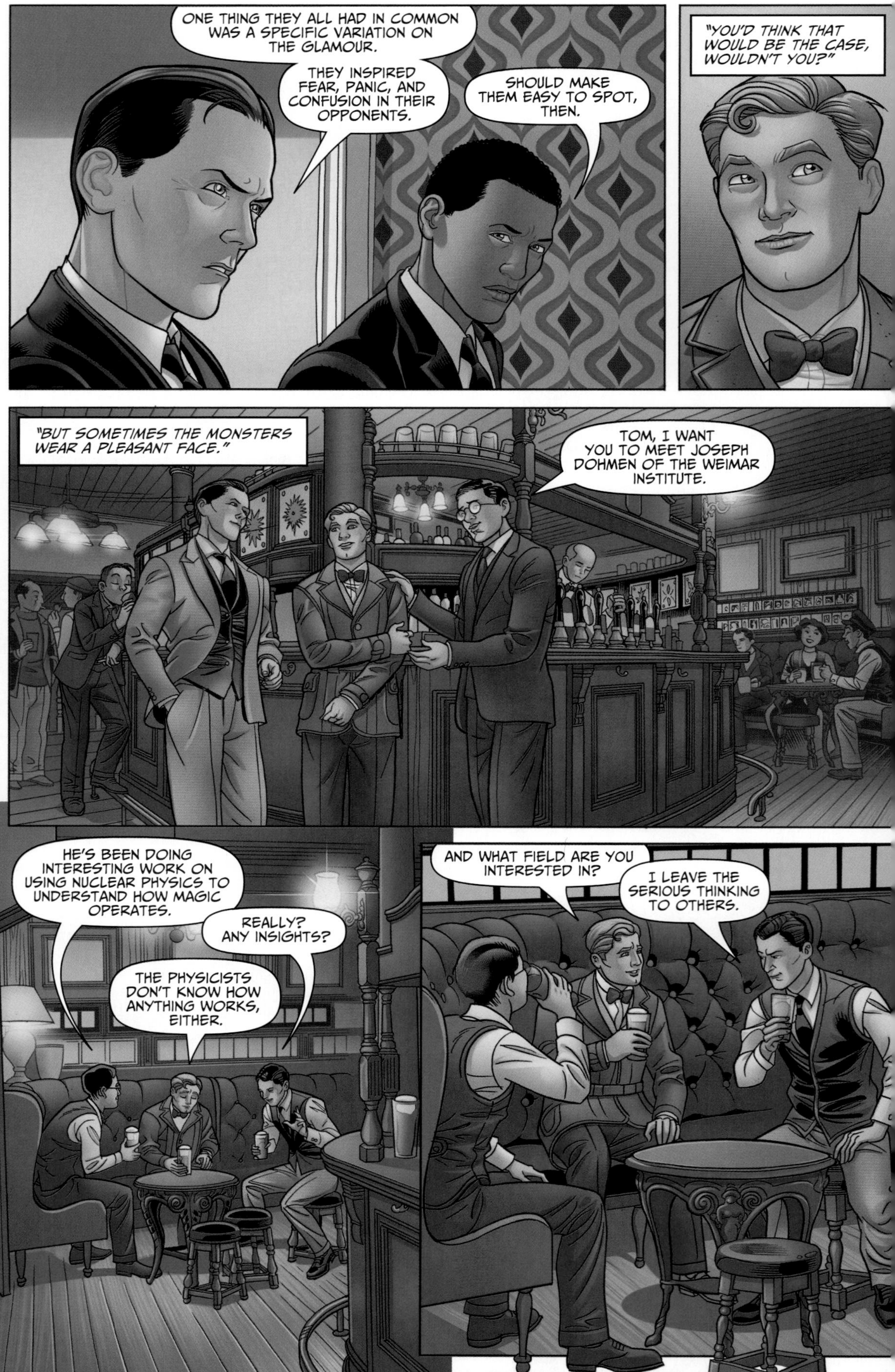
ONE THING THEY ALL HAD IN COMMON WAS A SPECIFIC VARIATION ON THE GLAMOUR.
THEY INSPIRED FEAR, PANIC, AND CONFUSION IN THEIR OPPONENTS.
SHOULD MAKE THEM EASY TO SPOT, THEN.
"YOU'D THINK THAT WOULD BE THE CASE, WOULDN'T YOU?"
"BUT SOMETIMES THE MONSTERS WEAR A PLEASANT FACE."
TOM, I WANT YOU TO MEET JOSEPH DOHMEN OF THE WEIMAR INSTITUTE.
HE'S BEEN DOING INTERESTING WORK ON USING NUCLEAR PHYSICS TO UNDERSTAND HOW MAGIC OPERATES.
REALLY? ANY INSIGHTS?
THE PHYSICISTS DON'T KNOW HOW ANYTHING WORKS, EITHER.
AND WHAT FIELD ARE YOU INTERESTED IN?
I LEAVE THE SERIOUS THINKING TO OTHERS.

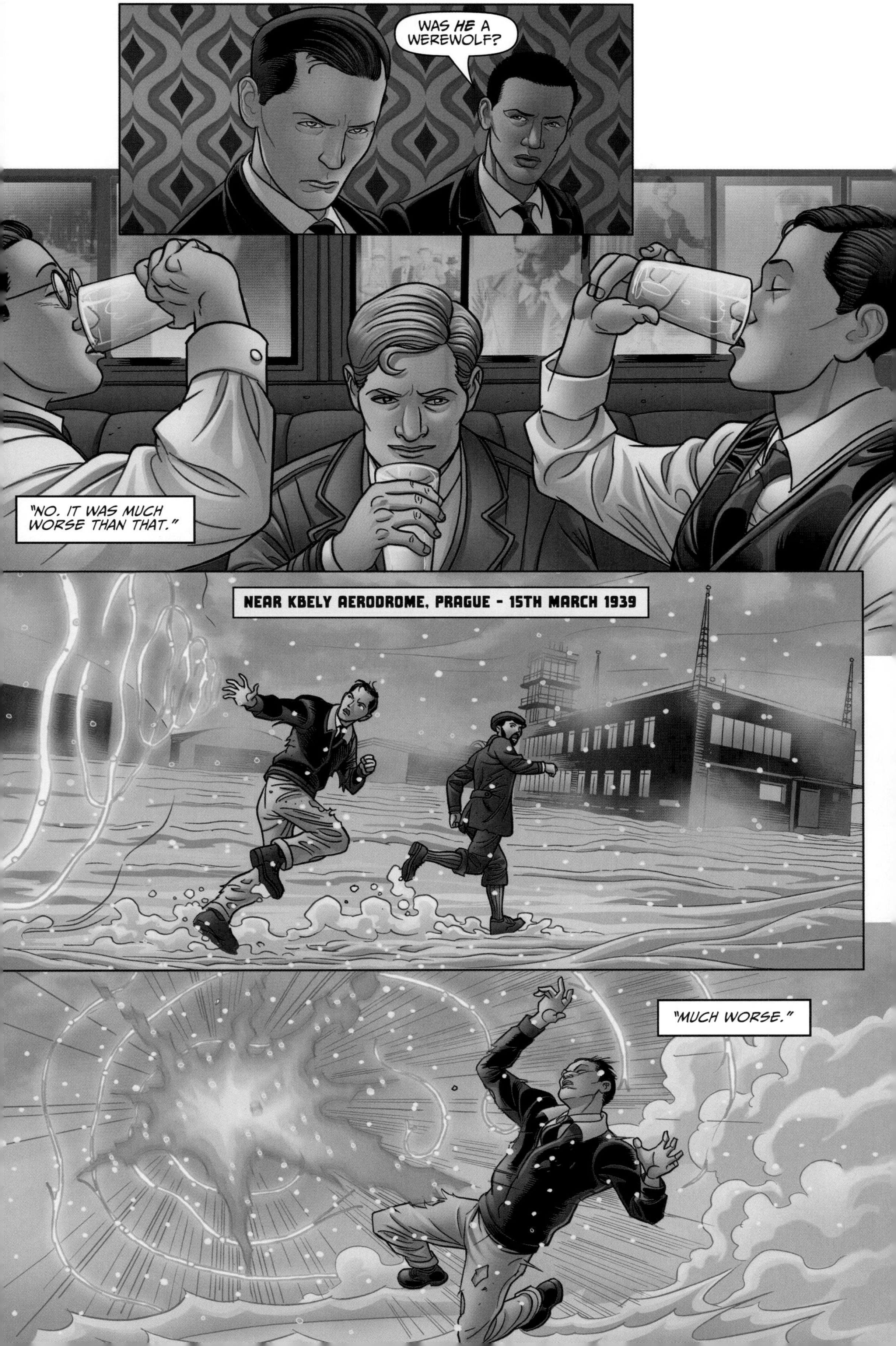
WAS HE A WEREWOLF?
"NO. IT WAS MUCH WORSE THAN THAT."
NEAR KBELY AERODROME, PRAGUE - 15TH MARCH 1939
"MUCH WORSE."

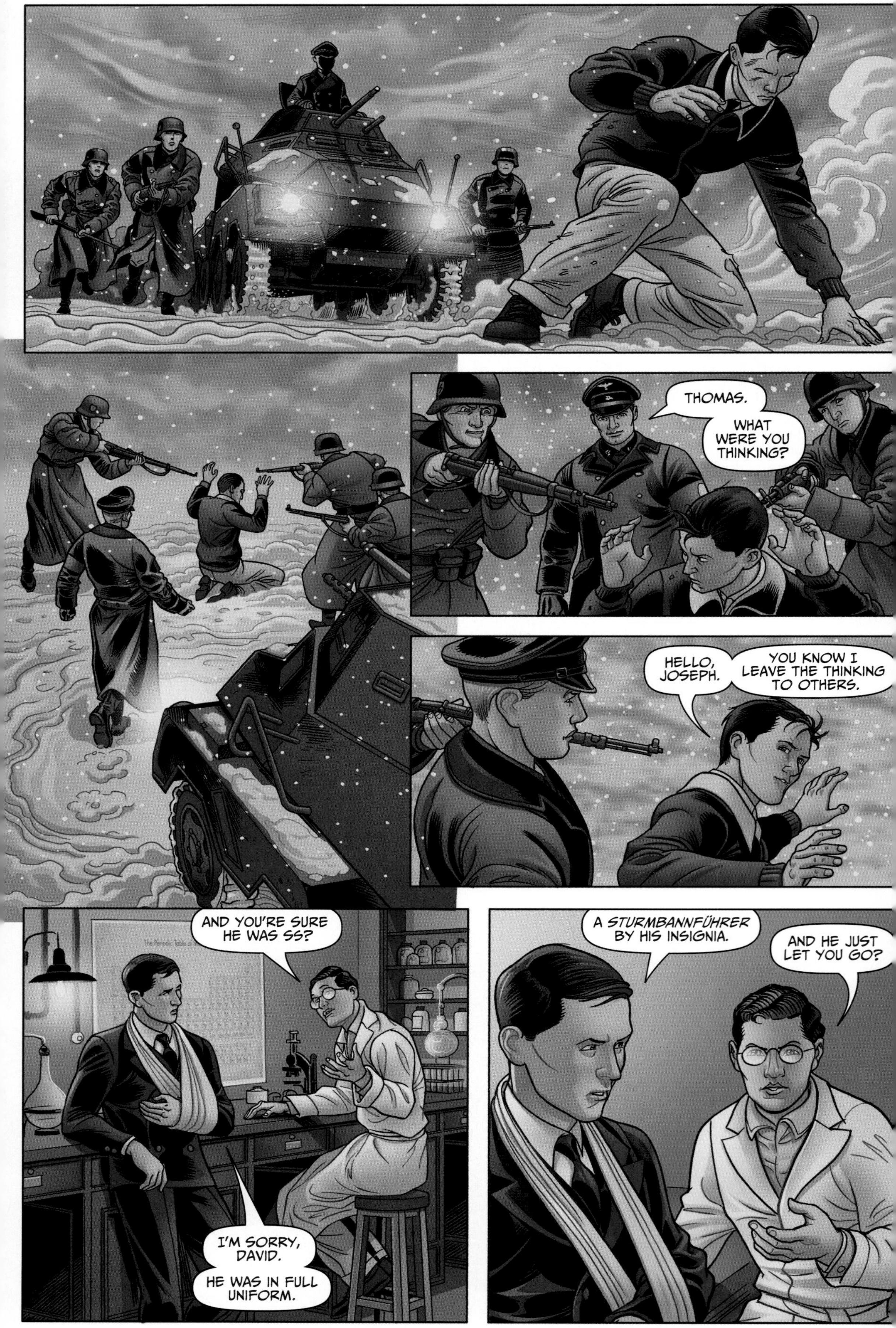
THOMAS.
WHAT WERE YOU THINKING?
HELLO, JOSEPH.
YOU KNOW I LEAVE THE THINKING TO OTHERS.
AND YOU'RE SURE HE WAS SS?
I'M SORRY, DAVID.
HE WAS IN FULL UNIFORM.
A *STURMBANNFÜHRER* BY HIS INSIGNIA.
AND HE JUST LET YOU GO?

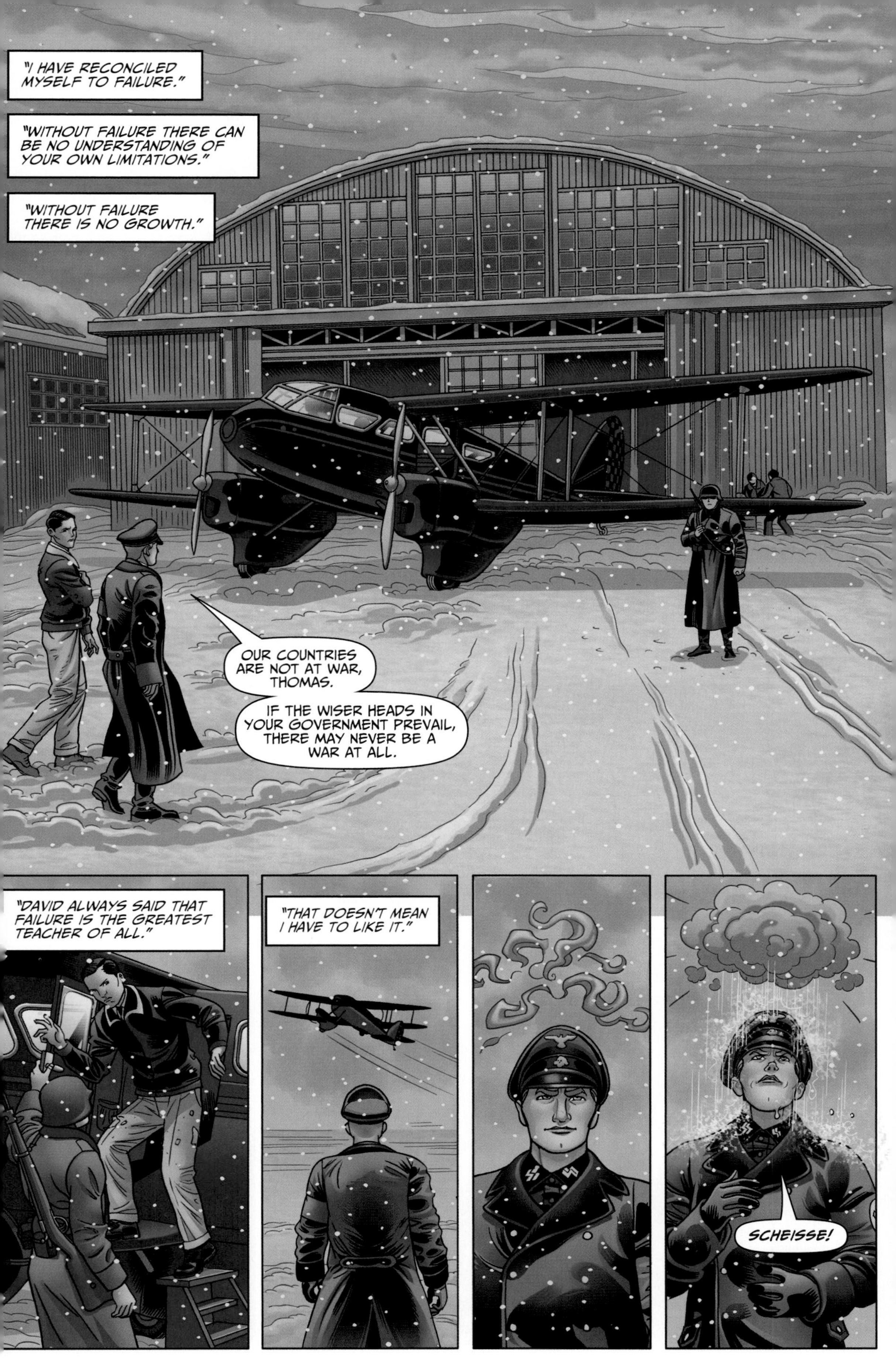
"I HAVE RECONCILED MYSELF TO FAILURE."
"WITHOUT FAILURE THERE CAN BE NO UNDERSTANDING OF YOUR OWN LIMITATIONS."
"WITHOUT FAILURE THERE IS NO GROWTH."
OUR COUNTRIES ARE NOT AT WAR, THOMAS.
IF THE WISER HEADS IN YOUR GOVERNMENT PREVAIL, THERE MAY NEVER BE A WAR AT ALL.
"DAVID ALWAYS SAID THAT FAILURE IS THE GREATEST TEACHER OF ALL."
"THAT DOESN'T MEAN I HAVE TO LIKE IT."
SCHEISSE!

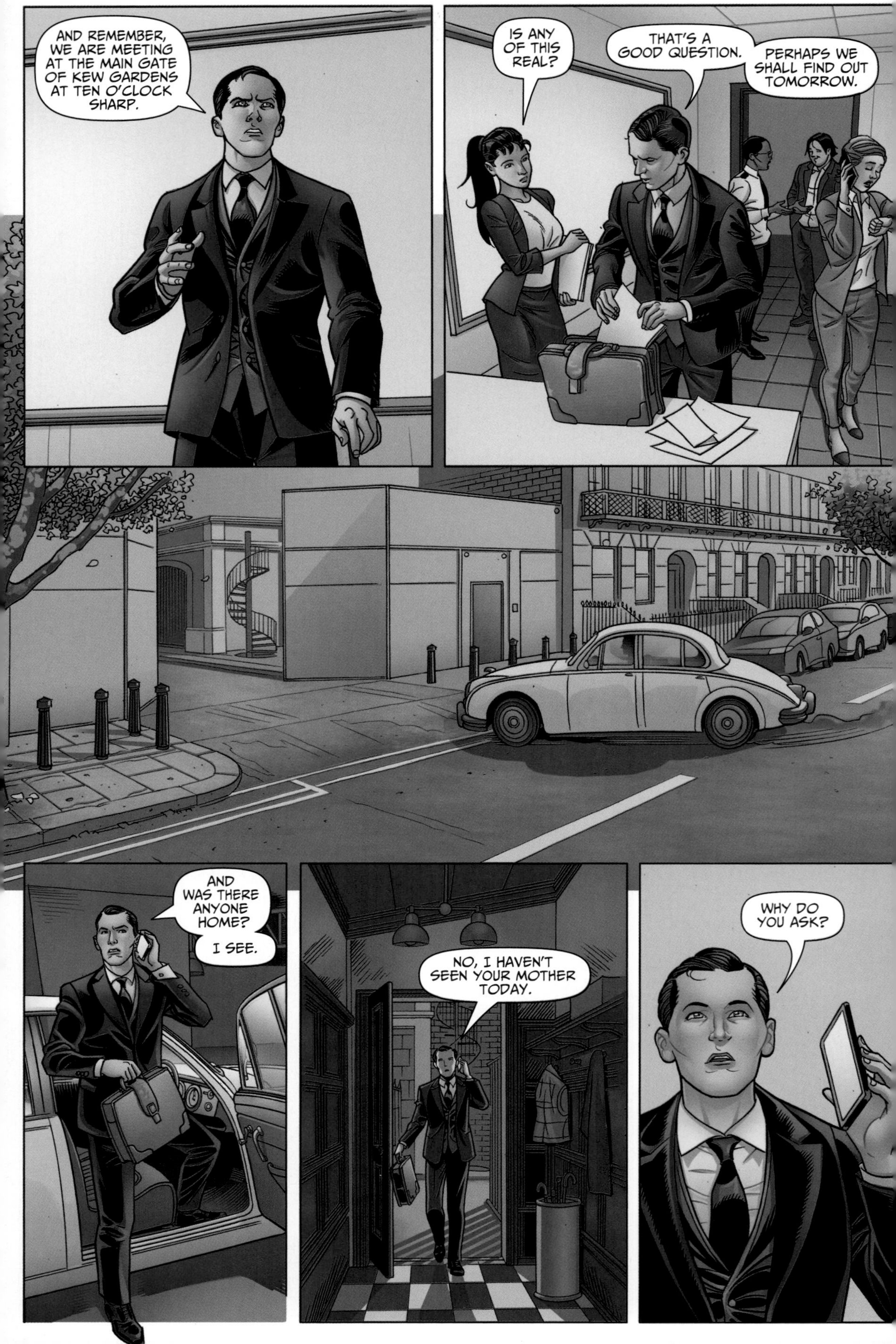
AND REMEMBER, WE ARE MEETING AT THE MAIN GATE OF KEW GARDENS AT TEN O'CLOCK SHARP.
IS ANY OF THIS REAL?
THAT'S A GOOD QUESTION.
PERHAPS WE SHALL FIND OUT TOMORROW.
AND WAS THERE ANYONE HOME?
I SEE.
NO, I HAVEN'T SEEN YOUR MOTHER TODAY.
WHY DO YOU ASK?

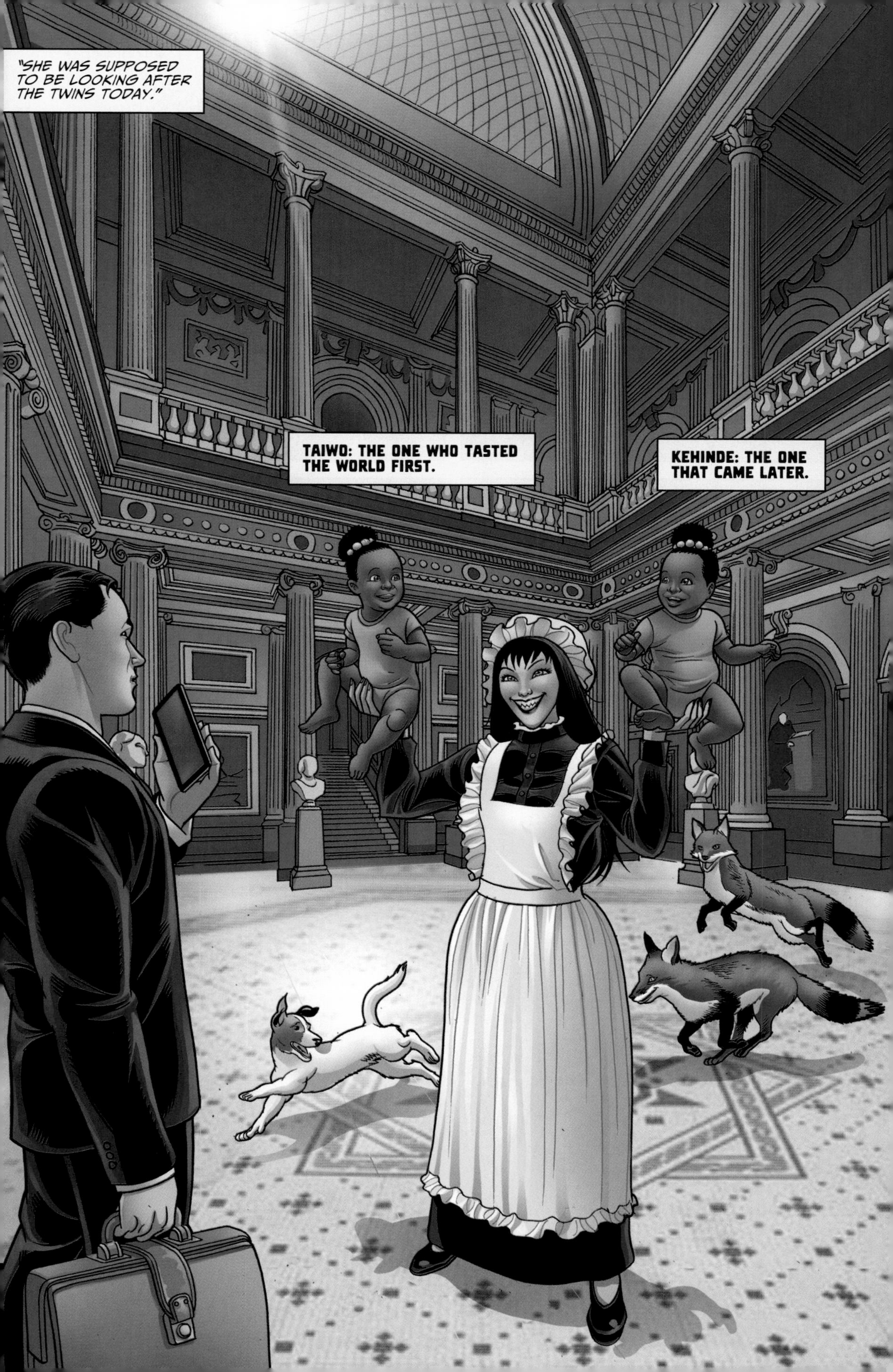
"SHE WAS SUPPOSED TO BE LOOKING AFTER THE TWINS TODAY."
TAIWO: THE ONE WHO TASTED THE WORLD FIRST.
KEHINDE: THE ONE THAT CAME LATER.

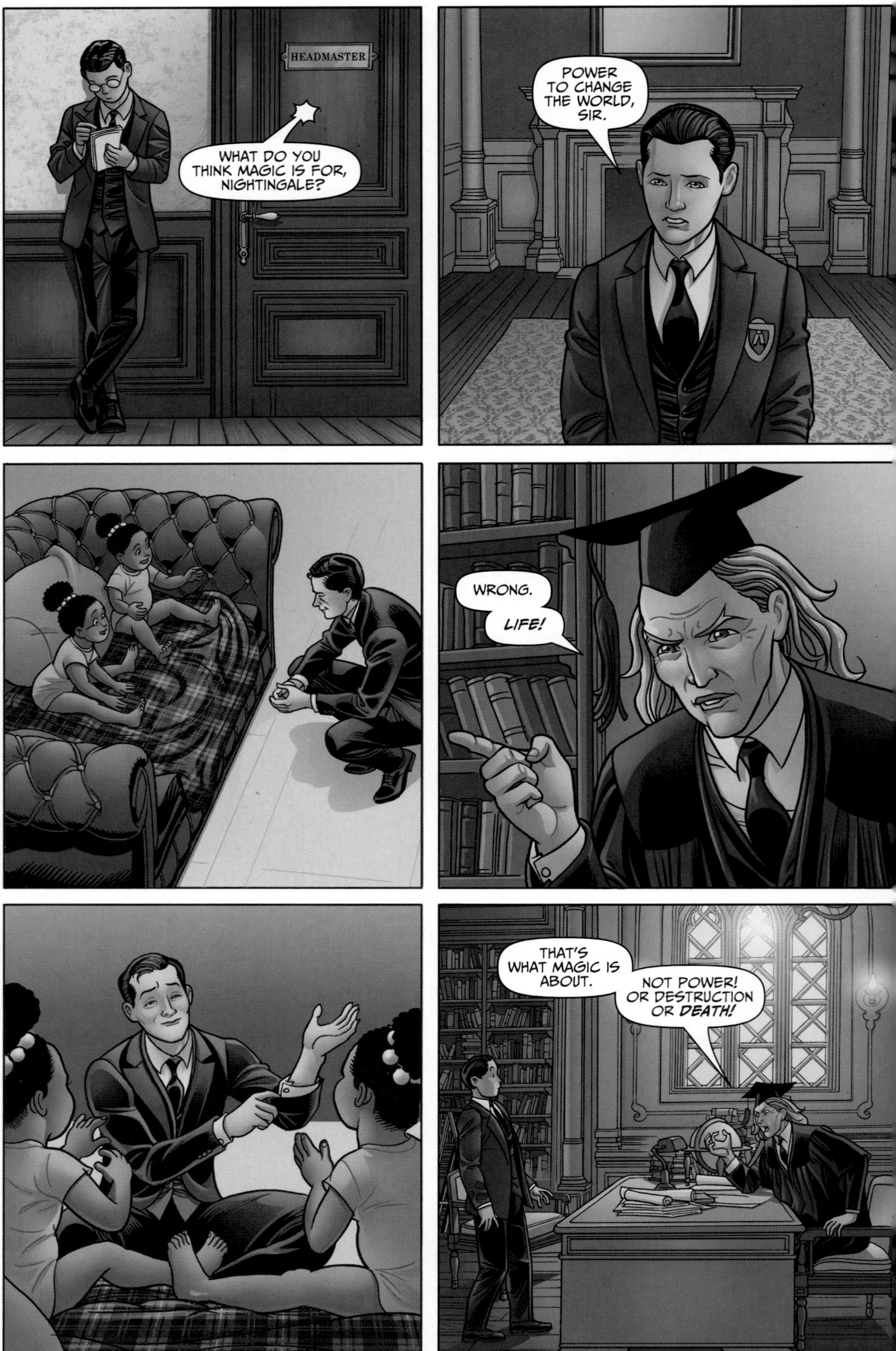
HEADMASTER
WHAT DO YOU THINK MAGIC IS FOR, NIGHTINGALE?
POWER TO CHANGE THE WORLD, SIR.
WRONG.
LIFE!
THAT'S WHAT MAGIC IS ABOUT.
NOT POWER! OR DESTRUCTION OR DEATH!

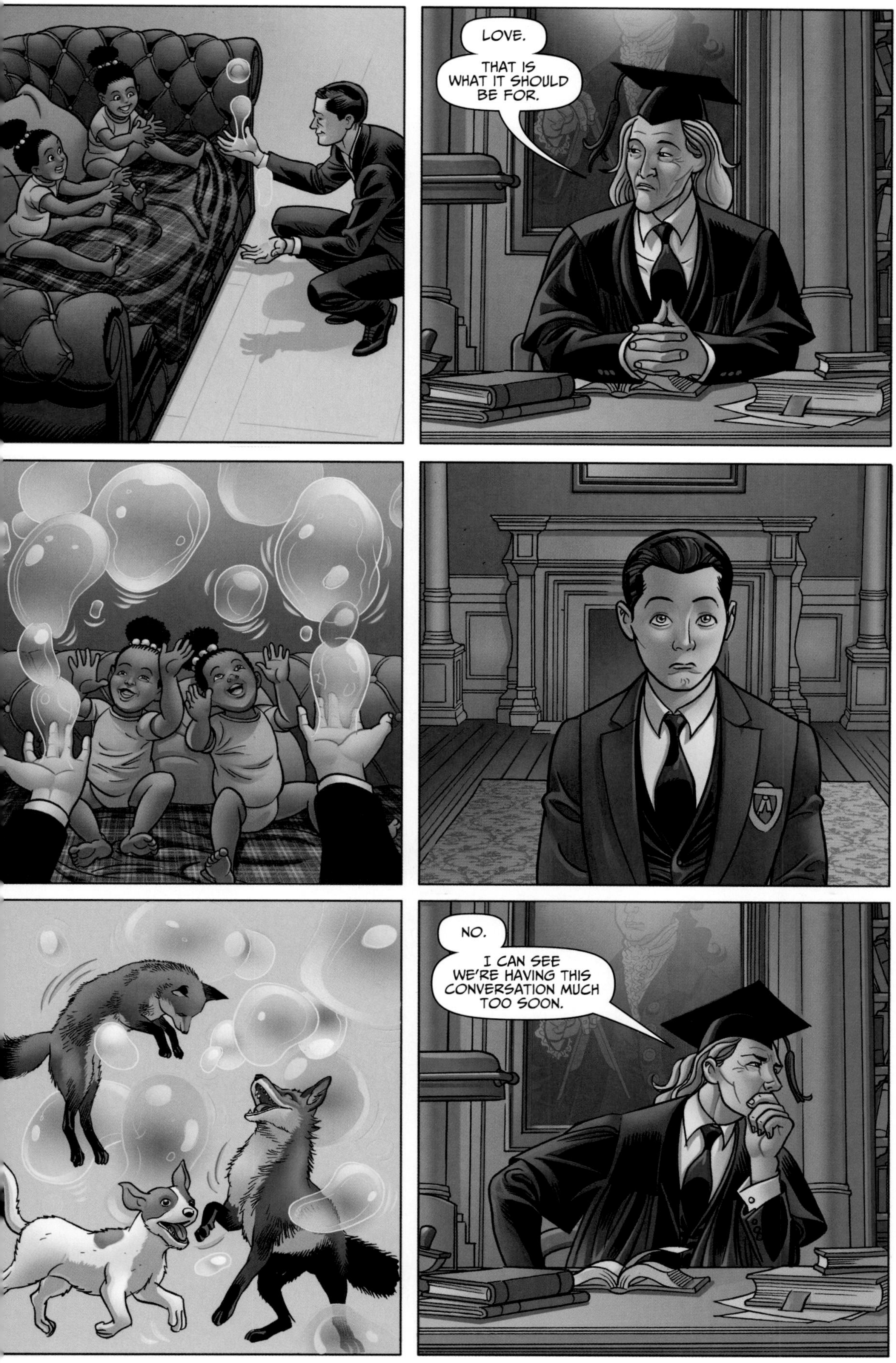
LOVE.
THAT IS WHAT IT SHOULD BE FOR.
NO.
I CAN SEE WE'RE HAVING THIS CONVERSATION MUCH TOO SOON.

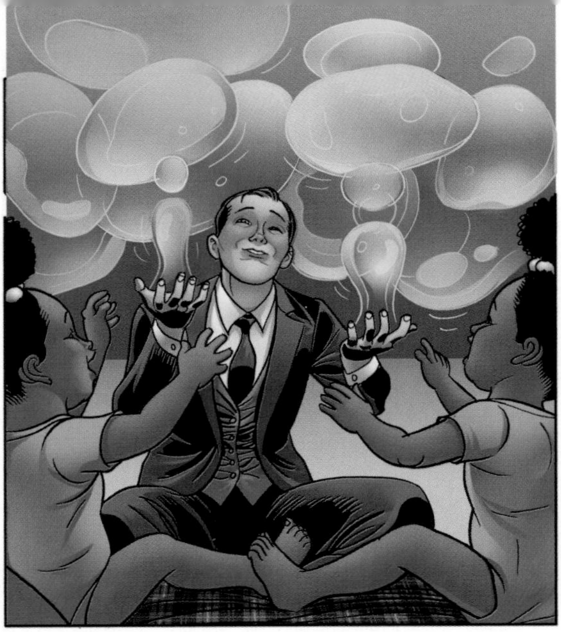

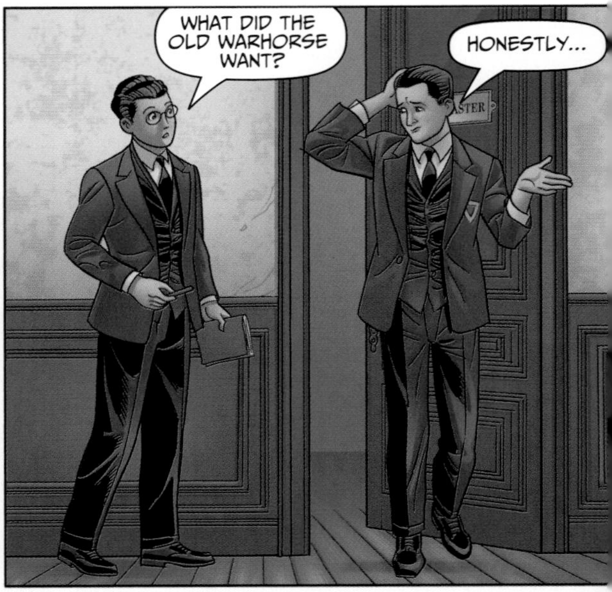
WHAT DID THE OLD WARHORSE WANT?
HONESTLY...

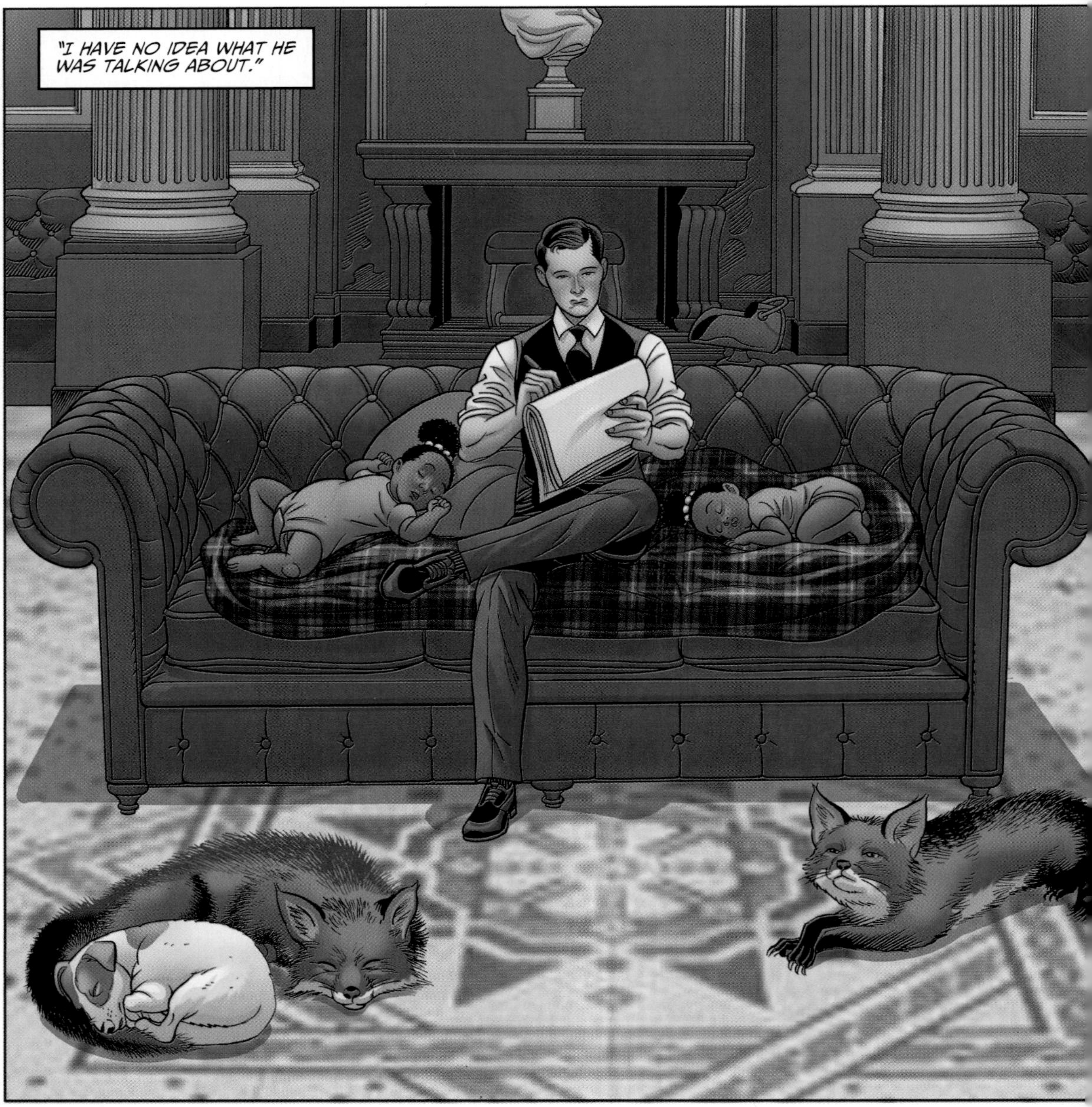
"I HAVE NO IDEA WHAT HE WAS TALKING ABOUT."

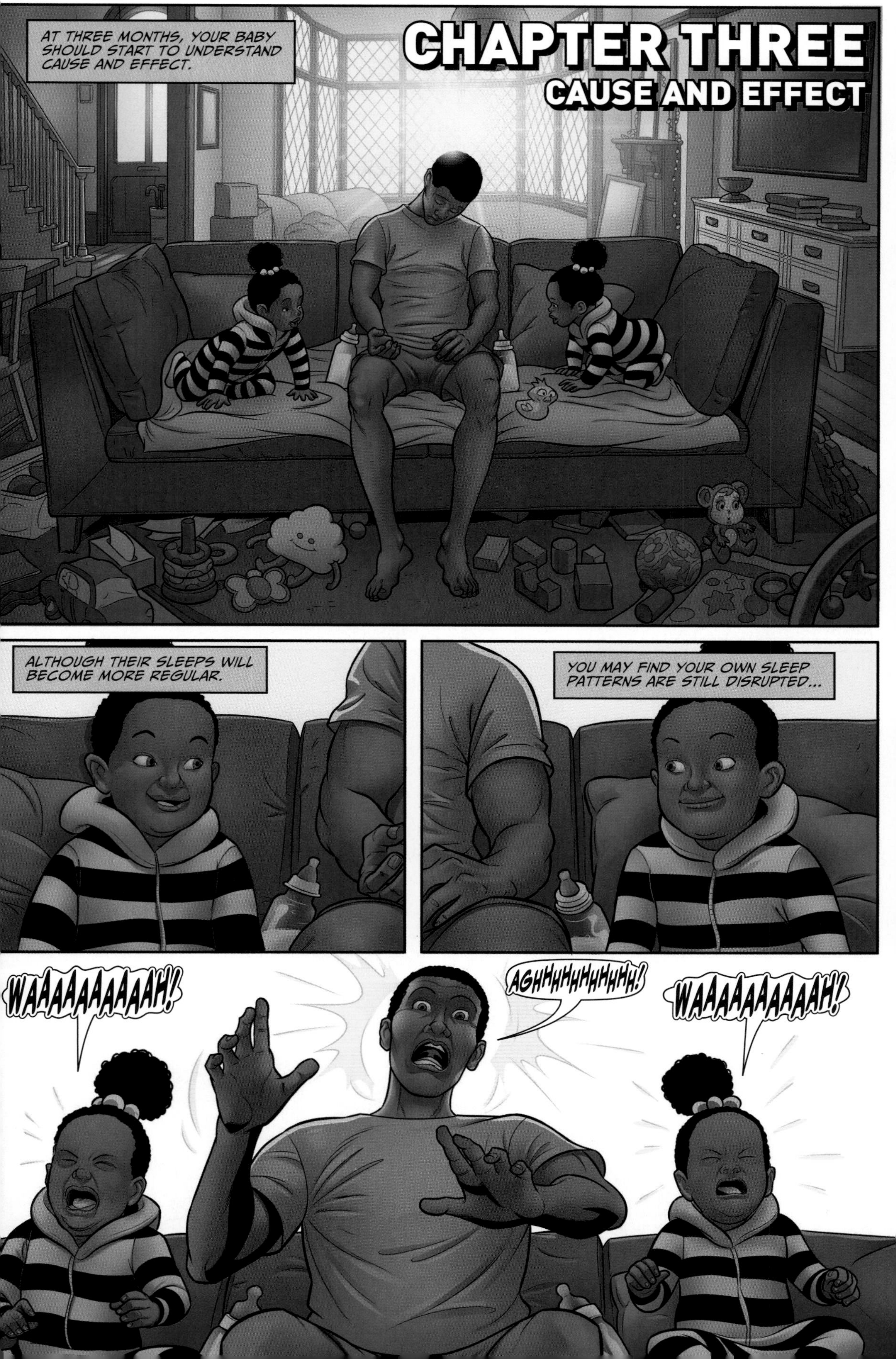
AT THREE MONTHS, YOUR BABY SHOULD START TO UNDERSTAND CAUSE AND EFFECT.
CHAPTER THREE
CAUSE AND EFFECT
ALTHOUGH THEIR SLEEPS WILL BECOME MORE REGULAR.
YOU MAY FIND YOUR OWN SLEEP PATTERNS ARE STILL DISRUPTED...
WAAAAAAAAAAH!
AGHHHHHHHHHHH!
WAAAAAAAAAAH!

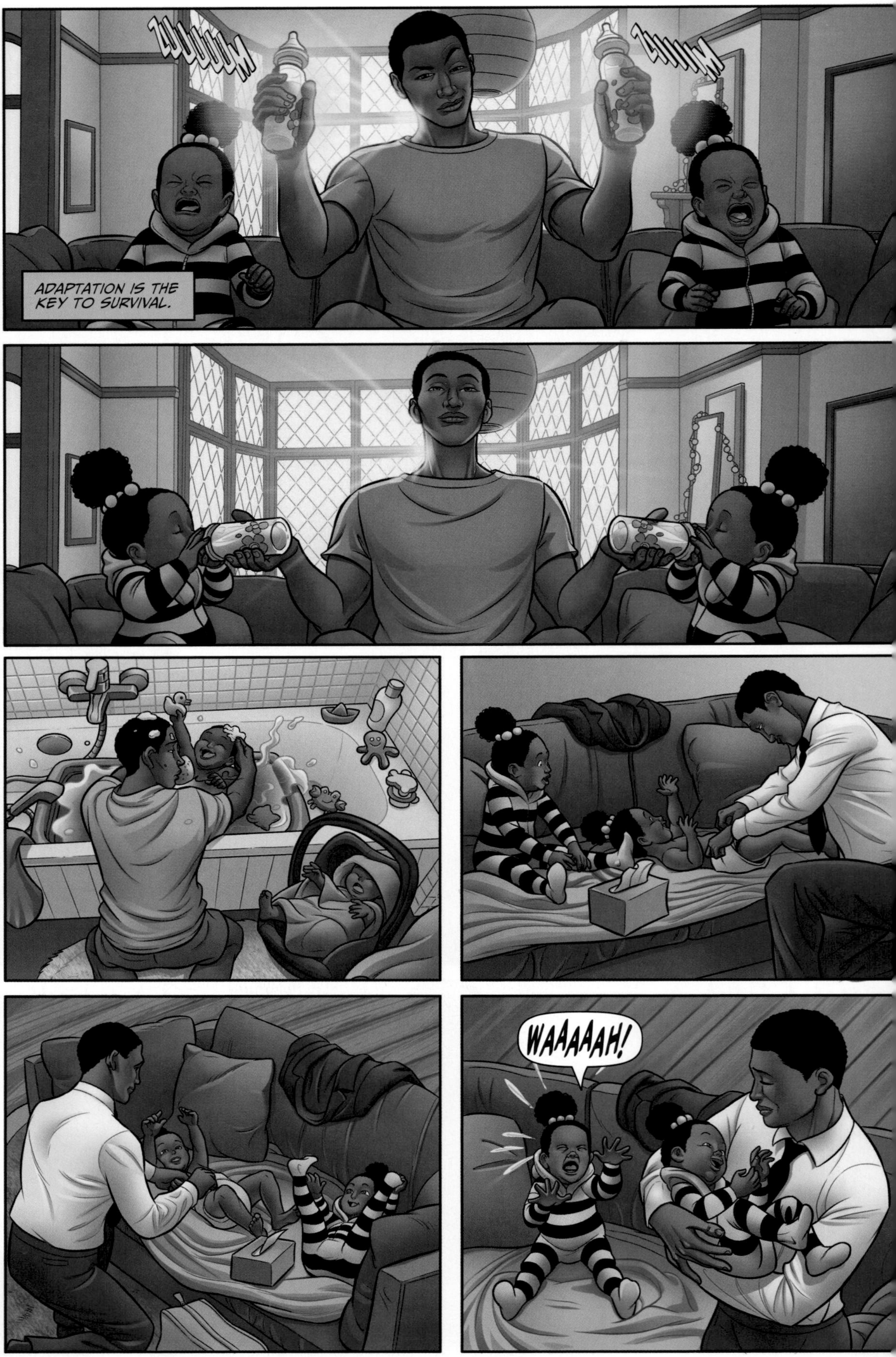
ZUUUUUM
ZUUUM
ADAPTATION IS THE KEY TO SURVIVAL.
WAAAAAH!

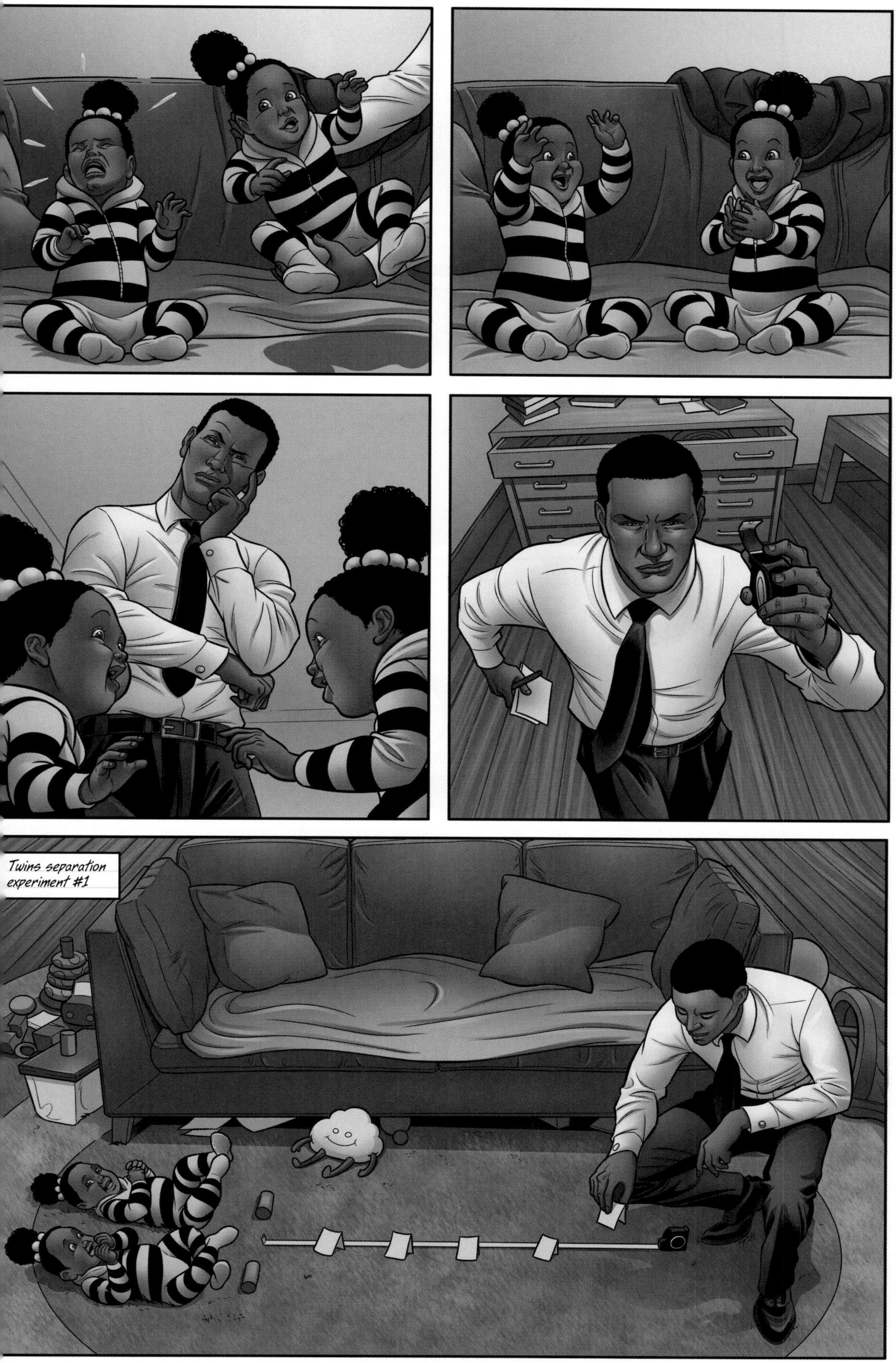
Twins separation experiment #1

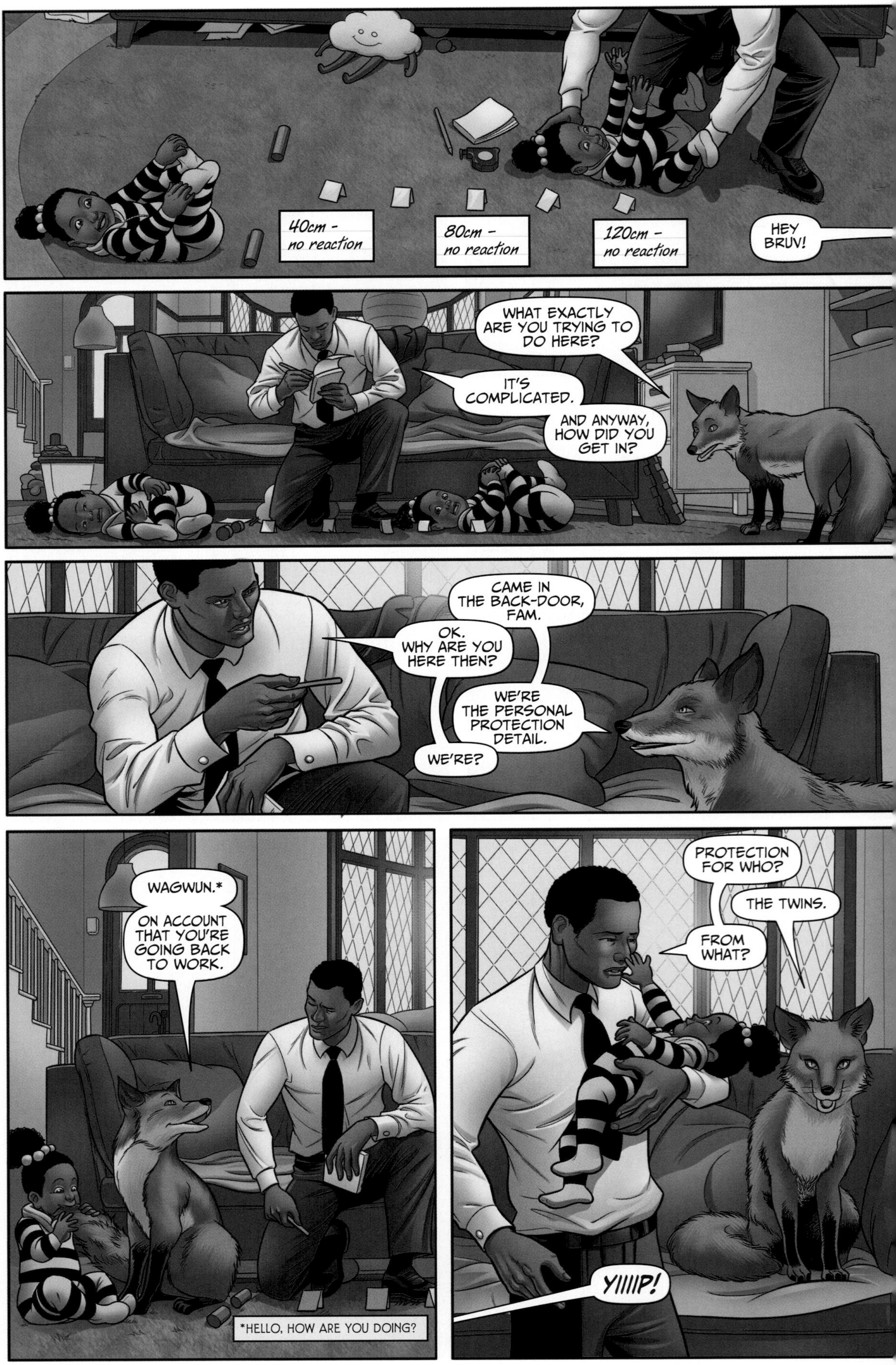
40cm - no reaction
80cm - no reaction
120cm - no reaction
HEY BRUV!
WHAT EXACTLY ARE YOU TRYING TO DO HERE?
IT'S COMPLICATED.
AND ANYWAY, HOW DID YOU GET IN?
CAME IN THE BACK-DOOR, FAM.
OK. WHY ARE YOU HERE THEN?
WE'RE THE PERSONAL PROTECTION DETAIL.
WE'RE?
WAGWUN.*
ON ACCOUNT THAT YOU'RE GOING BACK TO WORK.
*HELLO, HOW ARE YOU DOING?
PROTECTION FOR WHO?
THE TWINS.
FROM WHAT?
YIIIIP!

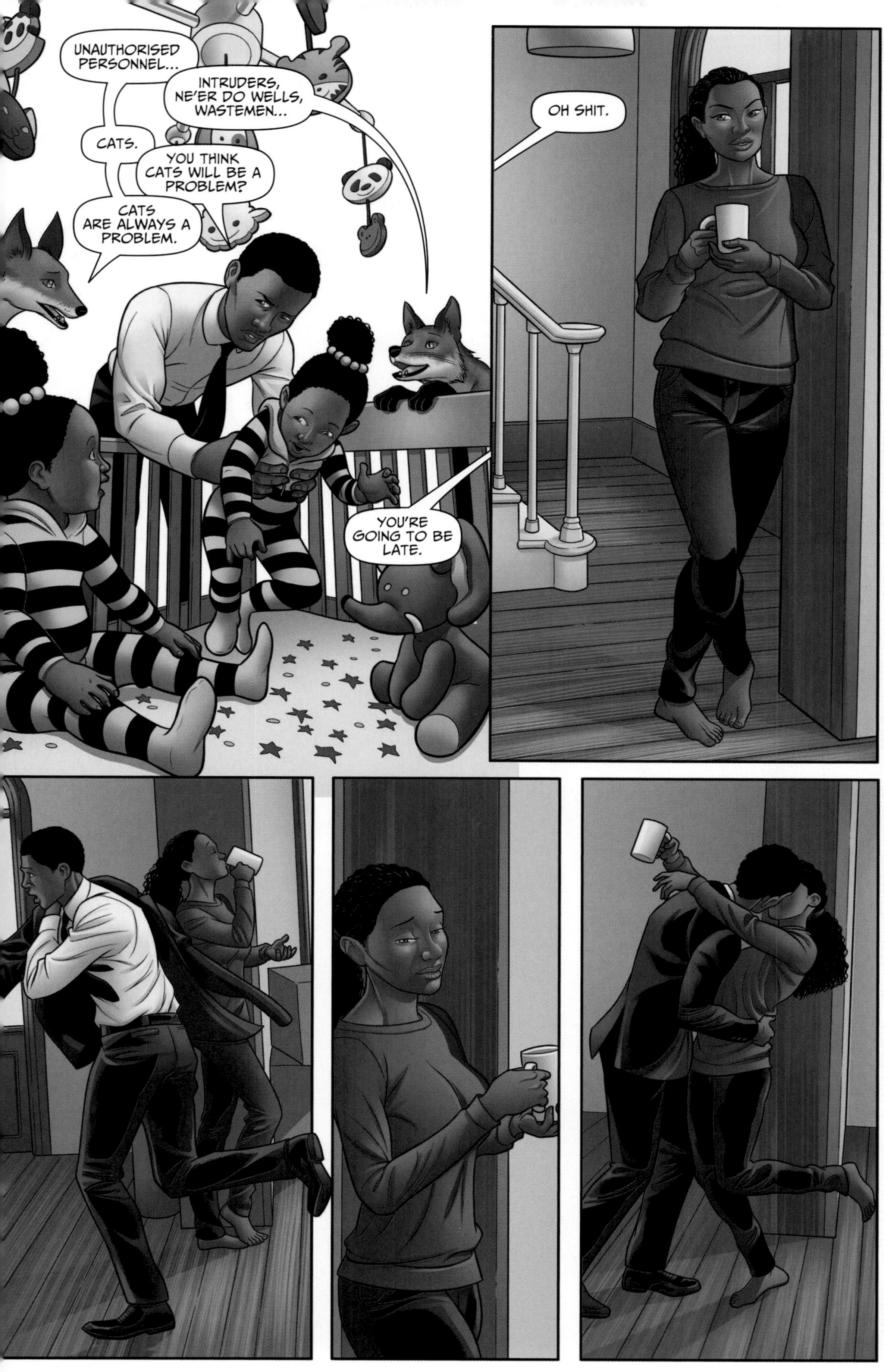
UNAUTHORISED PERSONNEL...
INTRUDERS, NE'ER DO WELLS, WASTEMEN...
CATS.
YOU THINK CATS WILL BE A PROBLEM?
CATS ARE ALWAYS A PROBLEM.
YOU'RE GOING TO BE LATE.
OH SHIT.

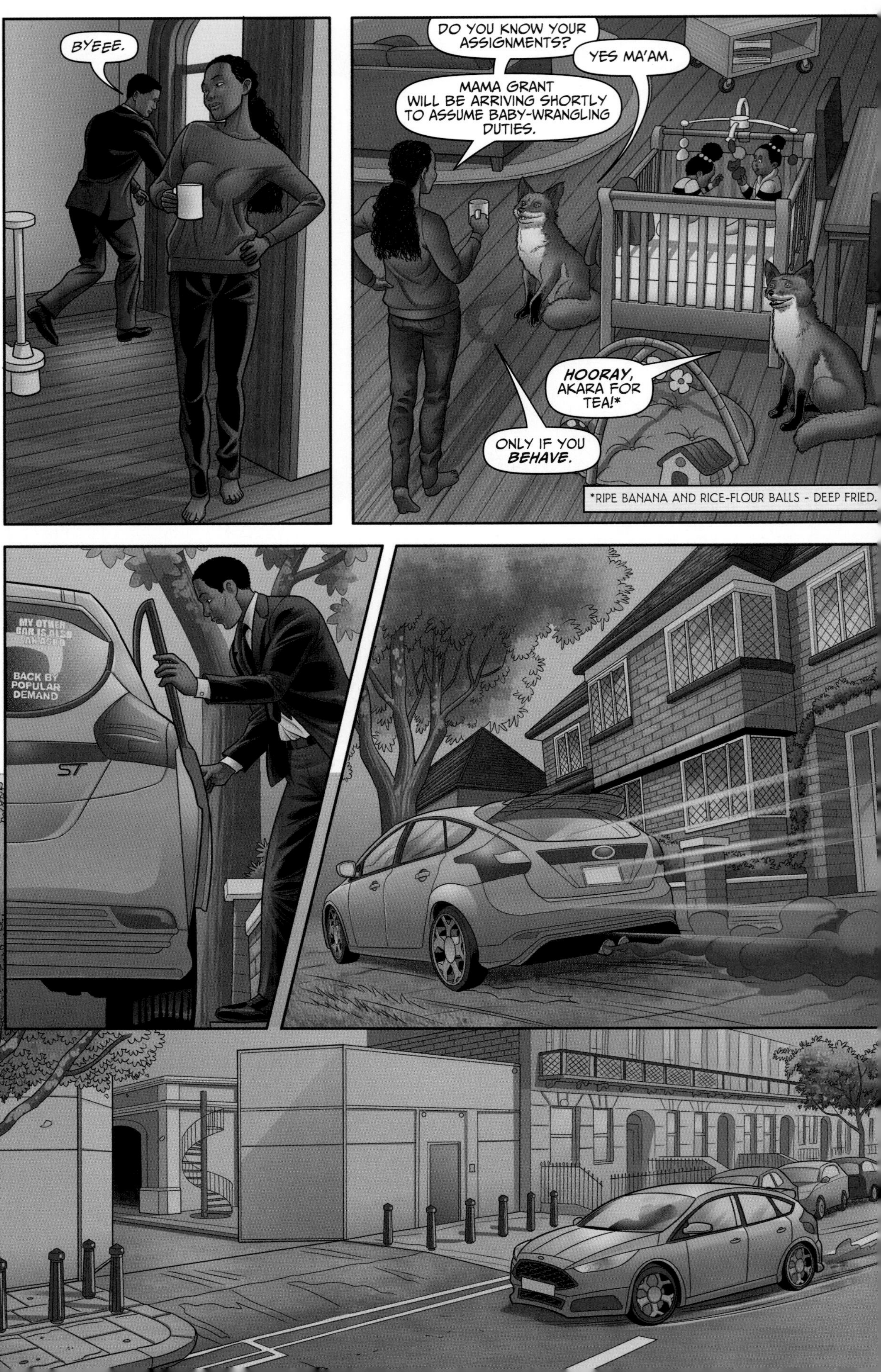
BYEEE.
DO YOU KNOW YOUR ASSIGNMENTS?
YES MA'AM.
MAMA GRANT WILL BE ARRIVING SHORTLY TO ASSUME BABY-WRANGLING DUTIES.
HOORAY, AKARA FOR TEA!*
ONLY IF YOU BEHAVE.
*RIPE BANANA AND RICE-FLOUR BALLS - DEEP FRIED.
MY OTHER CAR IS ALSO AN ASBO
BACK BY POPULAR DEMAND
ST

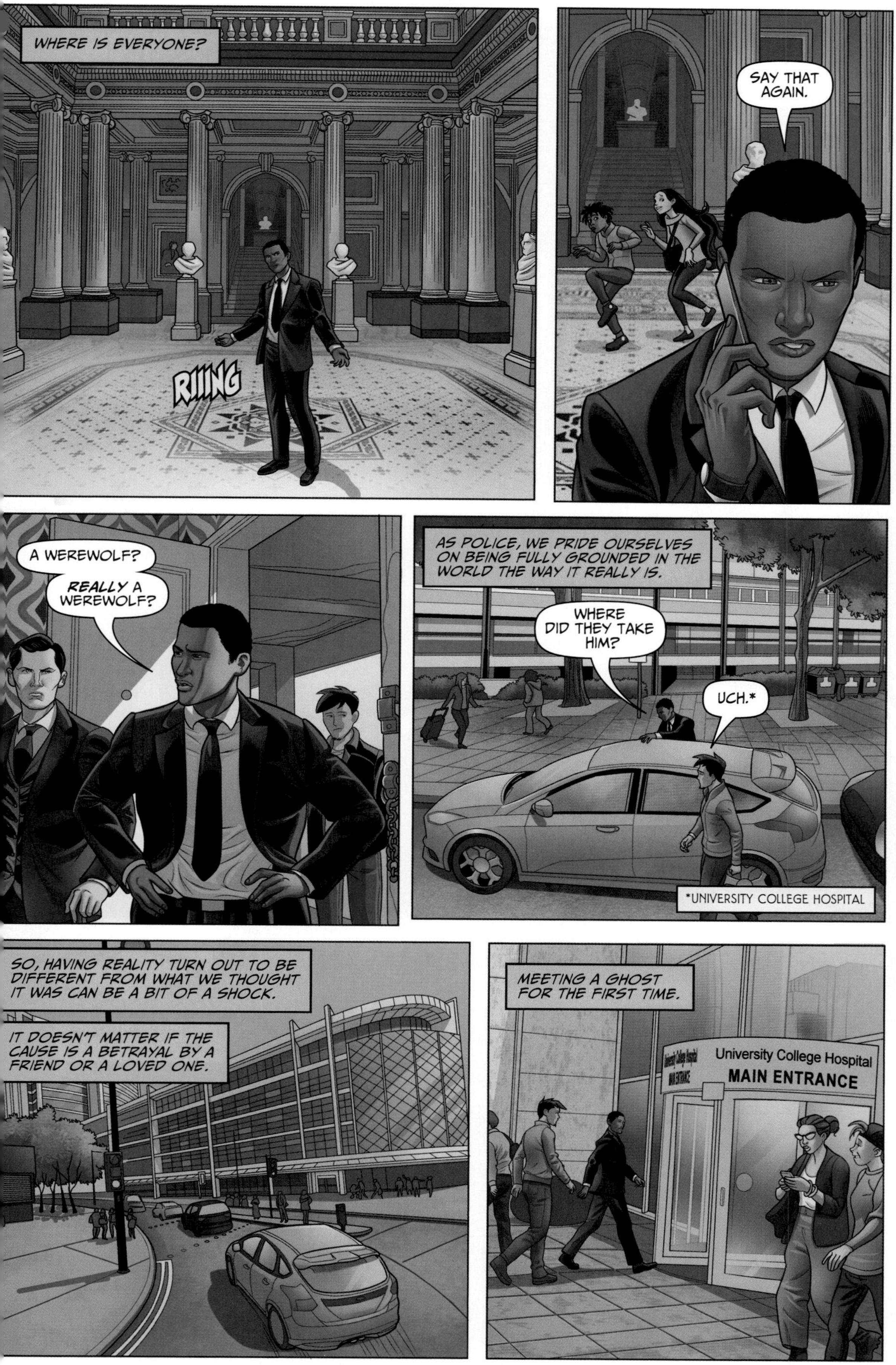
WHERE IS EVERYONE?
RIIING
SAY THAT AGAIN.
A WEREWOLF?
REALLY A WEREWOLF?
AS POLICE, WE PRIDE OURSELVES ON BEING FULLY GROUNDED IN THE WORLD THE WAY IT REALLY IS.
WHERE DID THEY TAKE HIM?
UCH.*
*UNIVERSITY COLLEGE HOSPITAL
SO, HAVING REALITY TURN OUT TO BE DIFFERENT FROM WHAT WE THOUGHT IT WAS CAN BE A BIT OF A SHOCK.
IT DOESN'T MATTER IF THE CAUSE IS A BETRAYAL BY A FRIEND OR A LOVED ONE.
MEETING A GHOST FOR THE FIRST TIME.
University College Hospital
MAIN ENTRANCE

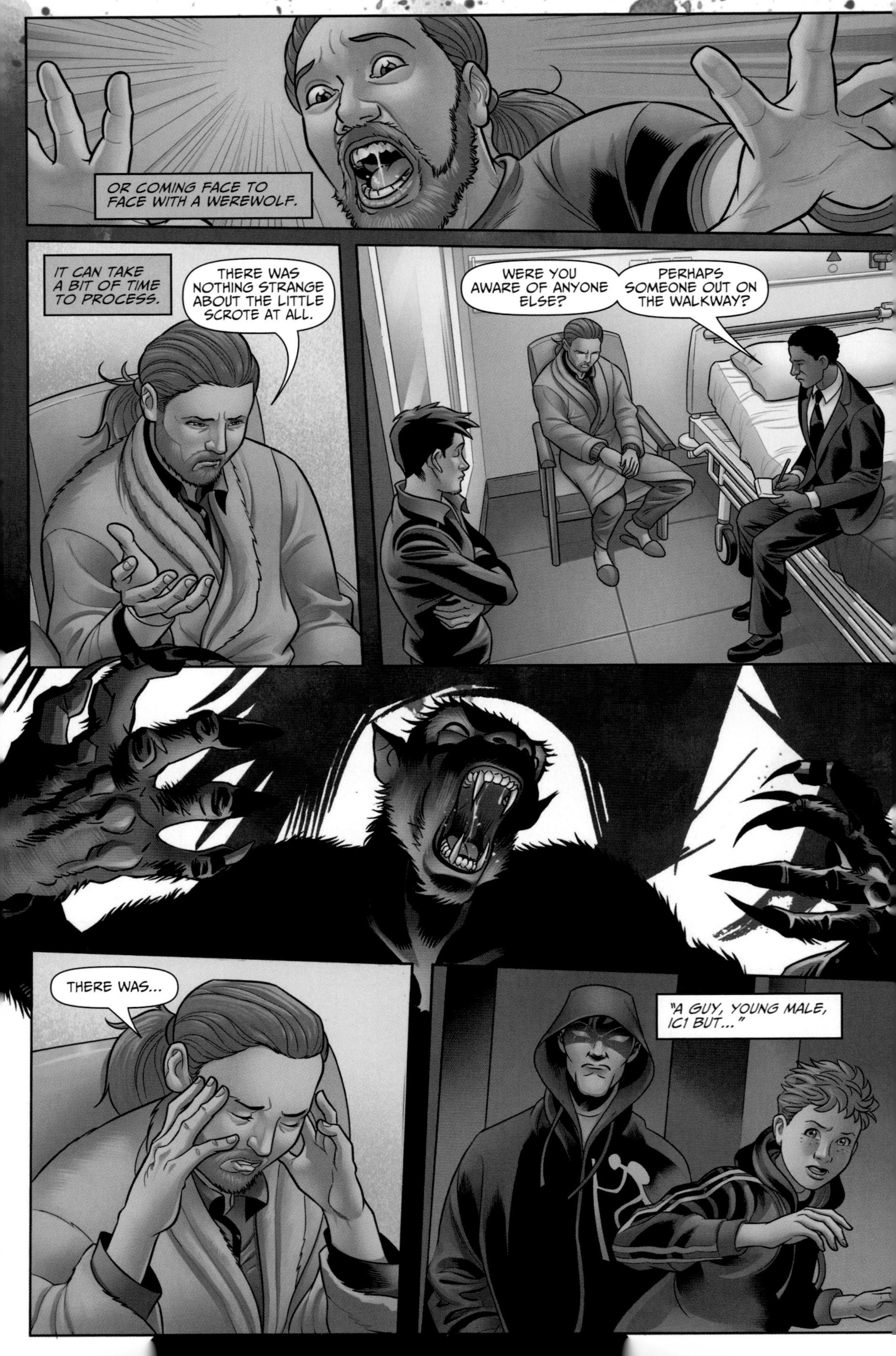
OR COMING FACE TO FACE WITH A WEREWOLF.
IT CAN TAKE A BIT OF TIME TO PROCESS.
THERE WAS NOTHING STRANGE ABOUT THE LITTLE SCROTE AT ALL.
WERE YOU AWARE OF ANYONE ELSE?
PERHAPS SOMEONE OUT ON THE WALKWAY?
THERE WAS...
"A GUY, YOUNG MALE, IC1 BUT..."

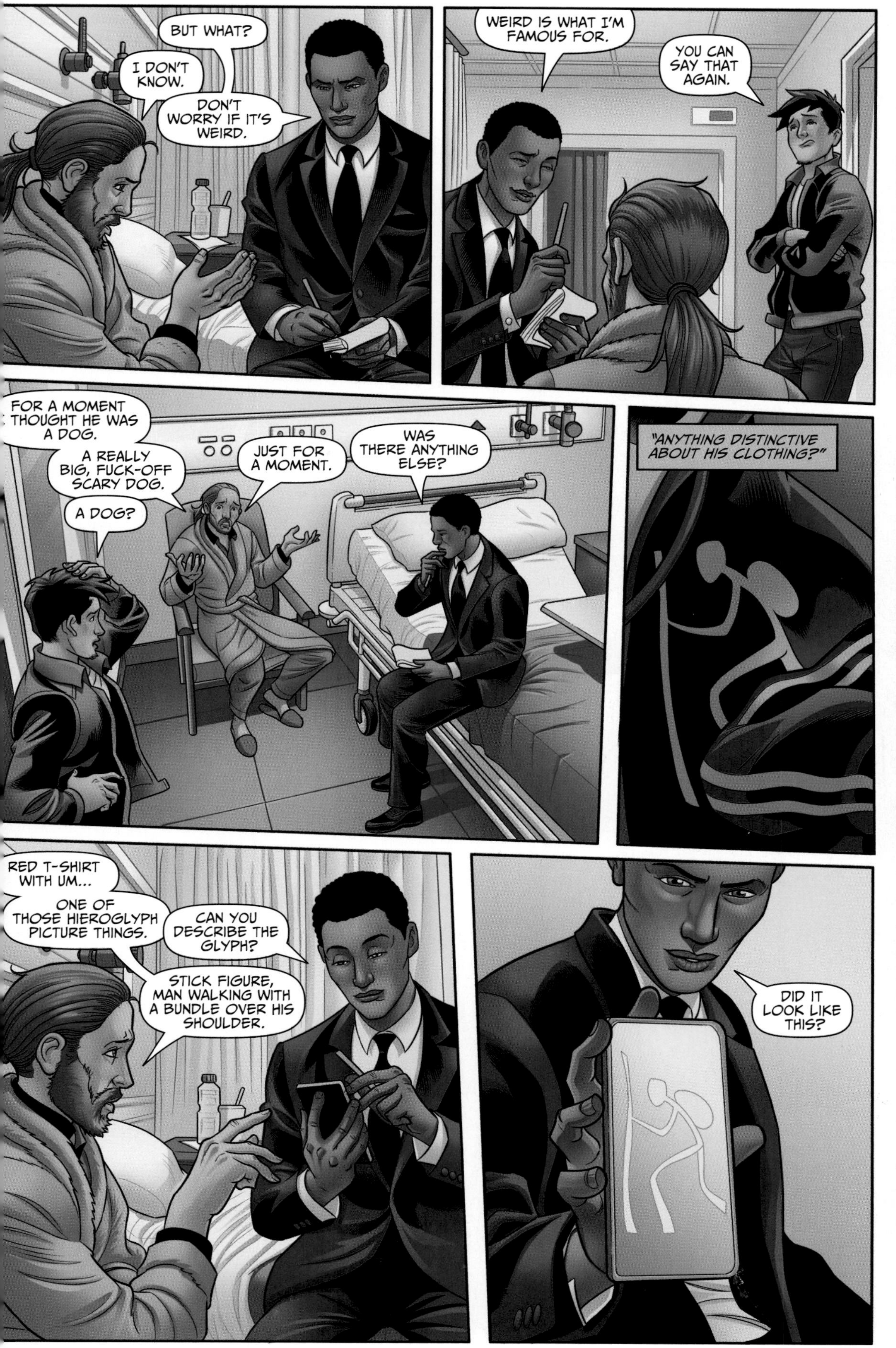
BUT WHAT?
I DON'T KNOW.
DON'T WORRY IF IT'S WEIRD.
WEIRD IS WHAT I'M FAMOUS FOR.
YOU CAN SAY THAT AGAIN.
FOR A MOMENT THOUGHT HE WAS A DOG.
A REALLY BIG, FUCK-OFF SCARY DOG.
A DOG?
JUST FOR A MOMENT.
WAS THERE ANYTHING ELSE?
"ANYTHING DISTINCTIVE ABOUT HIS CLOTHING?"
RED T-SHIRT WITH UM...
ONE OF THOSE HIEROGLYPH PICTURE THINGS.
CAN YOU DESCRIBE THE GLYPH?
STICK FIGURE, MAN WALKING WITH A BUNDLE OVER HIS SHOULDER.
DID IT LOOK LIKE THIS?

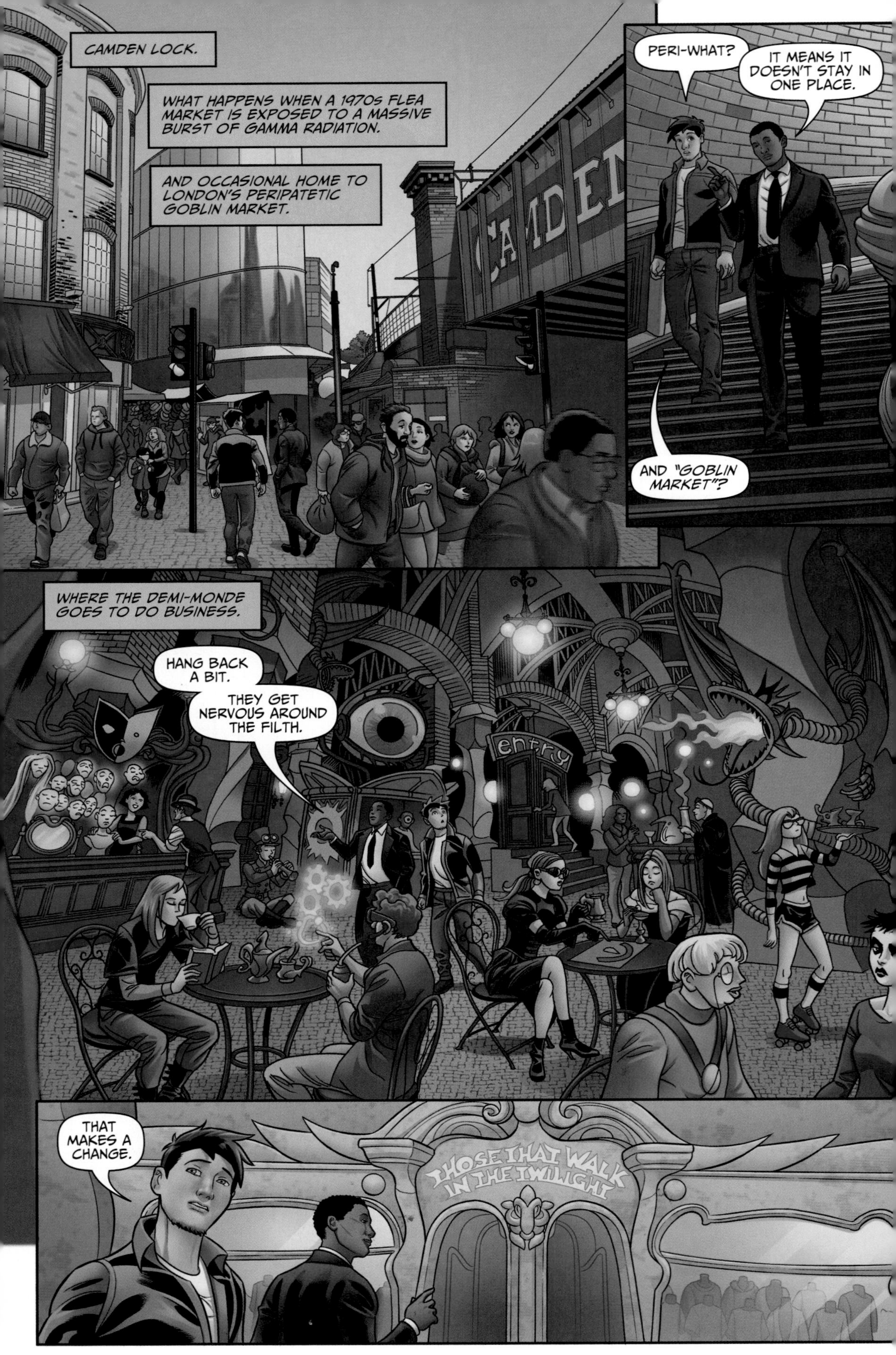
CAMDEN LOCK.
WHAT HAPPENS WHEN A 1970s FLEA MARKET IS EXPOSED TO A MASSIVE BURST OF GAMMA RADIATION.
AND OCCASIONAL HOME TO LONDON'S PERIPATETIC GOBLIN MARKET.
CAMDEN
PERI-WHAT?
IT MEANS IT DOESN'T STAY IN ONE PLACE.
AND "GOBLIN MARKET"?
WHERE THE DEMI-MONDE GOES TO DO BUSINESS.
HANG BACK A BIT.
THEY GET NERVOUS AROUND THE FILTH.
entry
THAT MAKES A CHANGE.
THOSE THAT WALK IN THE TWILIGHT

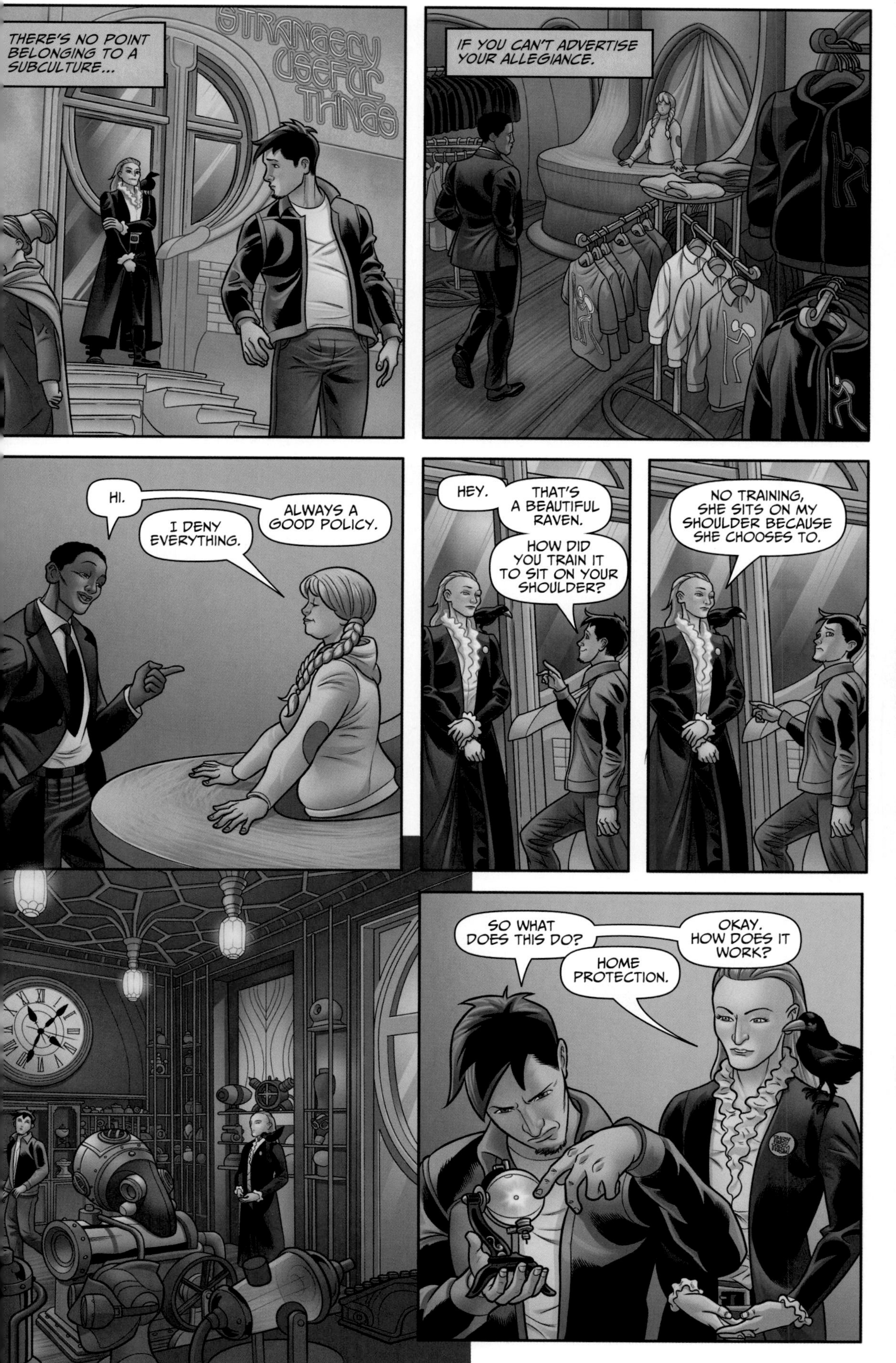
THERE'S NO POINT BELONGING TO A SUBCULTURE...
STRANGELY USEFUL THINGS
IF YOU CAN'T ADVERTISE YOUR ALLEGIANCE.
HI.
ALWAYS A GOOD POLICY.
I DENY EVERYTHING.
HEY.
THAT'S A BEAUTIFUL RAVEN.
HOW DID YOU TRAIN IT TO SIT ON YOUR SHOULDER?
NO TRAINING, SHE SITS ON MY SHOULDER BECAUSE SHE CHOOSES TO.
SO WHAT DOES THIS DO?
HOME PROTECTION.
OKAY. HOW DOES IT WORK?

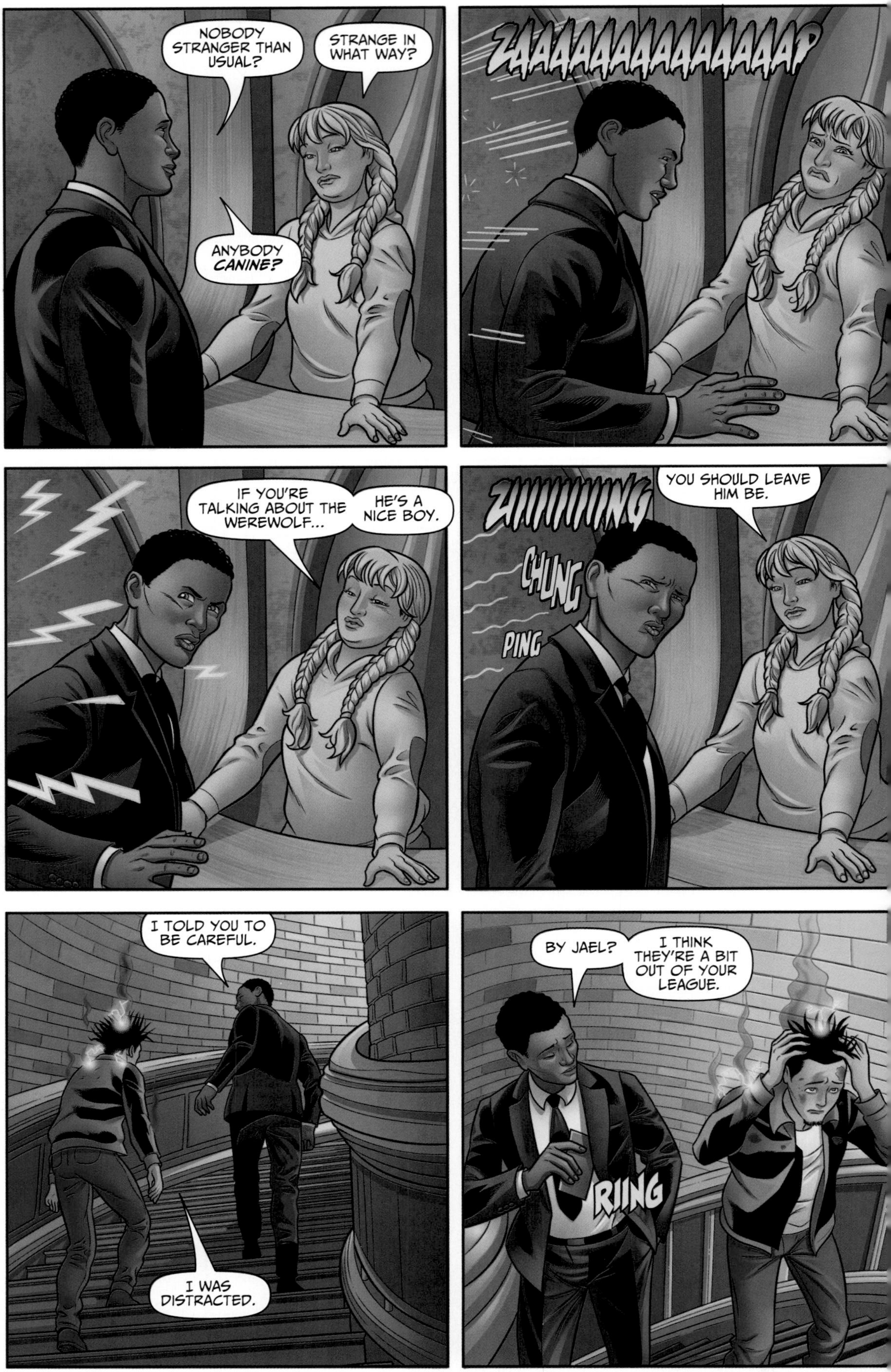
NOBODY STRANGER THAN USUAL?
STRANGE IN WHAT WAY?
ANYBODY CANINE?
ZAAAAAAAAAAAAAAP
IF YOU'RE TALKING ABOUT THE WEREWOLF...
HE'S A NICE BOY.
ZIIIIIIIIING
YOU SHOULD LEAVE HIM BE.
CHUNG
PING
I TOLD YOU TO BE CAREFUL.
I WAS DISTRACTED.
BY JAEL?
I THINK THEY'RE A BIT OUT OF YOUR LEAGUE.
RIING

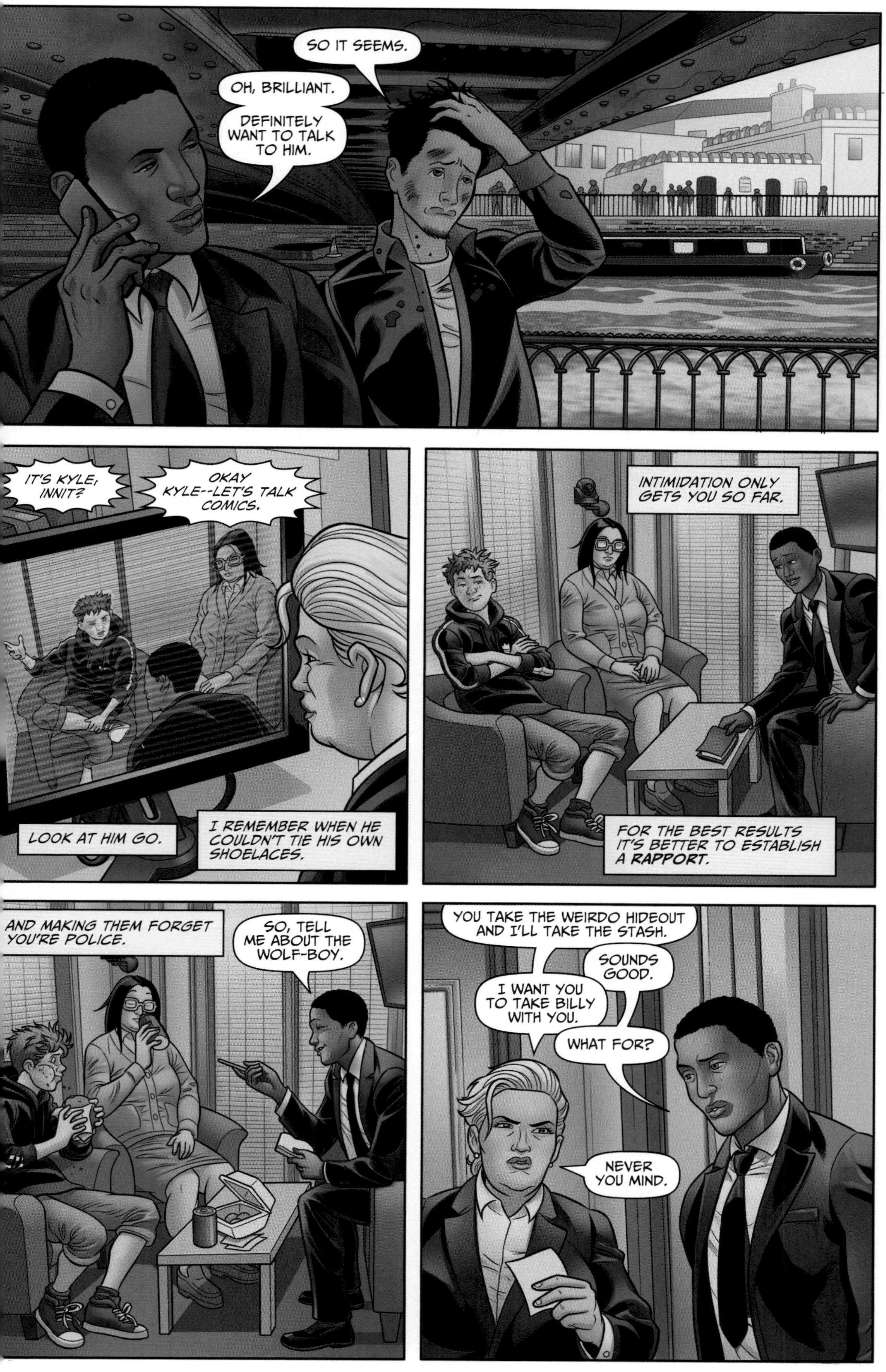
SO IT SEEMS.
OH, BRILLIANT.
DEFINITELY WANT TO TALK TO HIM.
IT'S KYLE, INNIT?
OKAY KYLE--LET'S TALK COMICS.
LOOK AT HIM GO.
I REMEMBER WHEN HE COULDN'T TIE HIS OWN SHOELACES.
INTIMIDATION ONLY GETS YOU SO FAR.
FOR THE BEST RESULTS IT'S BETTER TO ESTABLISH A RAPPORT.
AND MAKING THEM FORGET YOU'RE POLICE.
SO, TELL ME ABOUT THE WOLF-BOY.
YOU TAKE THE WEIRDO HIDEOUT AND I'LL TAKE THE STASH.
SOUNDS GOOD.
I WANT YOU TO TAKE BILLY WITH YOU.
WHAT FOR?
NEVER YOU MIND.

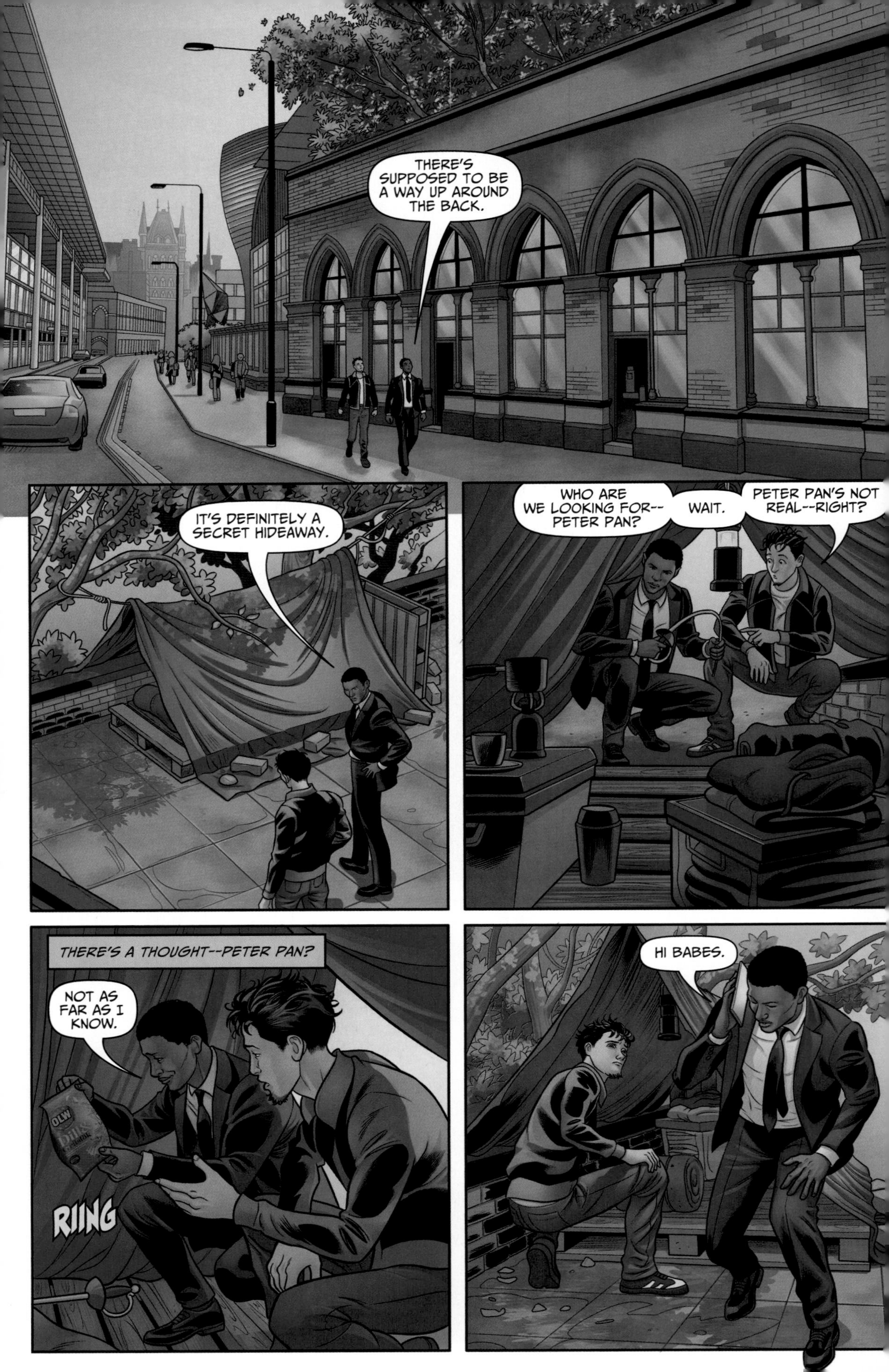
THERE'S SUPPOSED TO BE A WAY UP AROUND THE BACK.
IT'S DEFINITELY A SECRET HIDEAWAY.
WHO ARE WE LOOKING FOR-- PETER PAN?
WAIT.
PETER PAN'S NOT REAL--RIGHT?
THERE'S A THOUGHT--PETER PAN?
NOT AS FAR AS I KNOW.
RIING
HI BABES.

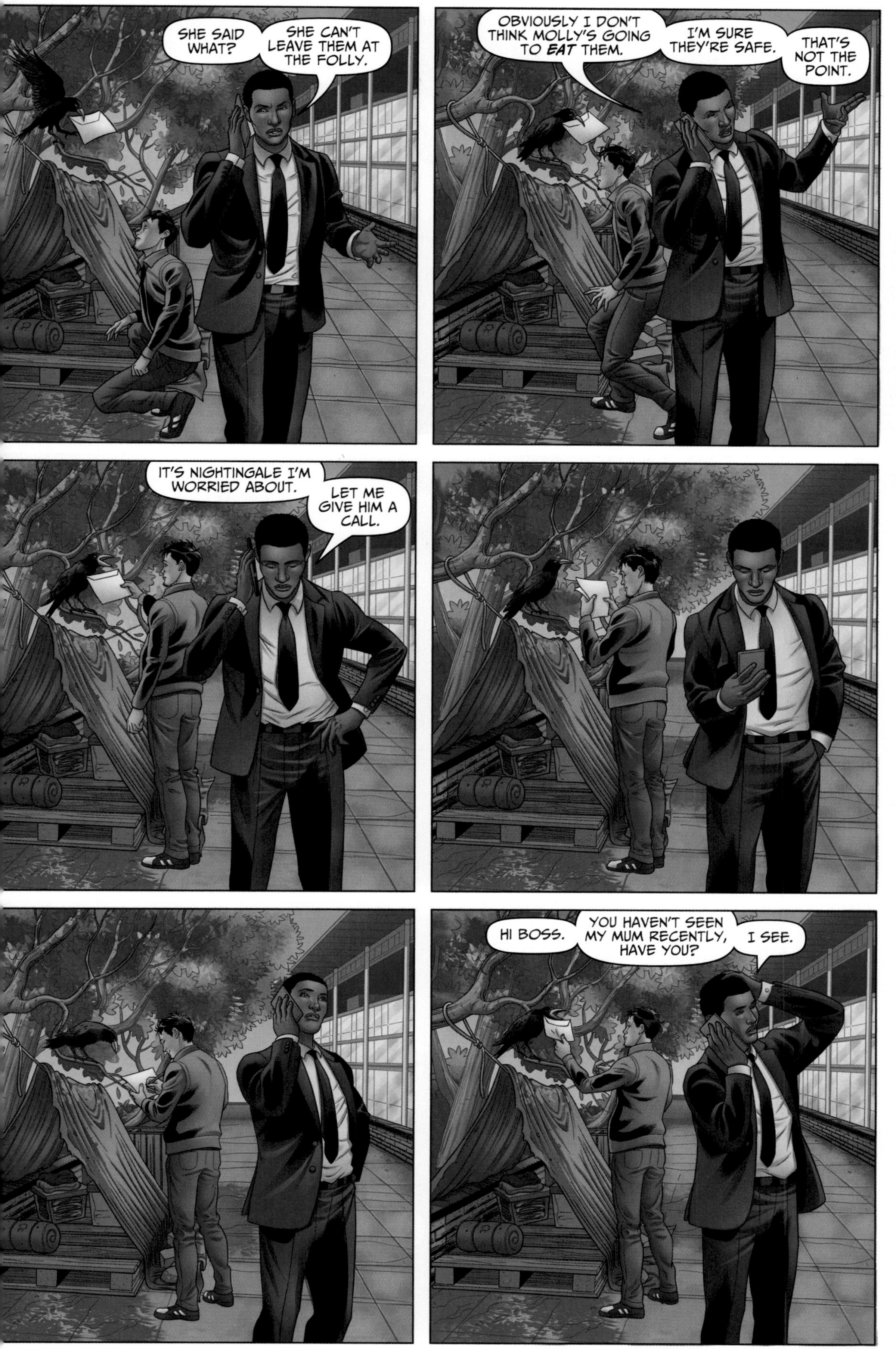
SHE SAID WHAT?
SHE CAN'T LEAVE THEM AT THE FOLLY.
OBVIOUSLY I DON'T THINK MOLLY'S GOING TO EAT THEM.
I'M SURE THEY'RE SAFE.
THAT'S NOT THE POINT.
IT'S NIGHTINGALE I'M WORRIED ABOUT.
LET ME GIVE HIM A CALL.
HI BOSS.
YOU HAVEN'T SEEN MY MUM RECENTLY, HAVE YOU?
I SEE.

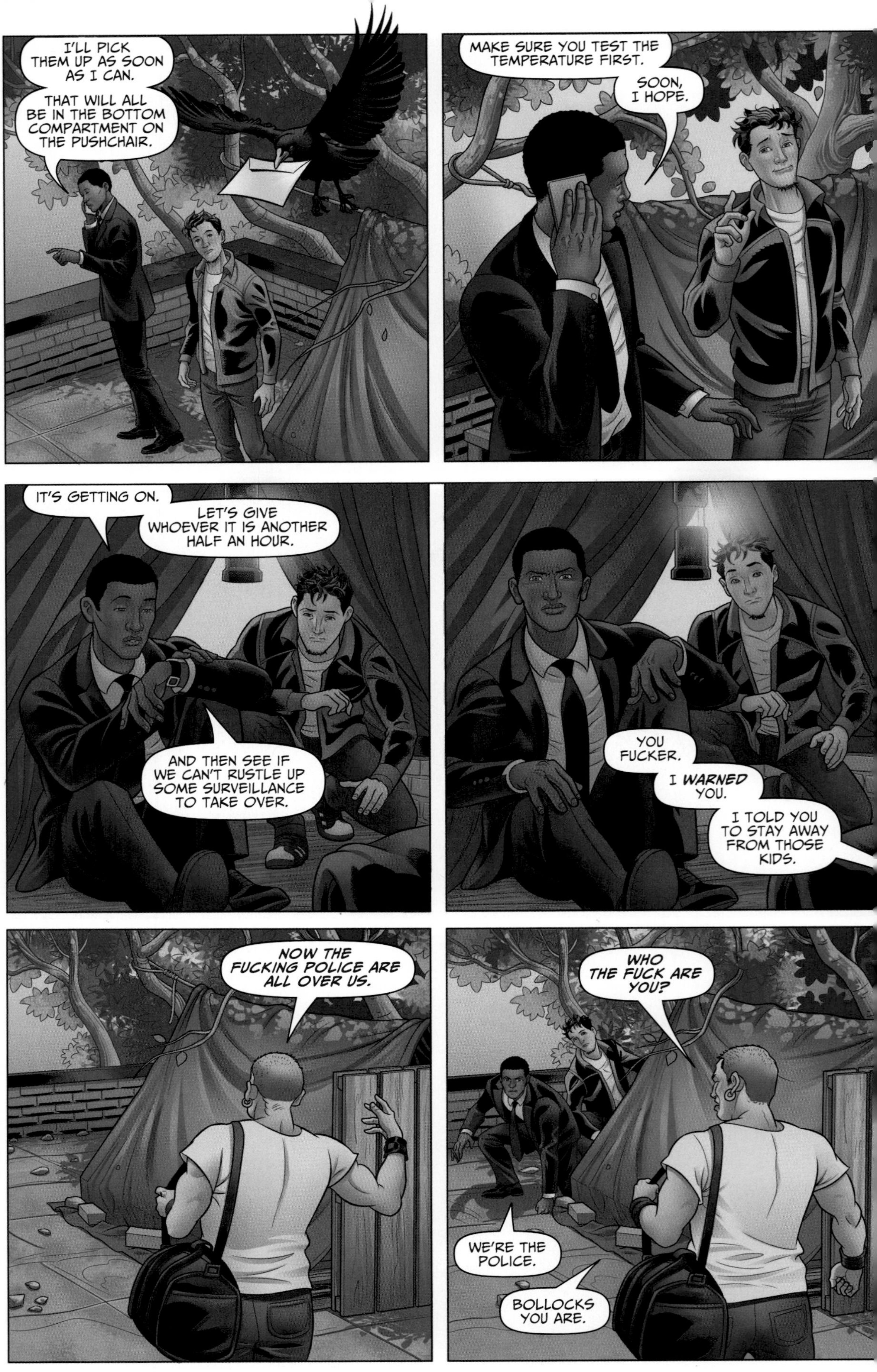
I'LL PICK THEM UP AS SOON AS I CAN.
THAT WILL ALL BE IN THE BOTTOM COMPARTMENT ON THE PUSHCHAIR.
MAKE SURE YOU TEST THE TEMPERATURE FIRST.
SOON, I HOPE.
IT'S GETTING ON.
LET'S GIVE WHOEVER IT IS ANOTHER HALF AN HOUR.
AND THEN SEE IF WE CAN'T RUSTLE UP SOME SURVEILLANCE TO TAKE OVER.
YOU FUCKER.
I *WARNED* YOU.
I TOLD YOU TO STAY AWAY FROM THOSE KIDS.
NOW THE FUCKING POLICE ARE ALL OVER US.
WHO THE FUCK ARE YOU?
WE'RE THE POLICE.
BOLLOCKS YOU ARE.

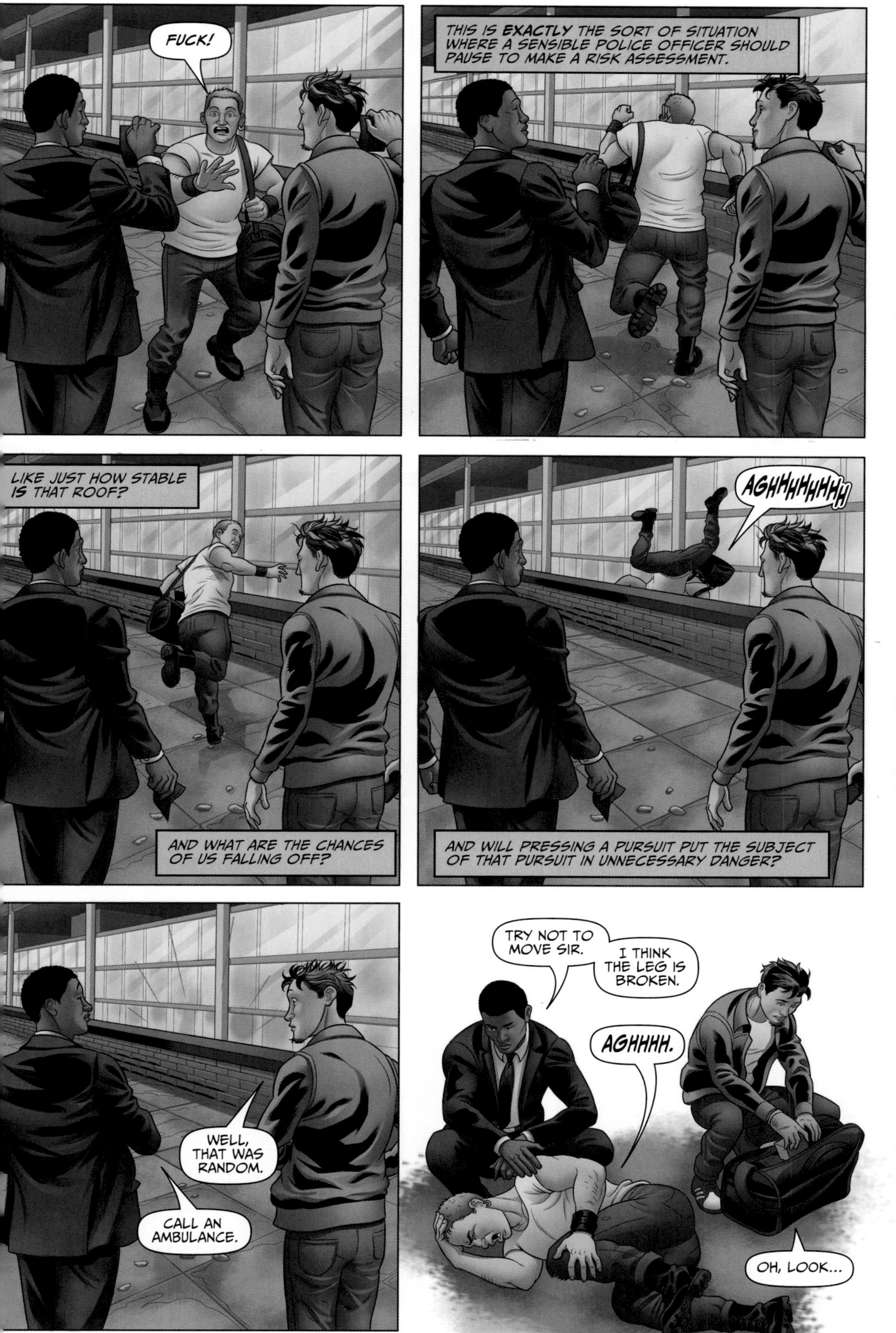
FUCK!
THIS IS EXACTLY THE SORT OF SITUATION WHERE A SENSIBLE POLICE OFFICER SHOULD PAUSE TO MAKE A RISK ASSESSMENT.
LIKE JUST HOW STABLE IS THAT ROOF?
AND WHAT ARE THE CHANCES OF US FALLING OFF?
AGHHHHHHHH
AND WILL PRESSING A PURSUIT PUT THE SUBJECT OF THAT PURSUIT IN UNNECESSARY DANGER?
WELL, THAT WAS RANDOM.
CALL AN AMBULANCE.
TRY NOT TO MOVE SIR.
I THINK THE LEG IS BROKEN.
AGHHHH.
OH, LOOK...

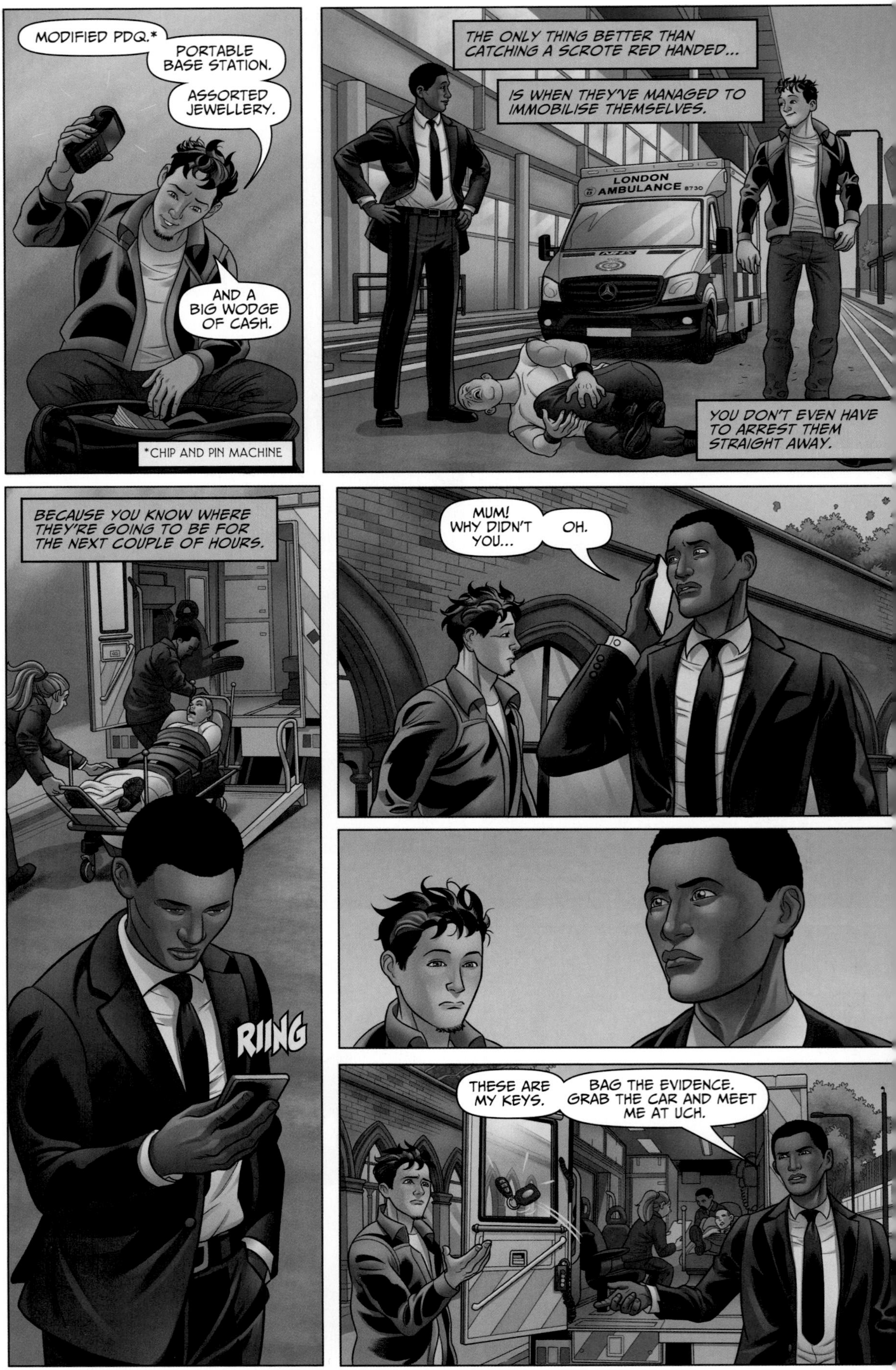
MODIFIED PDQ.*
PORTABLE BASE STATION.
ASSORTED JEWELLERY.
AND A BIG WODGE OF CASH.
*CHIP AND PIN MACHINE
THE ONLY THING BETTER THAN CATCHING A SCROTE RED HANDED...
IS WHEN THEY'VE MANAGED TO IMMOBILISE THEMSELVES.
LONDON AMBULANCE 8730
YOU DON'T EVEN HAVE TO ARREST THEM STRAIGHT AWAY.
BECAUSE YOU KNOW WHERE THEY'RE GOING TO BE FOR THE NEXT COUPLE OF HOURS.
RIING
MUM! WHY DIDN'T YOU...
OH.
THESE ARE MY KEYS.
BAG THE EVIDENCE. GRAB THE CAR AND MEET ME AT UCH.

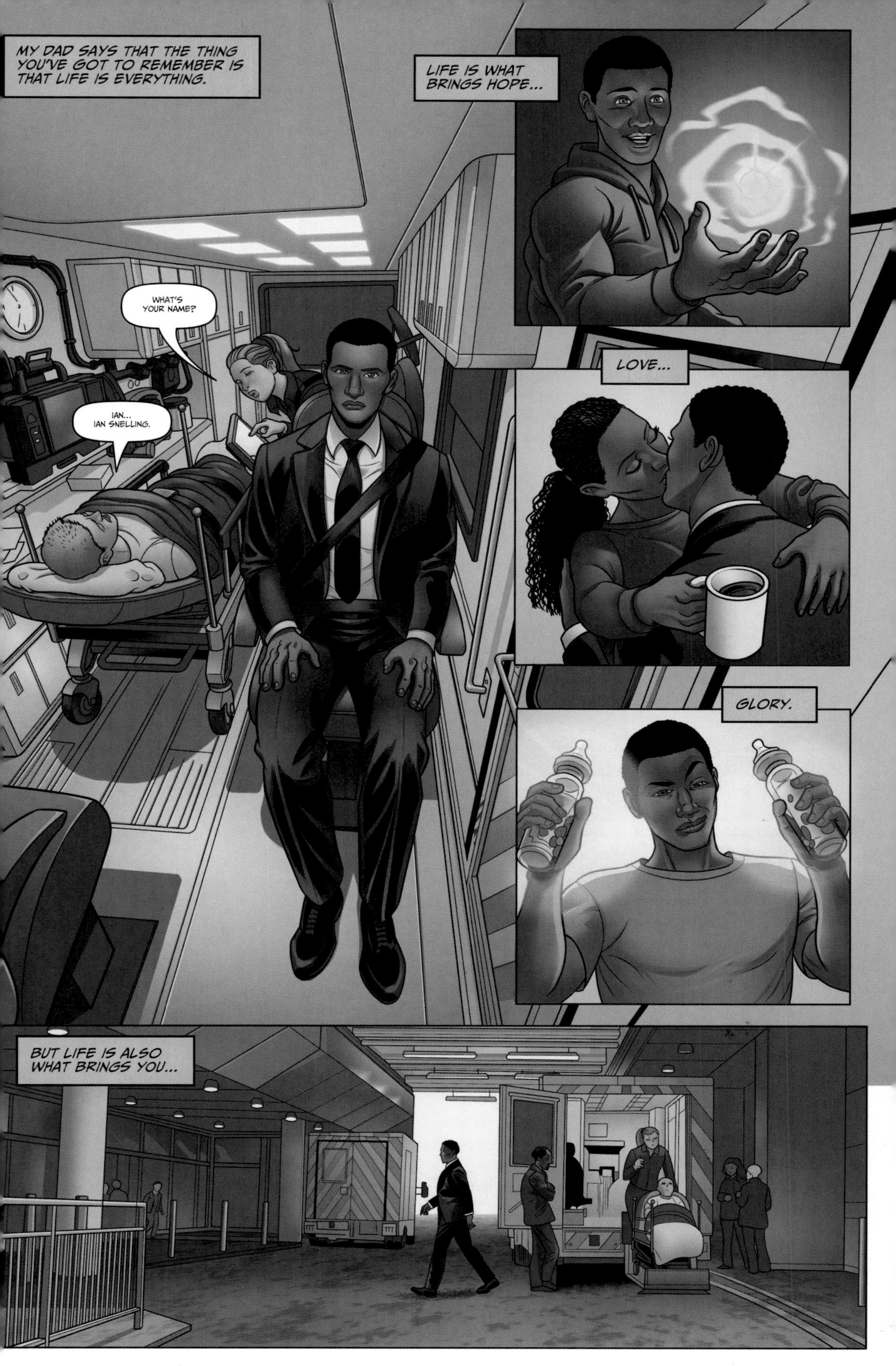
MY DAD SAYS THAT THE THING YOU'VE GOT TO REMEMBER IS THAT LIFE IS EVERYTHING.
WHAT'S YOUR NAME?
IAN... IAN SNELLING.
LIFE IS WHAT BRINGS HOPE...
LOVE...
GLORY.
BUT LIFE IS ALSO WHAT BRINGS YOU...

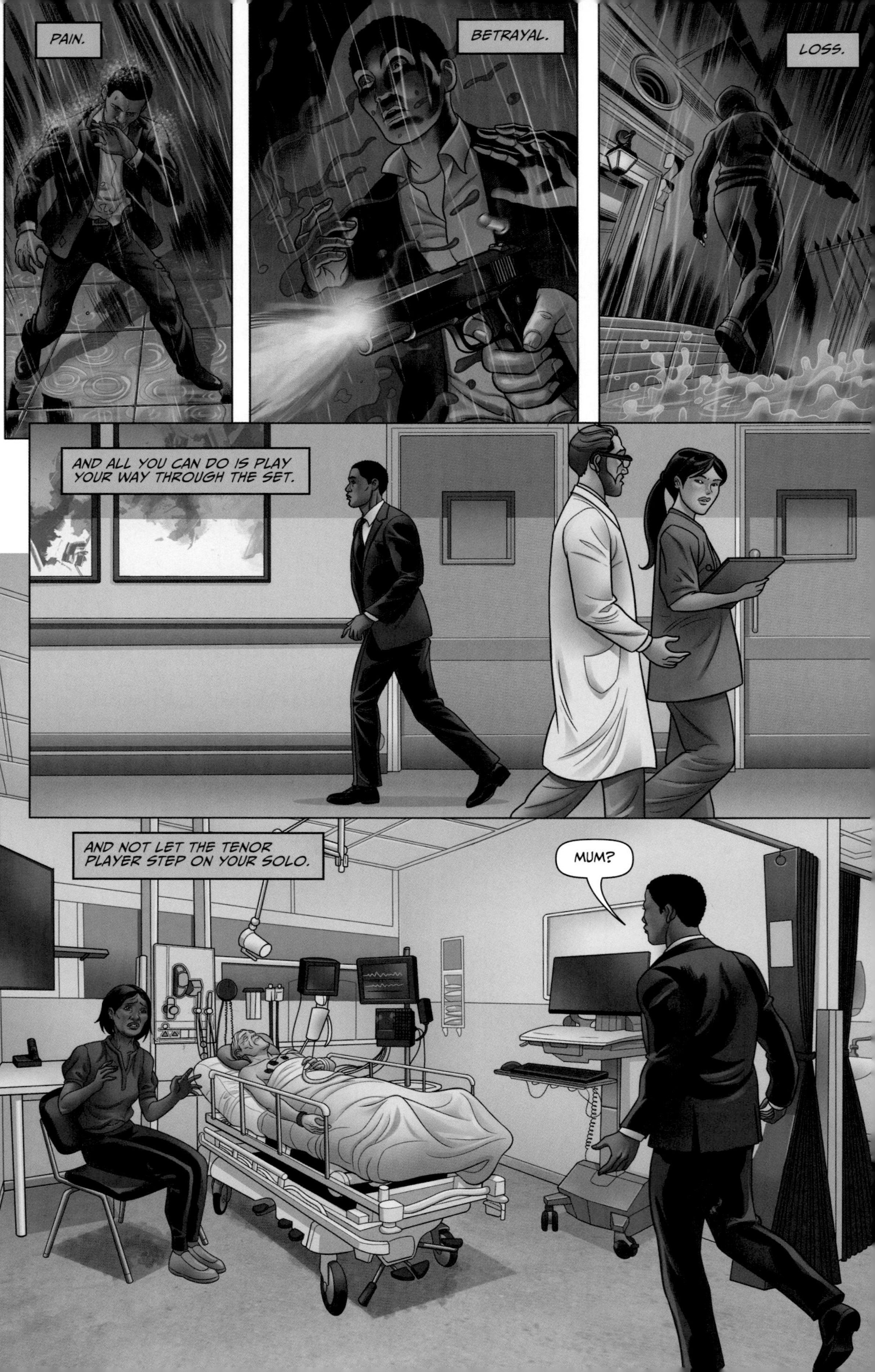
PAIN.
BETRAYAL.
LOSS.
AND ALL YOU CAN DO IS PLAY YOUR WAY THROUGH THE SET.
AND NOT LET THE TENOR PLAYER STEP ON YOUR SOLO.
MUM?

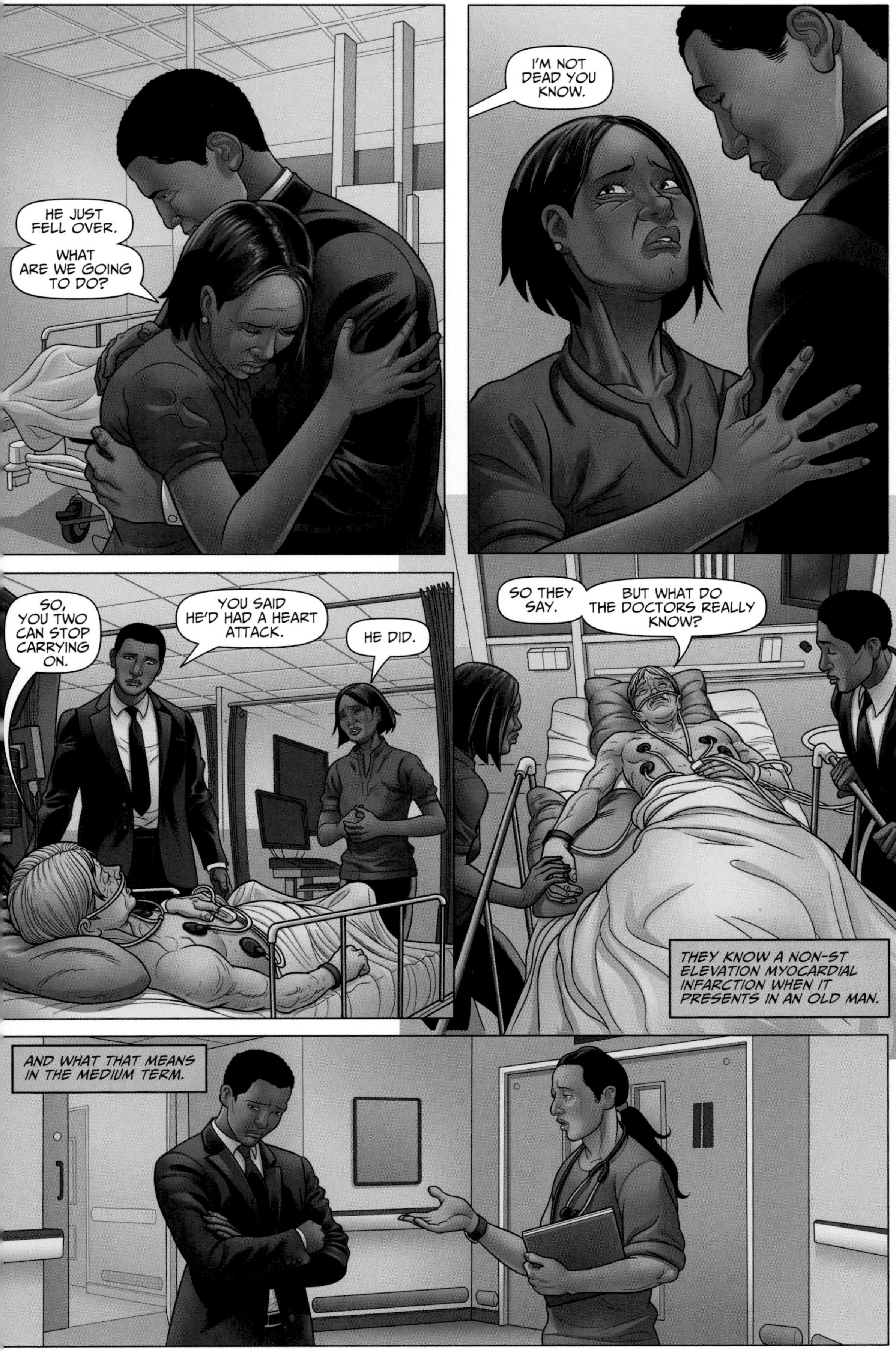
HE JUST FELL OVER.
WHAT ARE WE GOING TO DO?
I'M NOT DEAD YOU KNOW.
SO, YOU TWO CAN STOP CARRYING ON.
YOU SAID HE'D HAD A HEART ATTACK.
HE DID.
SO THEY SAY.
BUT WHAT DO THE DOCTORS REALLY KNOW?
THEY KNOW A NON-ST ELEVATION MYOCARDIAL INFARCTION WHEN IT PRESENTS IN AN OLD MAN.
AND WHAT THAT MEANS IN THE MEDIUM TERM.

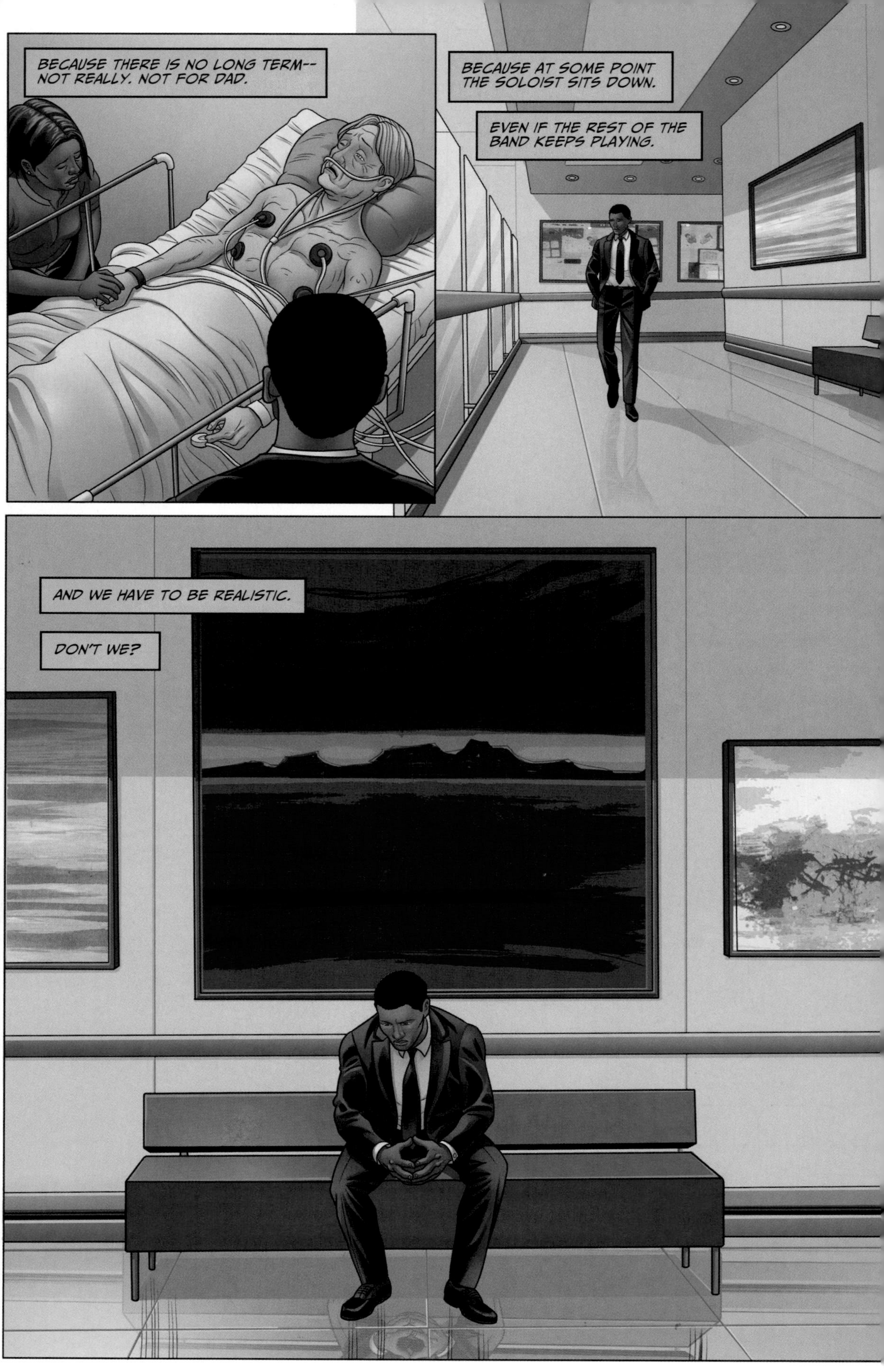
BECAUSE THERE IS NO LONG TERM--NOT REALLY. NOT FOR DAD.
BECAUSE AT SOME POINT THE SOLOIST SITS DOWN.
EVEN IF THE REST OF THE BAND KEEPS PLAYING.
AND WE HAVE TO BE REALISTIC.
DON'T WE?

CHAPTER FOUR
PAINTING IN THE BACKGROUND

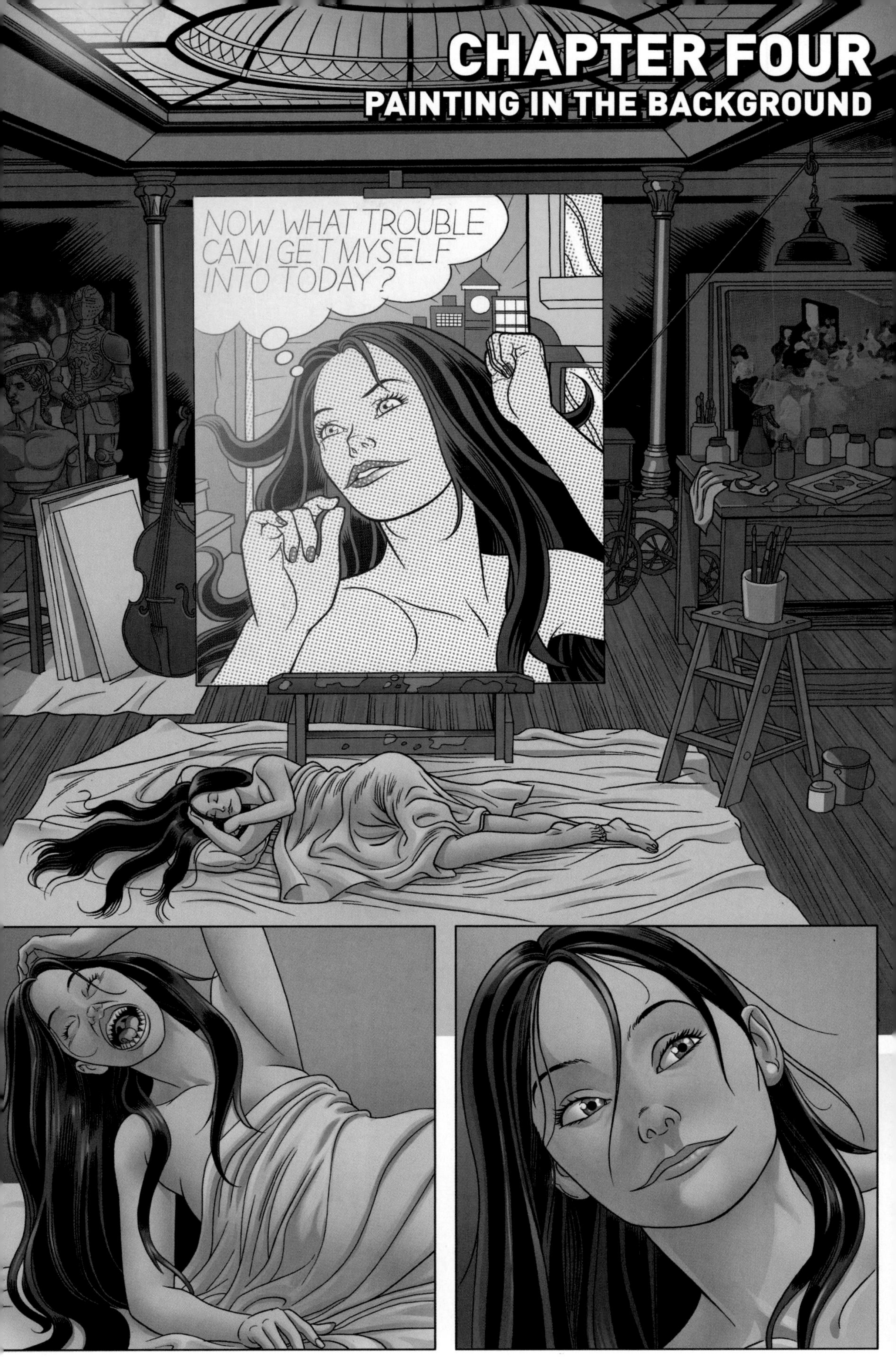
NOW WHAT TROUBLE CAN I GET MYSELF INTO TODAY?

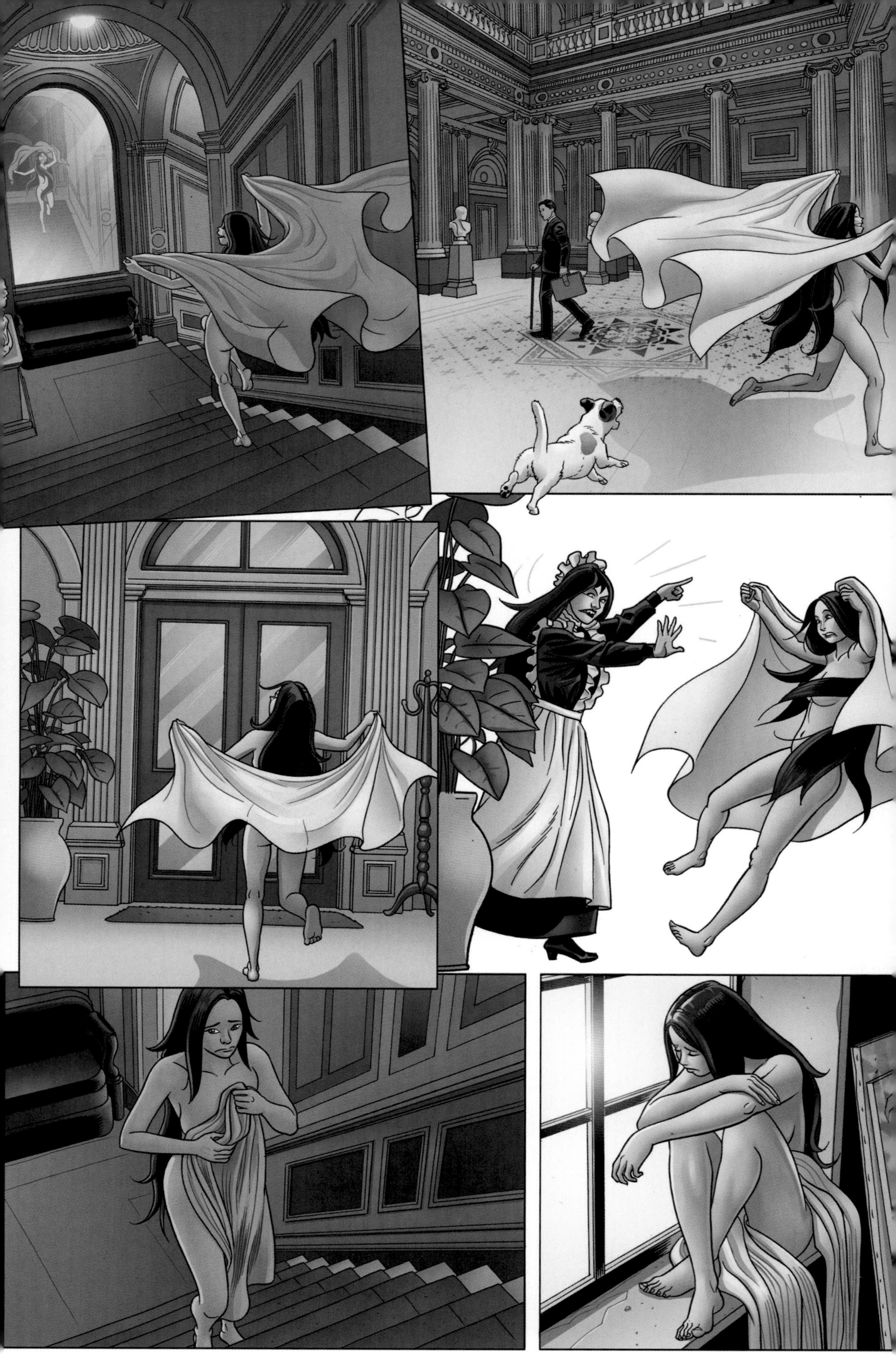

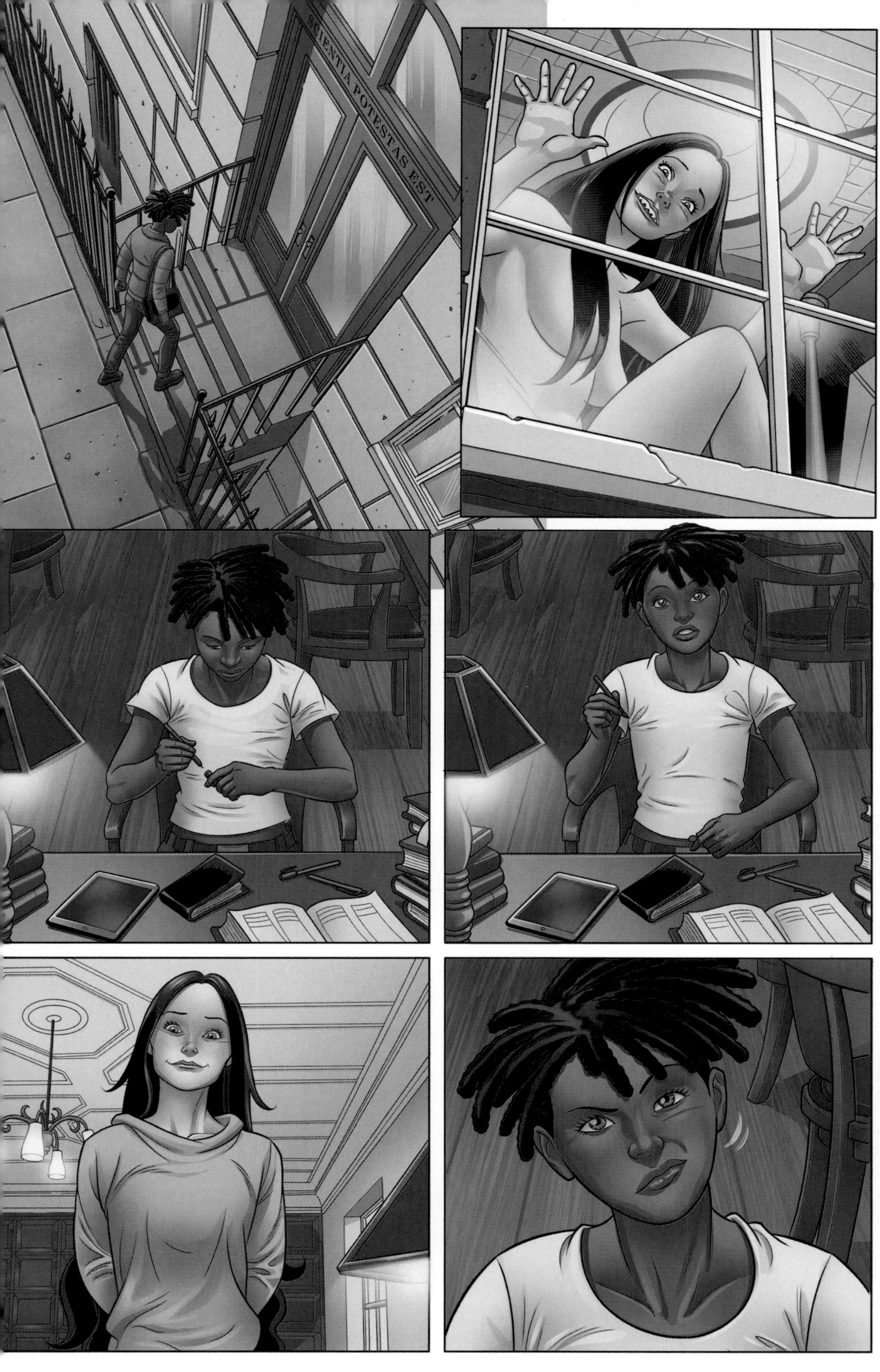
SCIENTIA POTESTAS EST

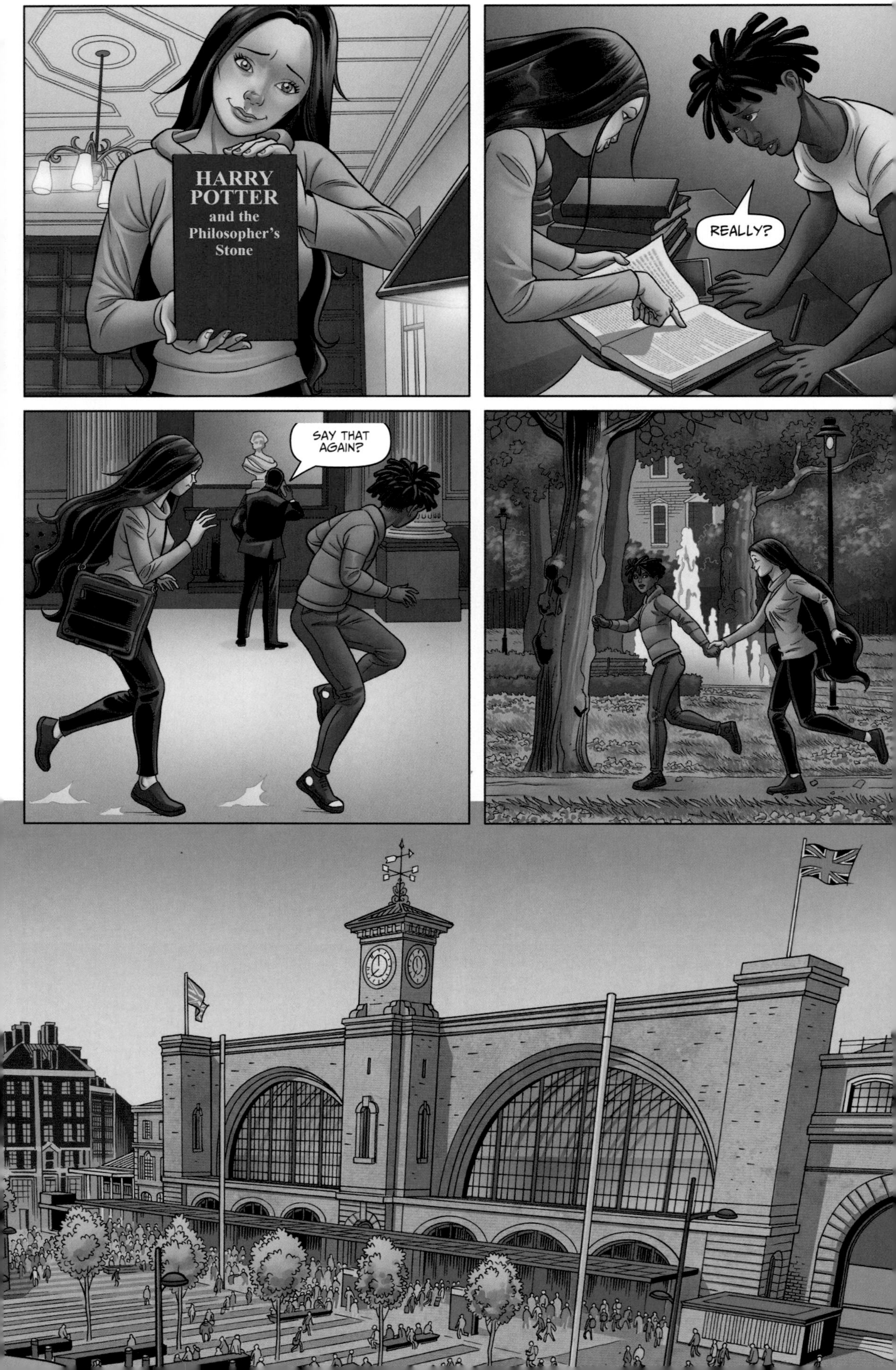
HARRY POTTER and the Philosopher's Stone
REALLY?
SAY THAT AGAIN?

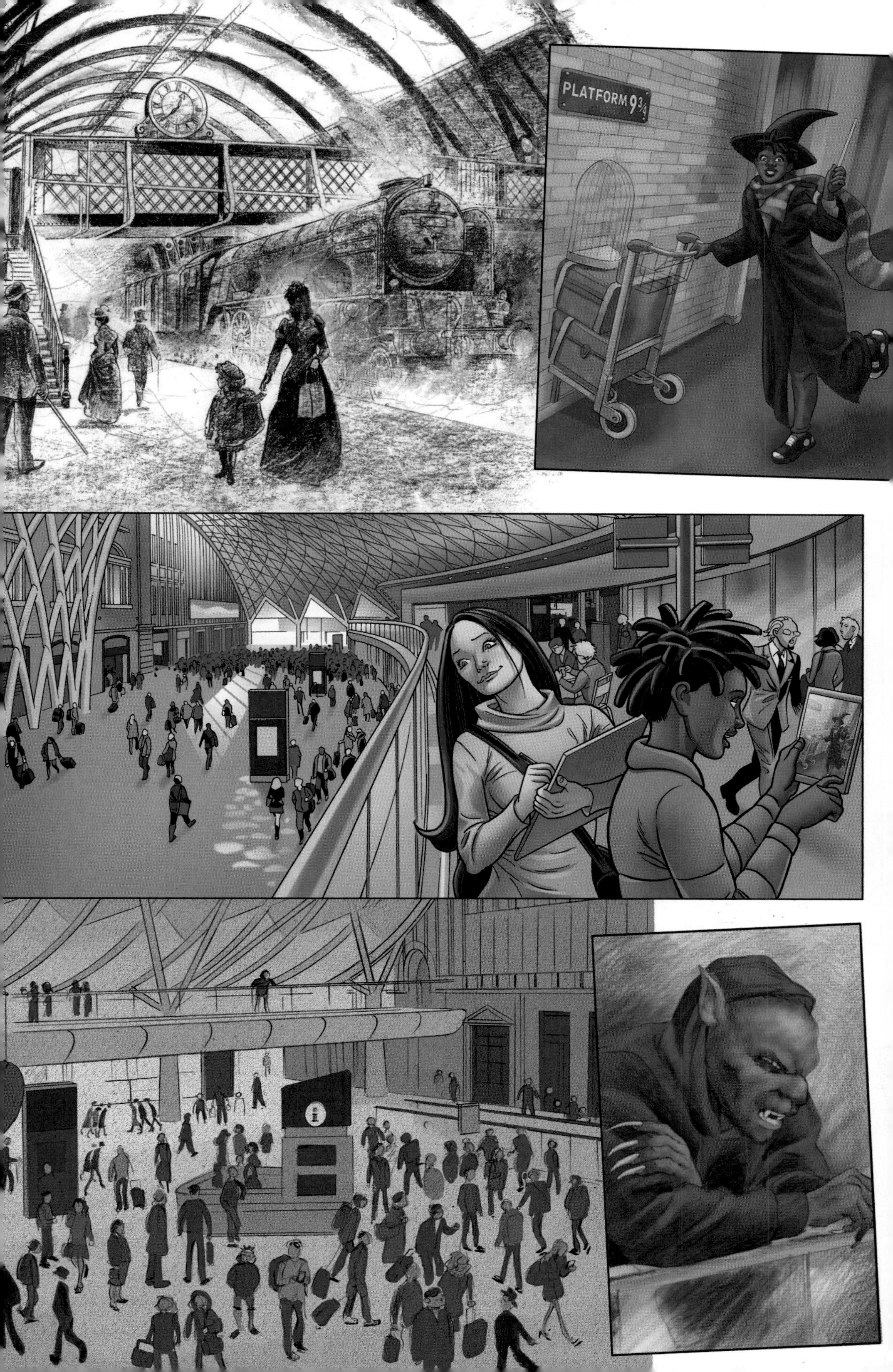
PLATFORM 9 3/4

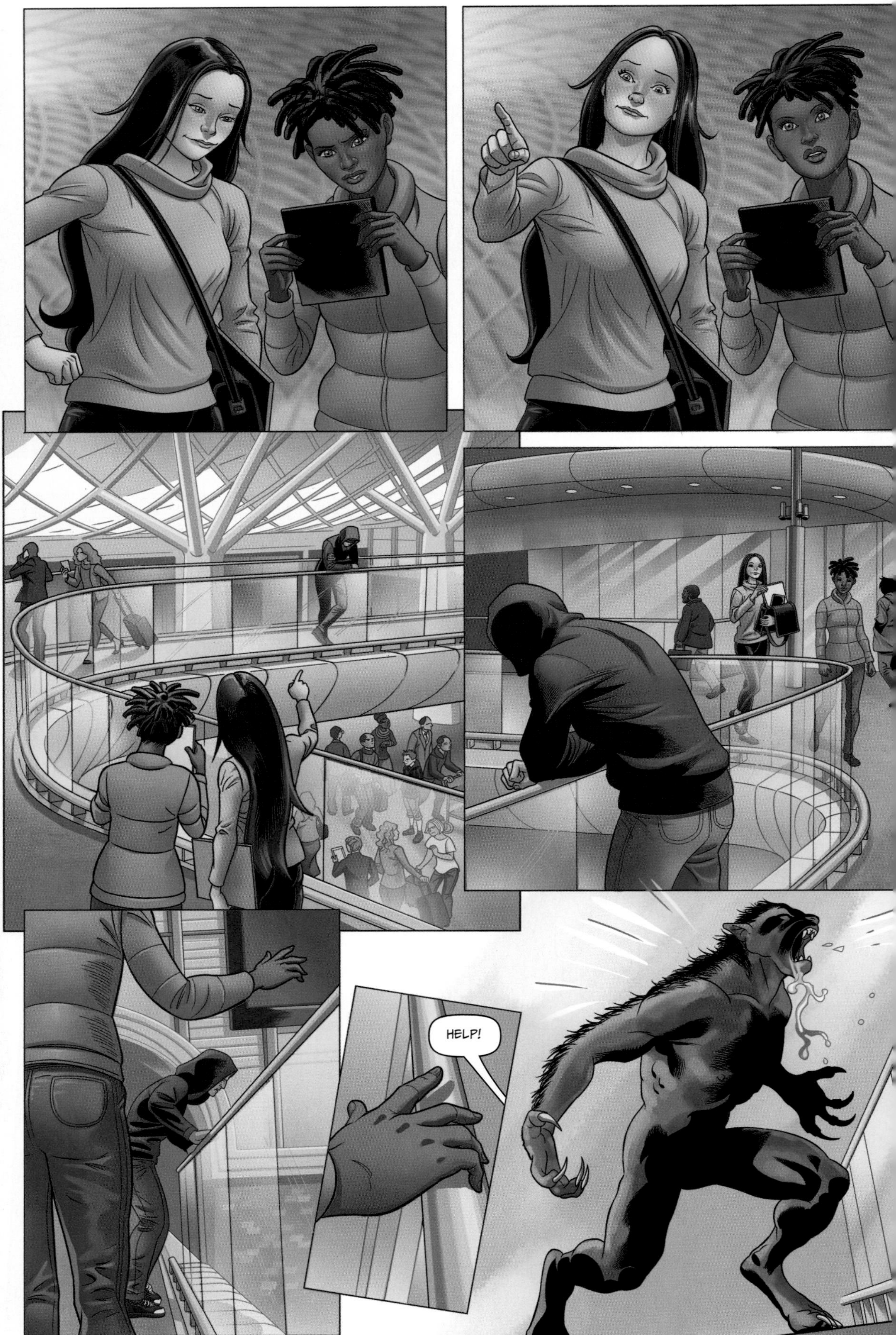
HELP!

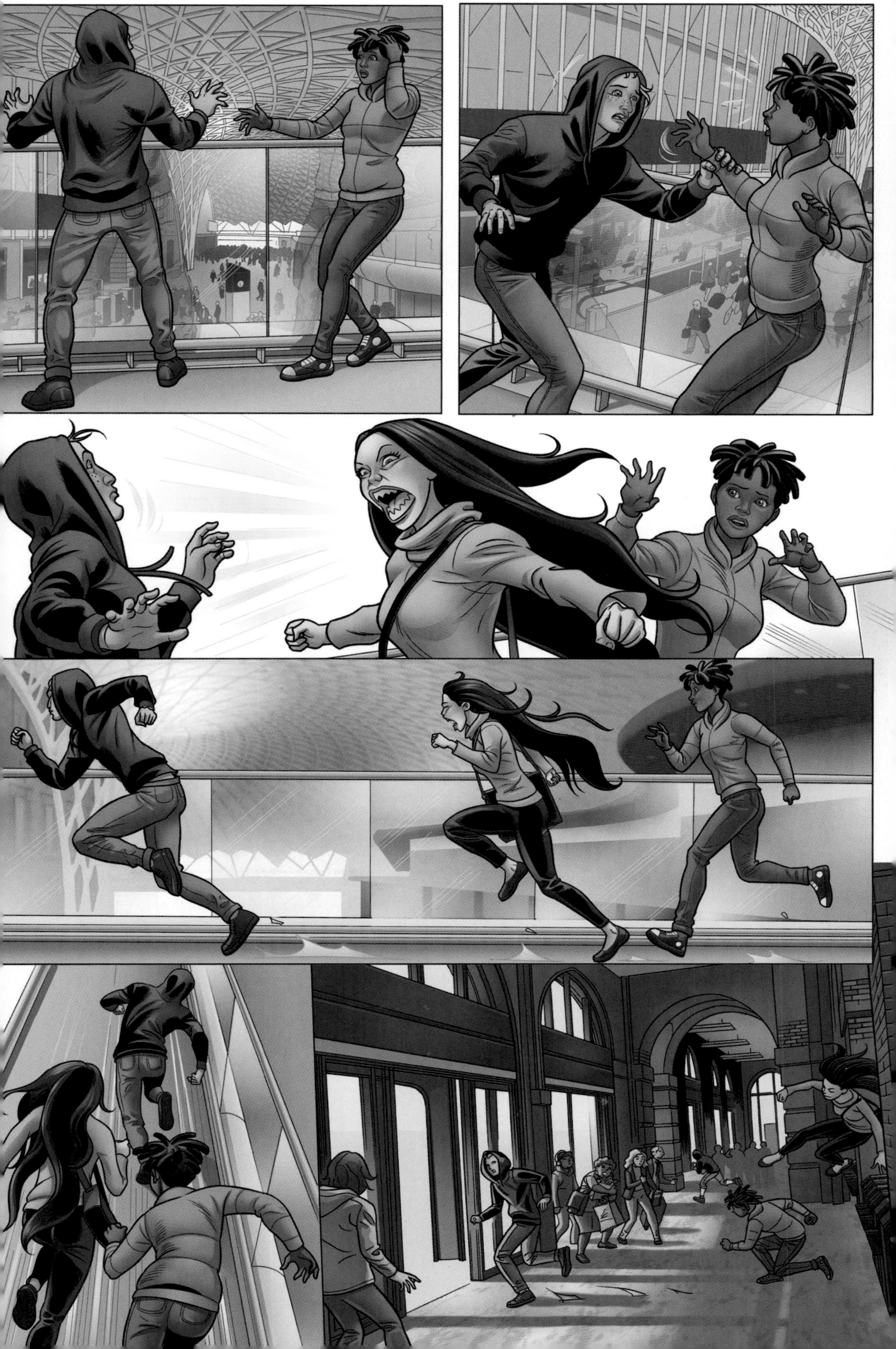

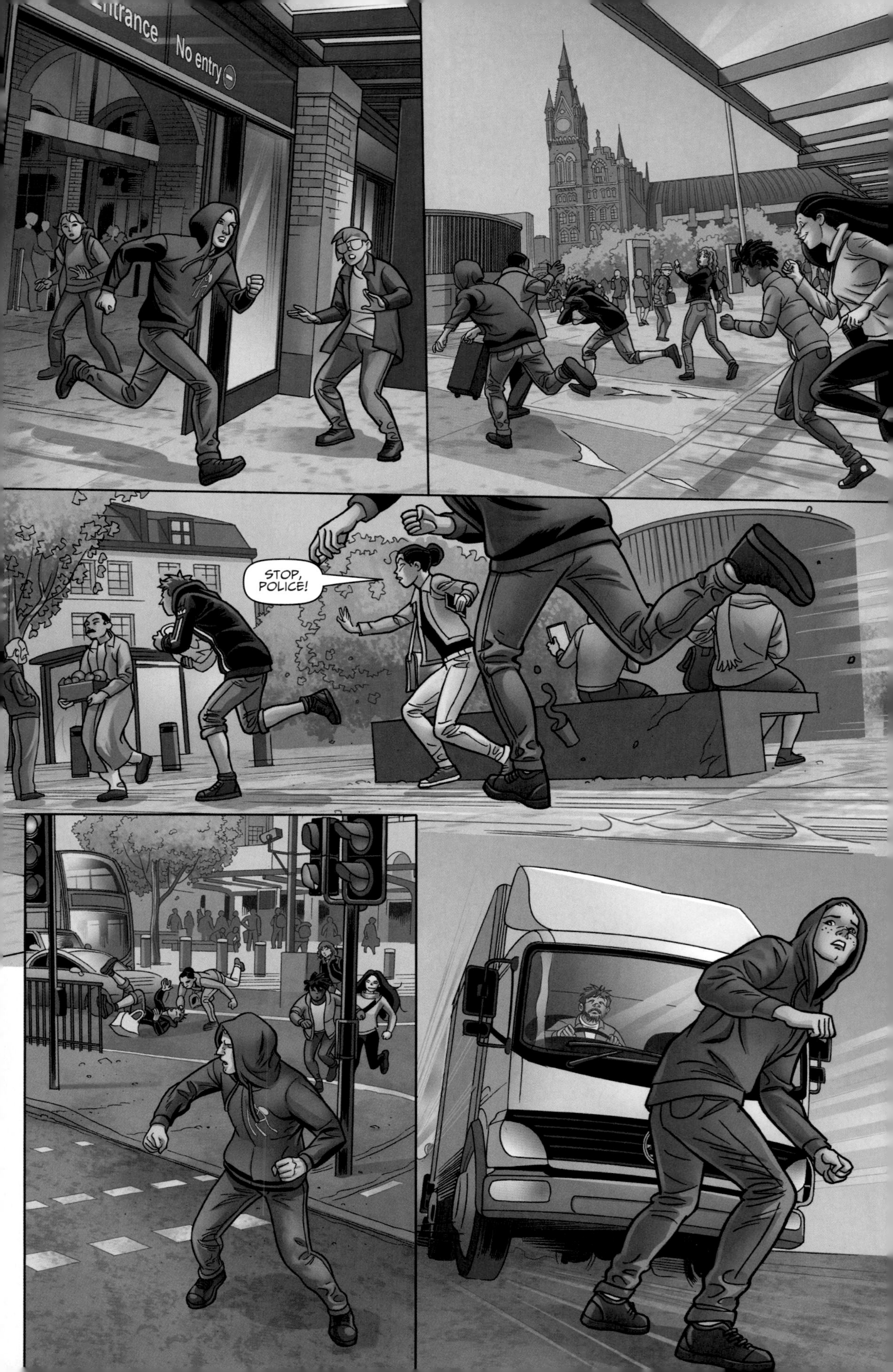
Entrance
No entry
STOP, POLICE!

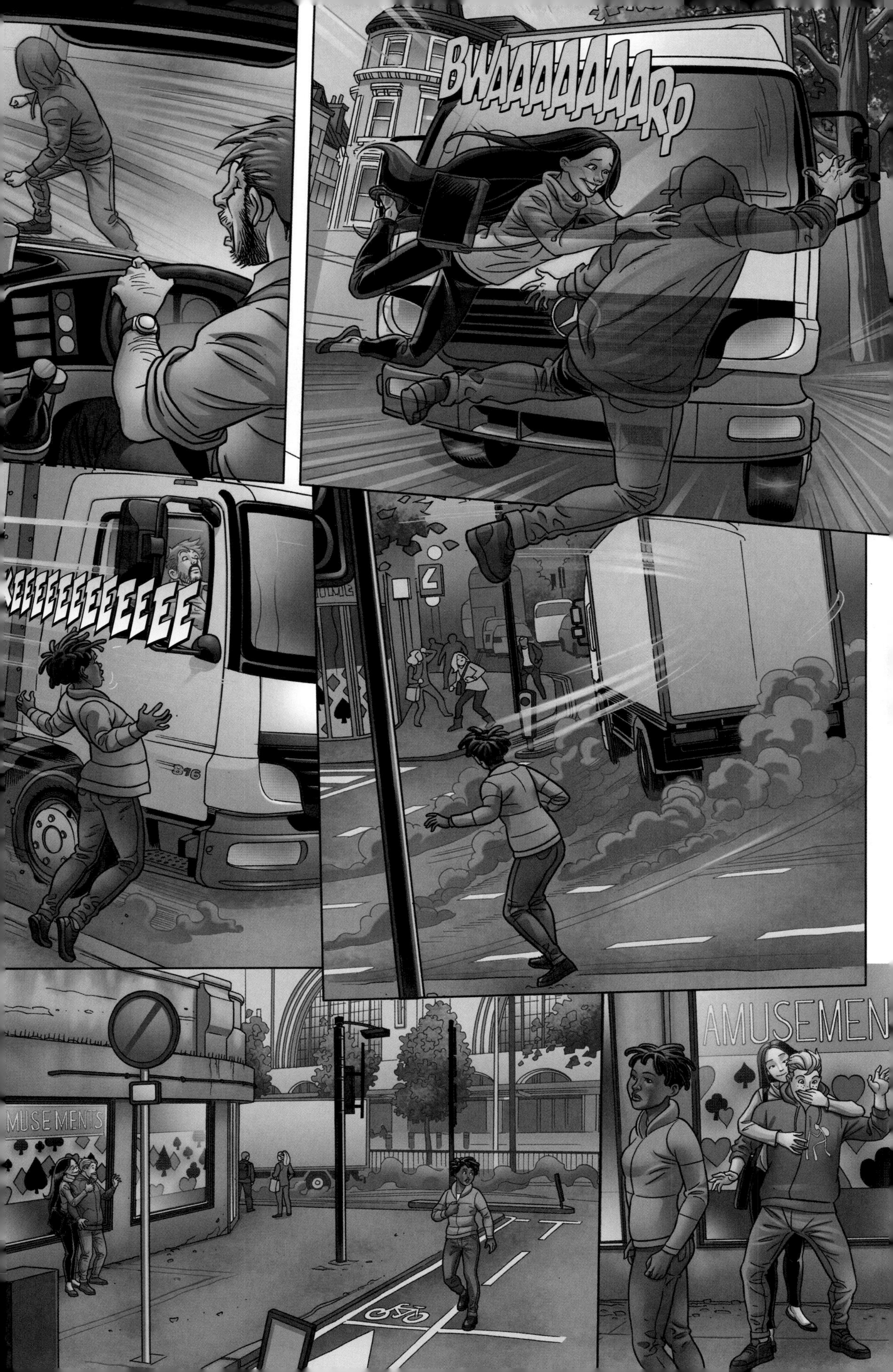
BWAAAAAAAARP
EEEEEEEEEEEEE
MUSEMENTS
AMUSEMEN

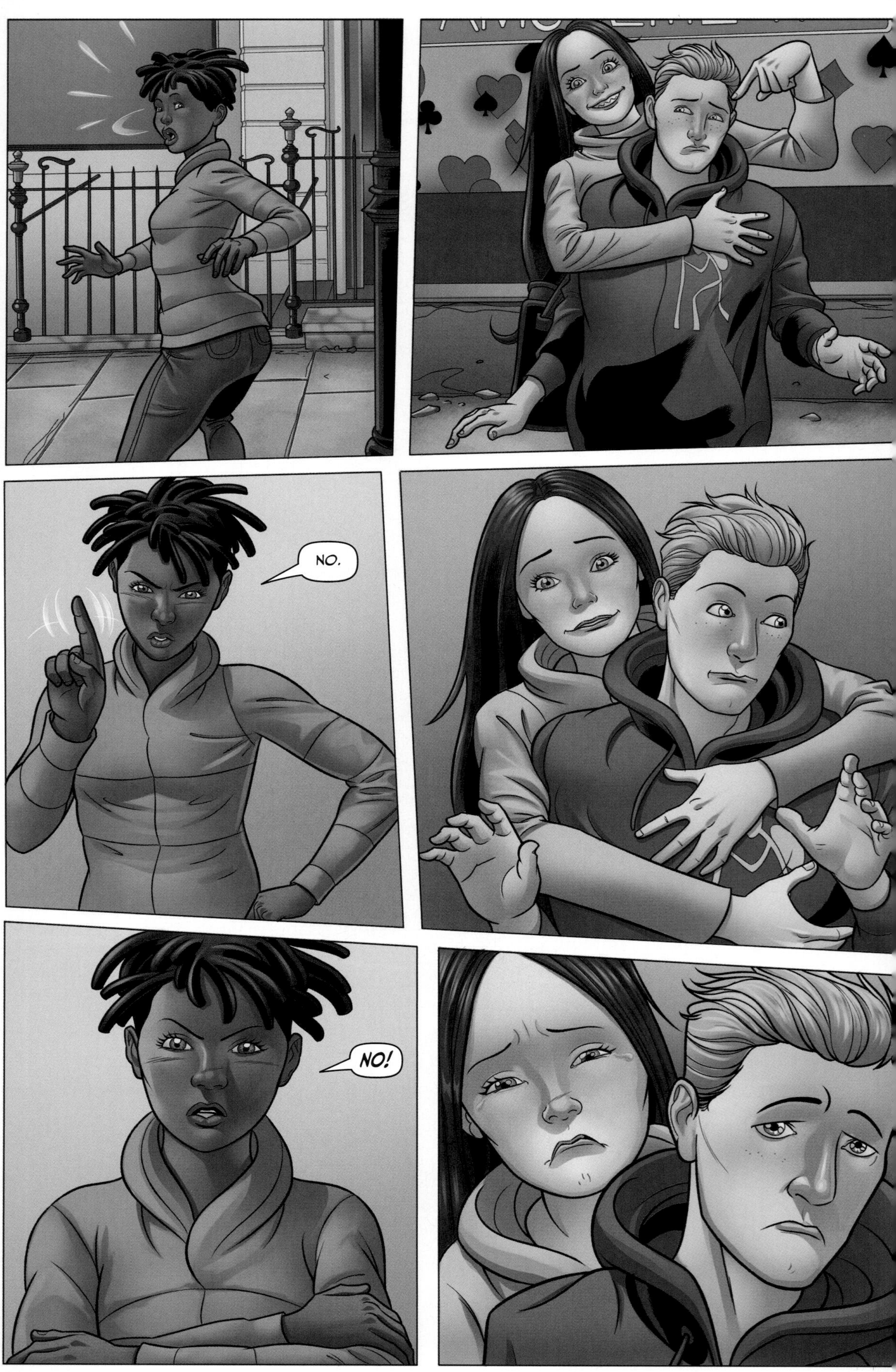
NO.
NO!

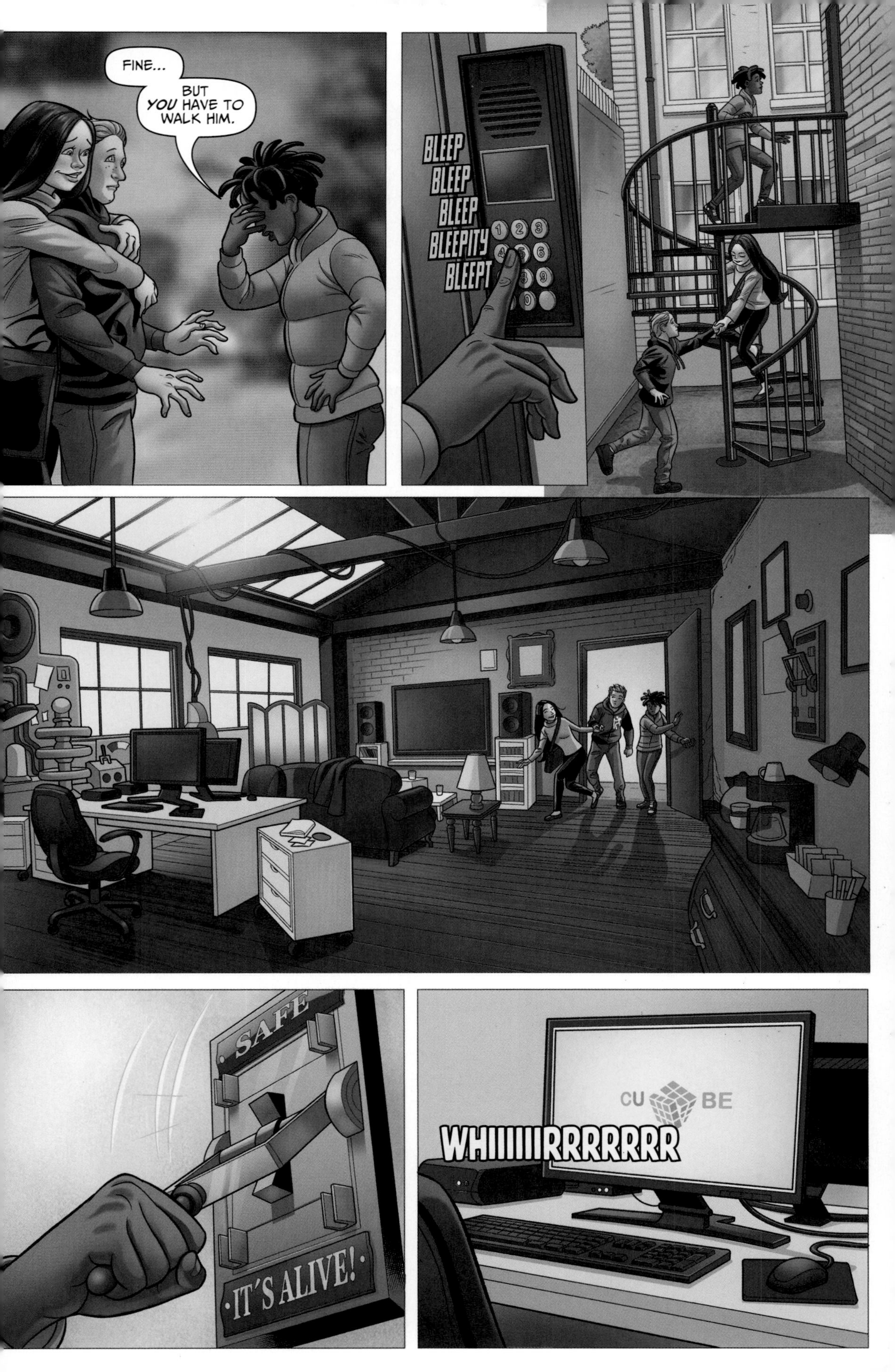
FINE...
BUT YOU HAVE TO WALK HIM.
BLEEP
BLEEP
BLEEP
BLEEPITY
BLEEPT
SAFE
IT'S ALIVE!
CU BE
WHIIIIIIRRRRRRR

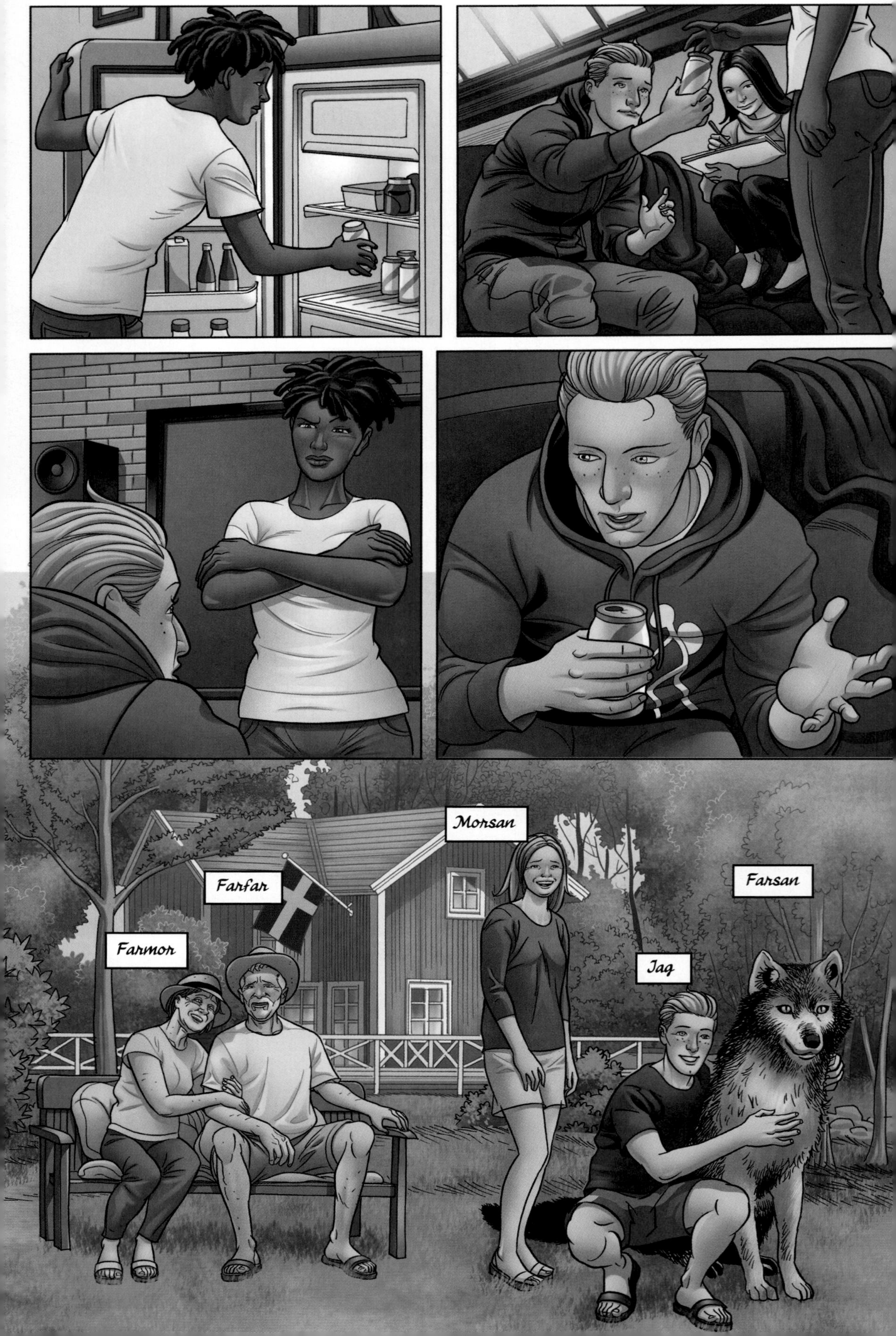
Morsan
Farfar
Farsan
Farmor
Jag

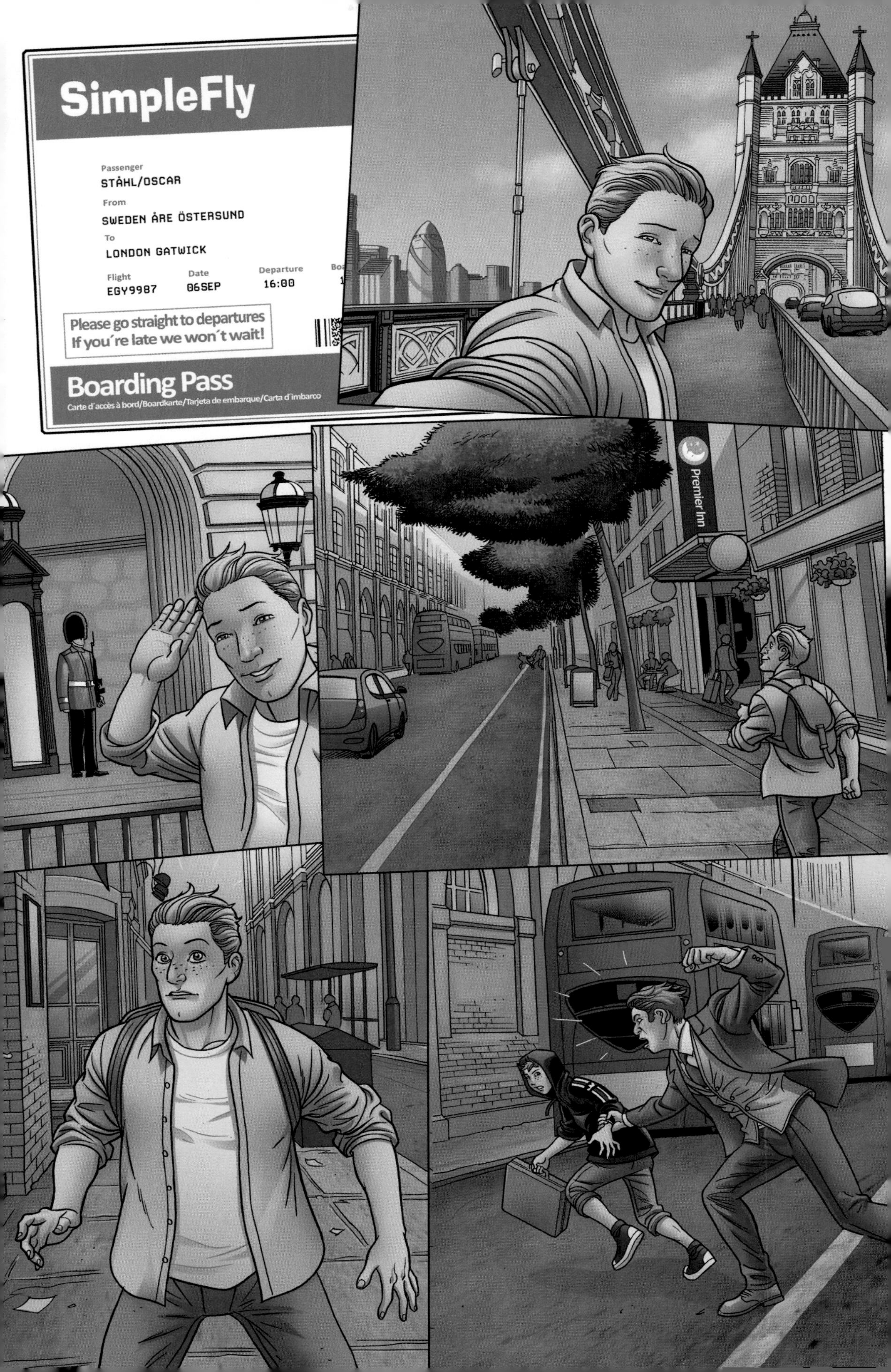
SimpleFly
Passenger
STÅHL/OSCAR
From
SWEDEN ÅRE ÖSTERSUND
To
LONDON GATWICK
Flight
EGY9987
Date
06SEP
Departure
16:00
Please go straight to departures
If you´re late we won´t wait!
Boarding Pass
Carte d´accès à bord/Boardkarte/Tarjeta de embarque/Carta d´imbarco
Premier Inn

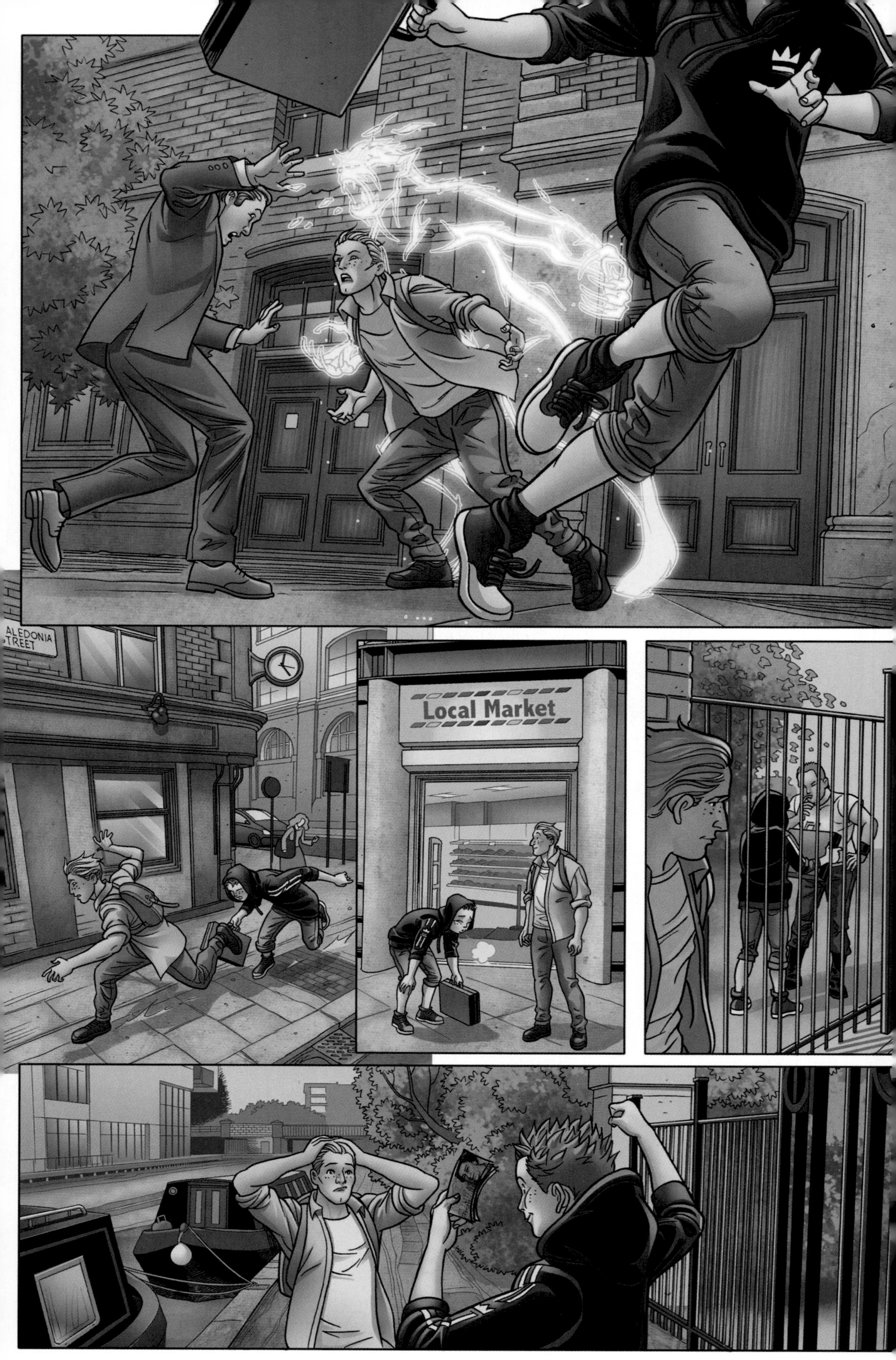
ALEDONIA
TREET
Local Market

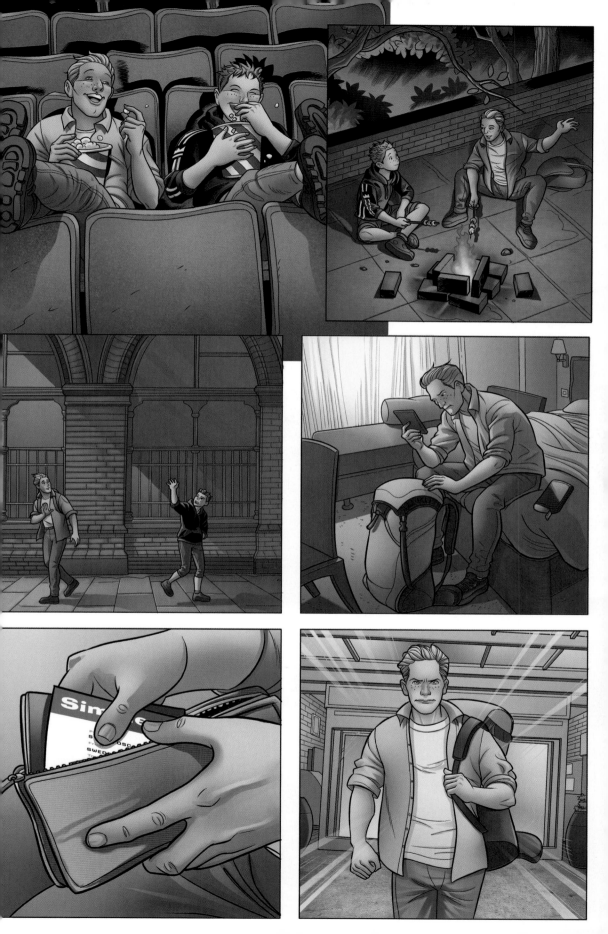

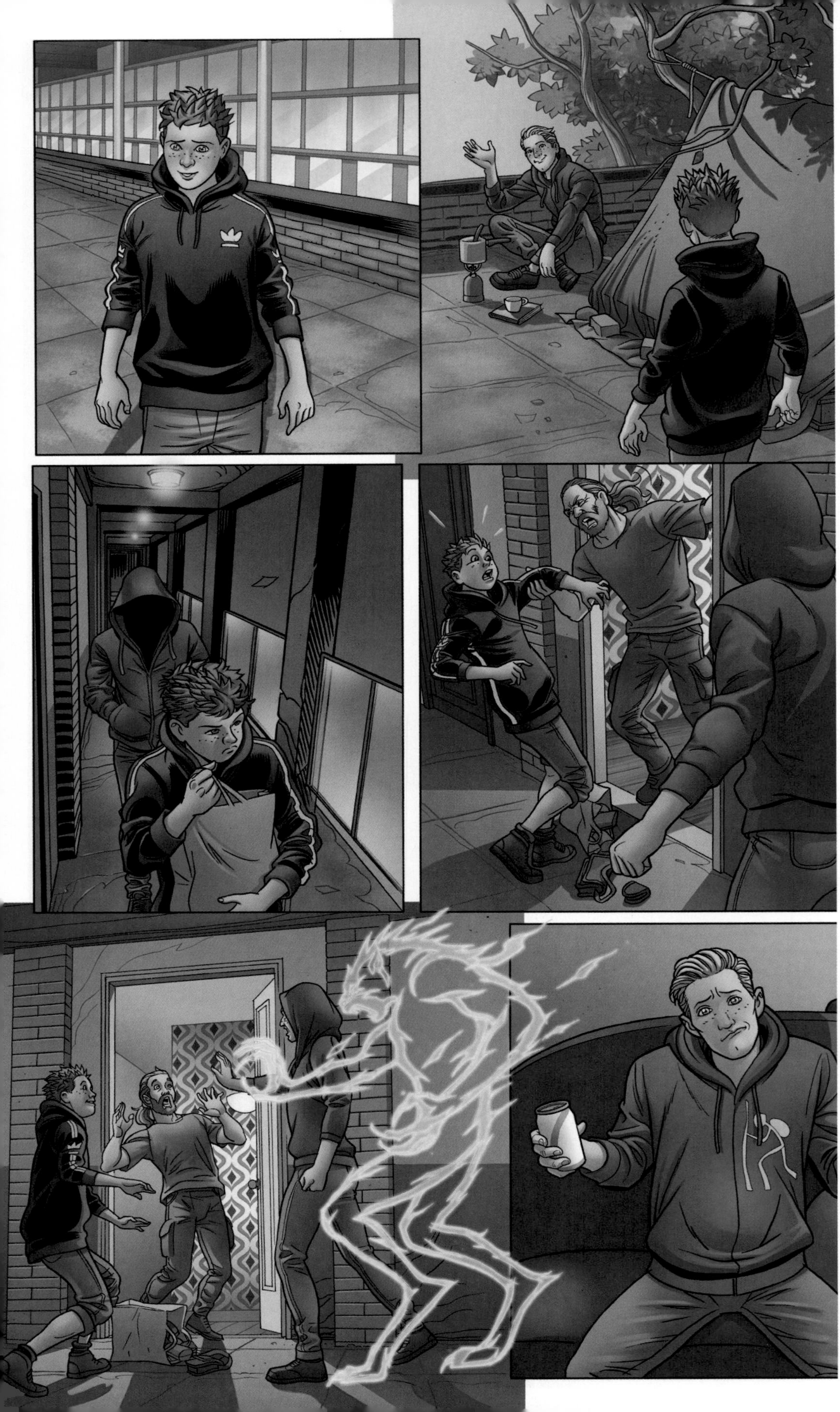

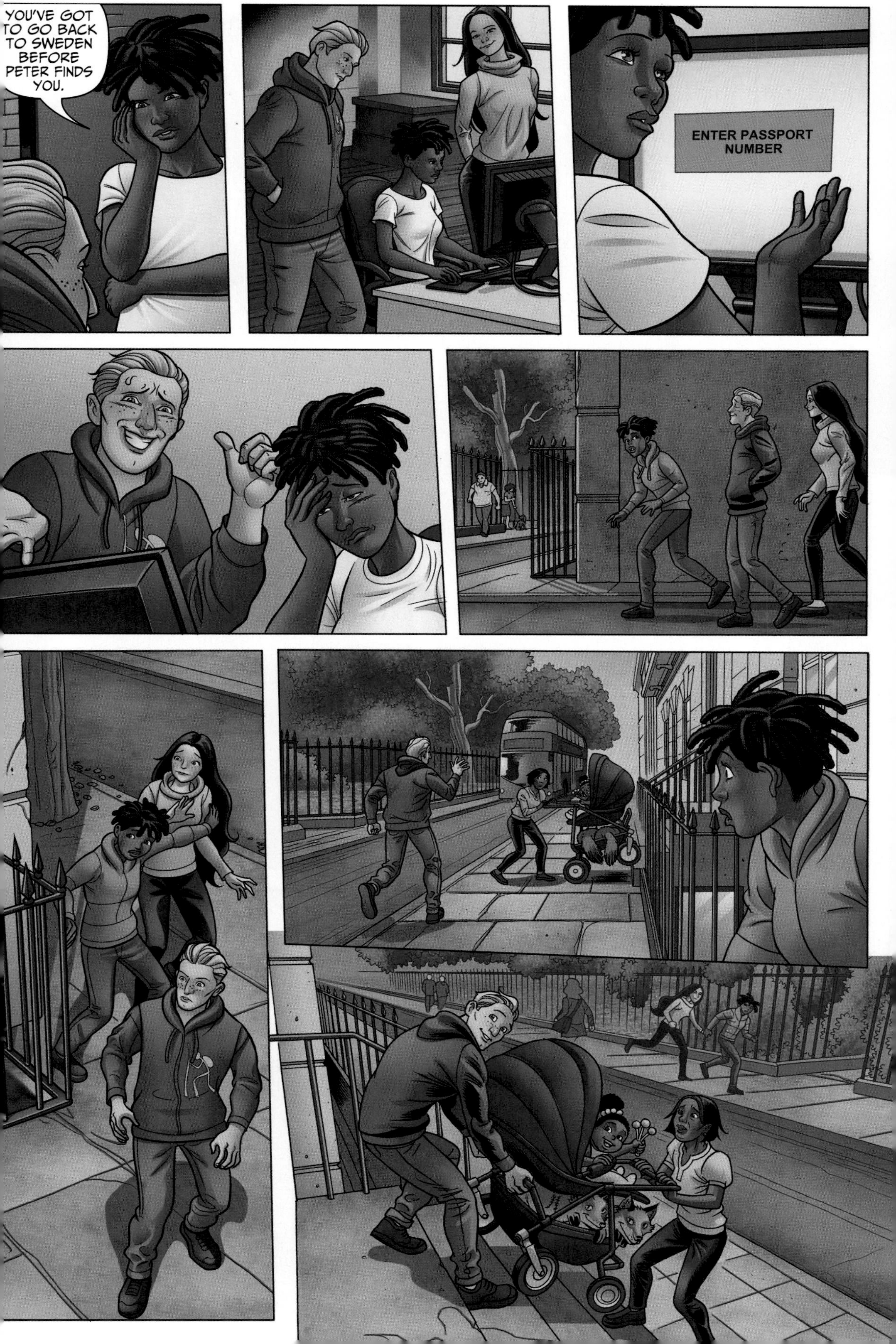
YOU'VE GOT TO GO BACK TO SWEDEN BEFORE PETER FINDS YOU.
ENTER PASSPORT NUMBER

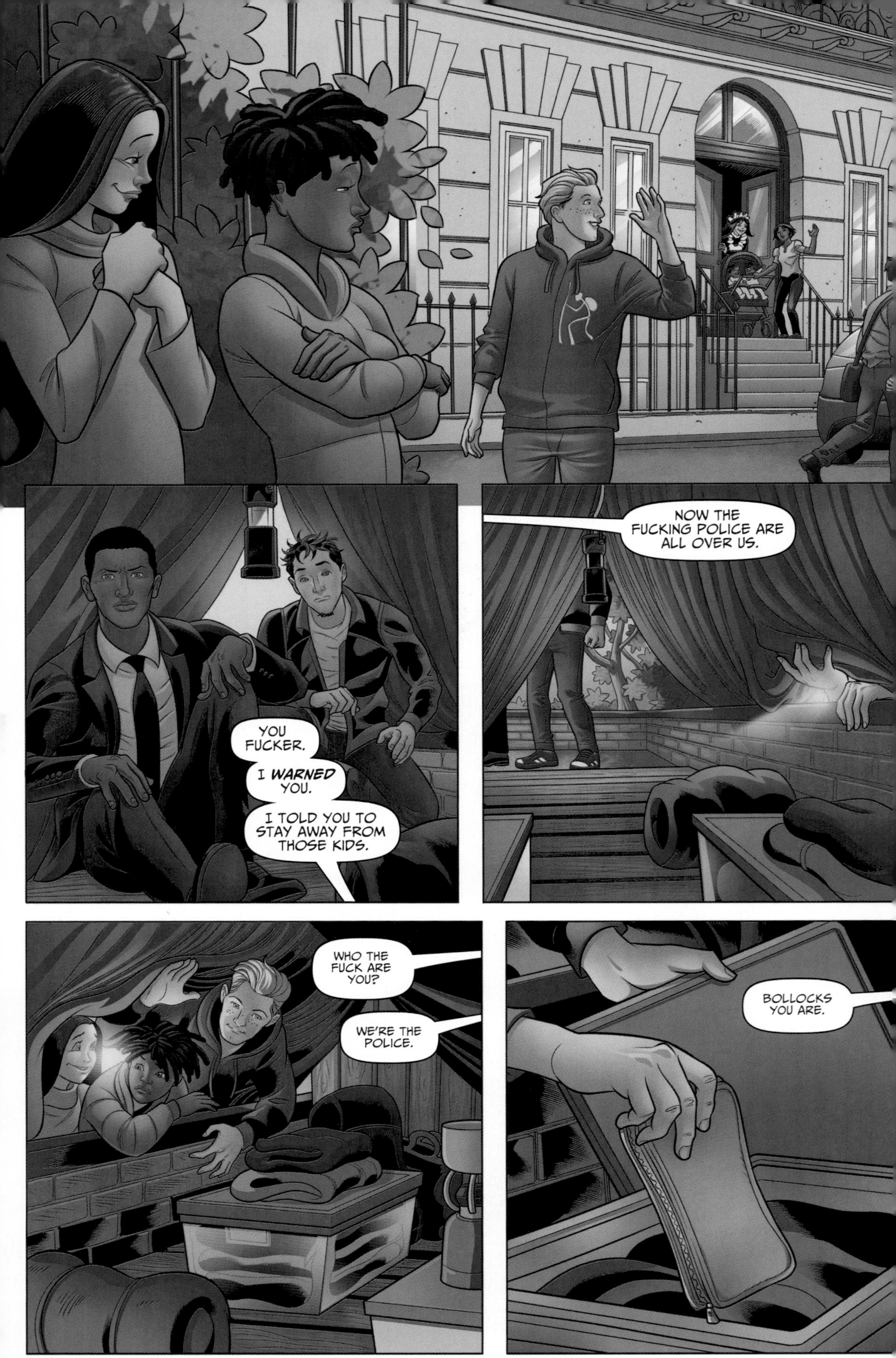
YOU FUCKER.
I WARNED YOU.
I TOLD YOU TO STAY AWAY FROM THOSE KIDS.
NOW THE FUCKING POLICE ARE ALL OVER US.
WHO THE FUCK ARE YOU?
WE'RE THE POLICE.
BOLLOCKS YOU ARE.

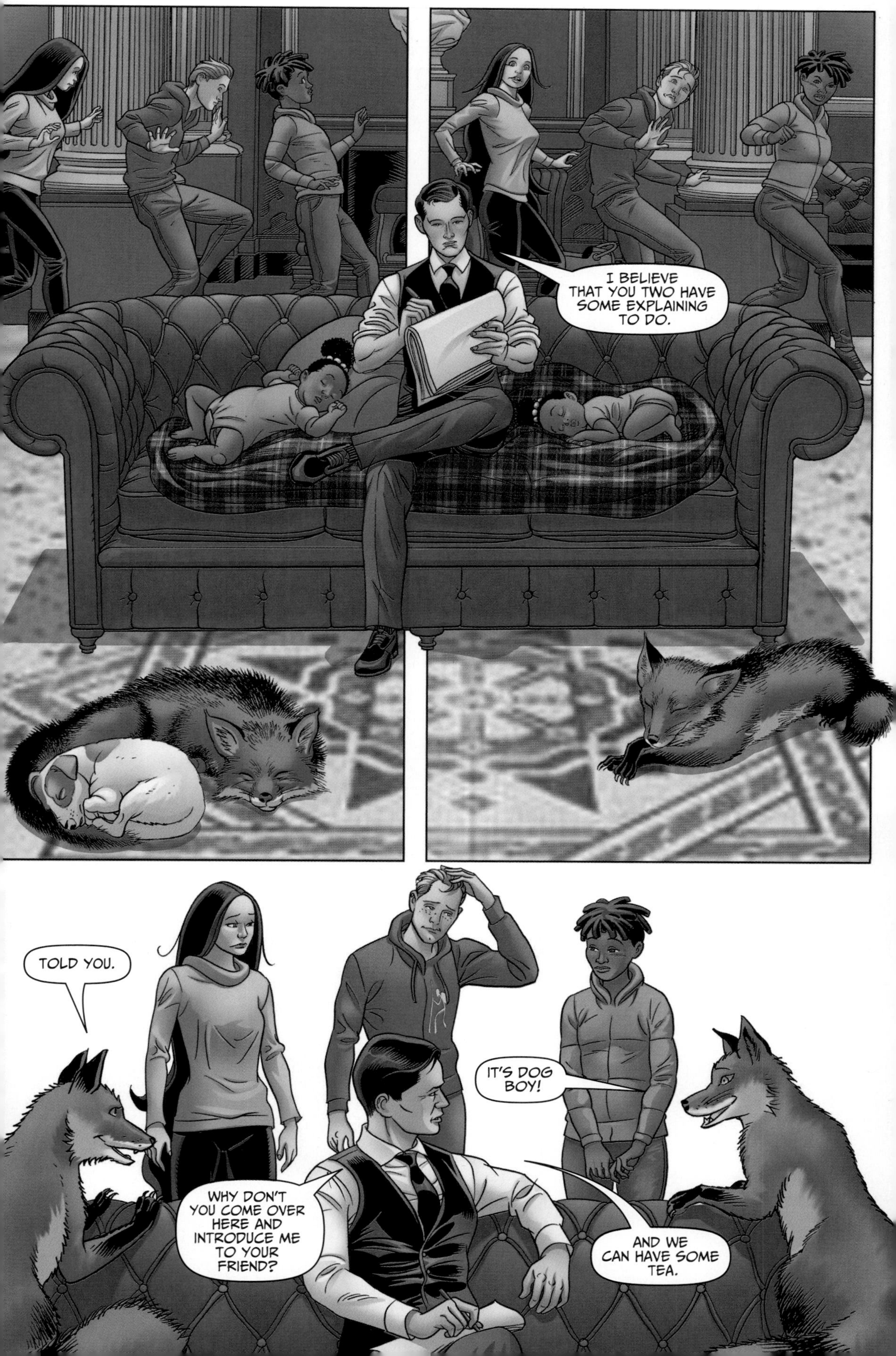
I BELIEVE THAT YOU TWO HAVE SOME EXPLAINING TO DO.
TOLD YOU.
IT'S DOG BOY!
WHY DON'T YOU COME OVER HERE AND INTRODUCE ME TO YOUR FRIEND?
AND WE CAN HAVE SOME TEA.

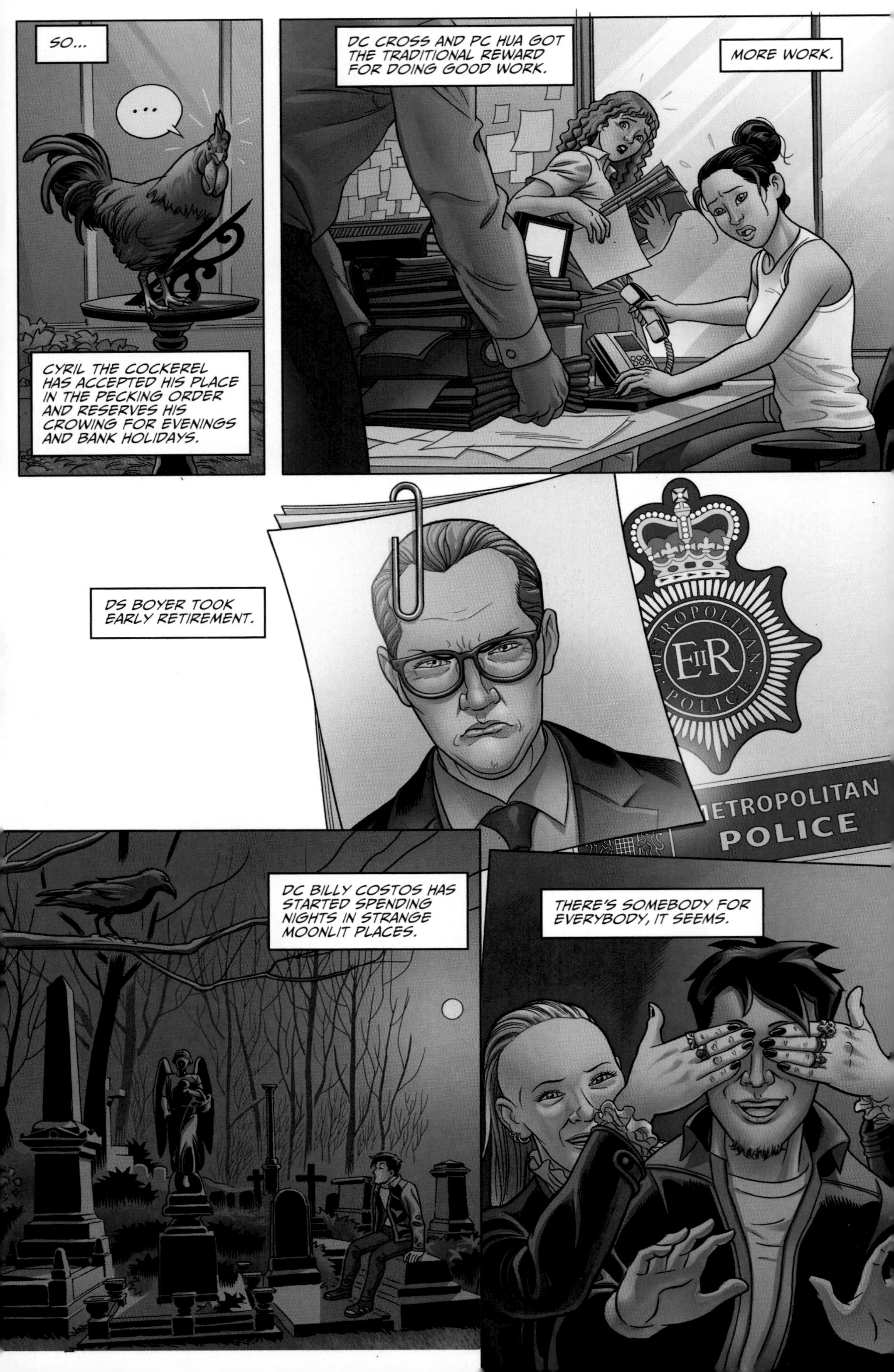
SO...
...
CYRIL THE COCKEREL HAS ACCEPTED HIS PLACE IN THE PECKING ORDER AND RESERVES HIS CROWING FOR EVENINGS AND BANK HOLIDAYS.
DC CROSS AND PC HUA GOT THE TRADITIONAL REWARD FOR DOING GOOD WORK.
MORE WORK.
DS BOYER TOOK EARLY RETIREMENT.
METROPOLITAN POLICE
EIIR
METROPOLITAN POLICE
DC BILLY COSTOS HAS STARTED SPENDING NIGHTS IN STRANGE MOONLIT PLACES.
THERE'S SOMEBODY FOR EVERYBODY, IT SEEMS.

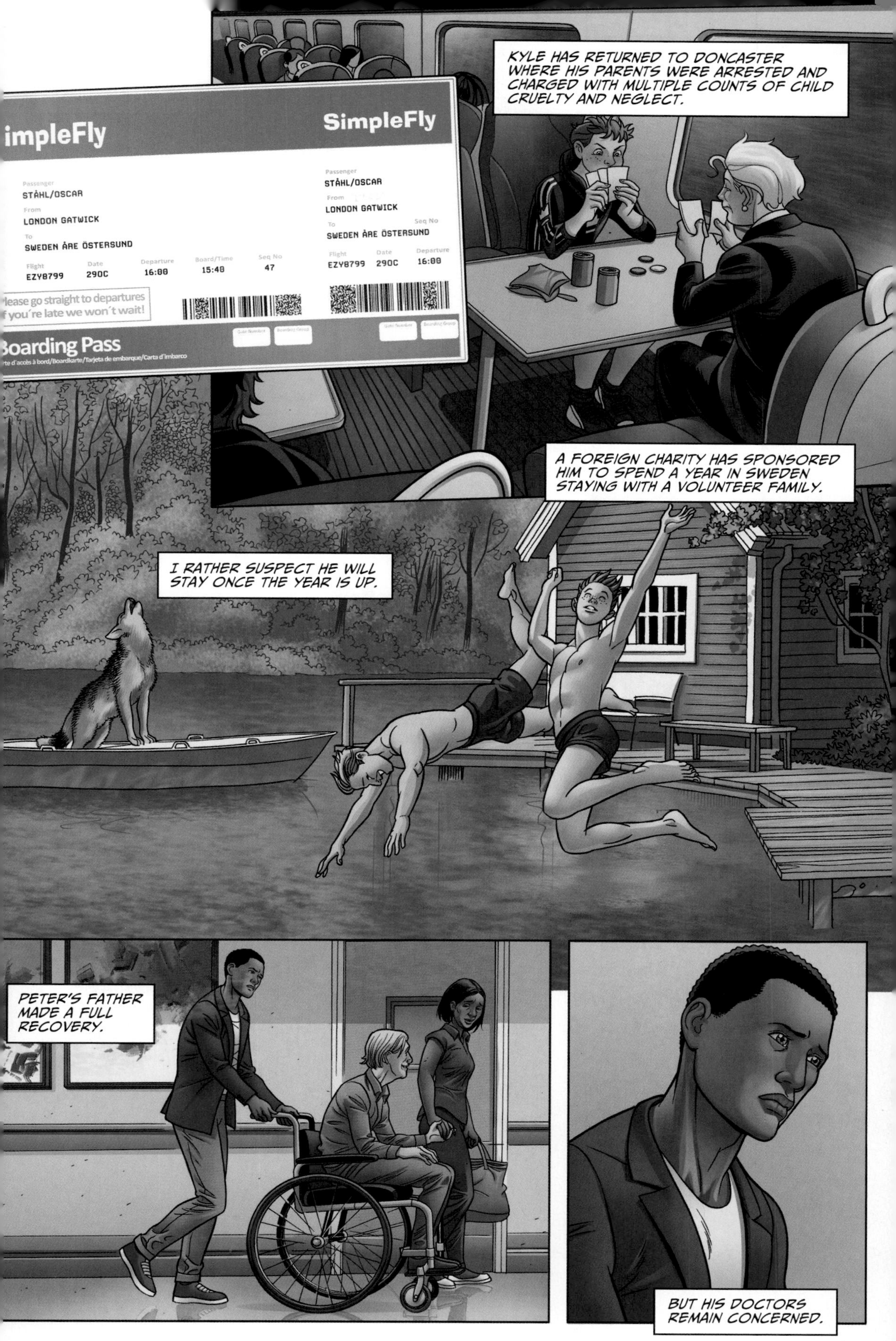
impleFly
SimpleFly
Passenger
STÅHL/OSCAR
From
LONDON GATWICK
To
SWEDEN ÅRE ÖSTERSUND
Flight
EZY8799
Date
29OC
Departure
16:00
Board/Time
15:40
Seq No
47
Please go straight to departures
if you´re late we won´t wait!
Boarding Pass
rte d'accès à bord/Boardkarte/Tarjeta de embarque/Carta d'imbarco
Passenger
STÅHL/OSCAR
From
LONDON GATWICK
To
Seq No
SWEDEN ÅRE ÖSTERSUND
Flight
EZY8799
Date
29OC
Departure
16:00
KYLE HAS RETURNED TO DONCASTER WHERE HIS PARENTS WERE ARRESTED AND CHARGED WITH MULTIPLE COUNTS OF CHILD CRUELTY AND NEGLECT.
A FOREIGN CHARITY HAS SPONSORED HIM TO SPEND A YEAR IN SWEDEN STAYING WITH A VOLUNTEER FAMILY.
I RATHER SUSPECT HE WILL STAY ONCE THE YEAR IS UP.
PETER'S FATHER MADE A FULL RECOVERY.
BUT HIS DOCTORS REMAIN CONCERNED.

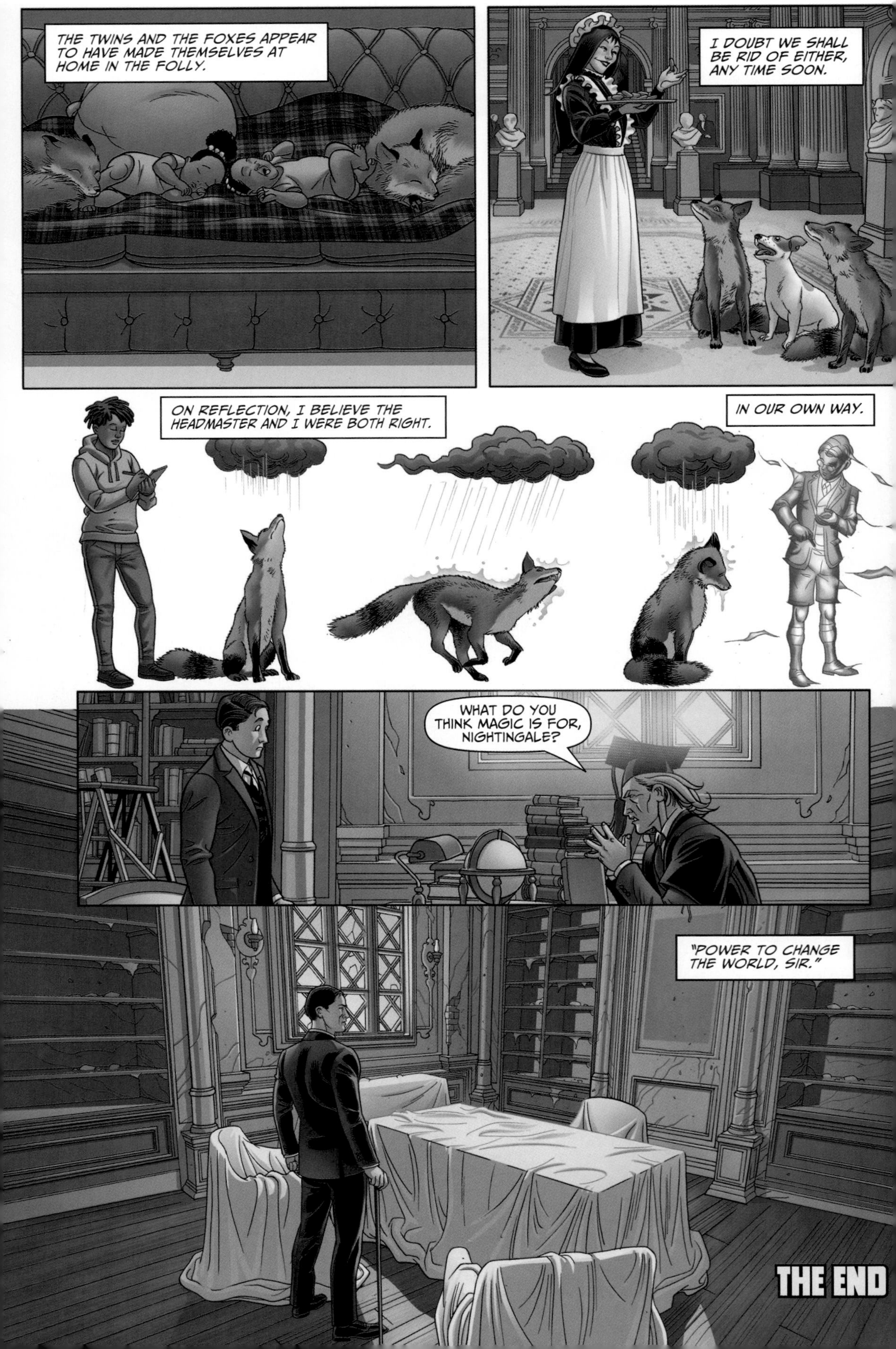
THE TWINS AND THE FOXES APPEAR TO HAVE MADE THEMSELVES AT HOME IN THE FOLLY.
I DOUBT WE SHALL BE RID OF EITHER, ANY TIME SOON.
ON REFLECTION, I BELIEVE THE HEADMASTER AND I WERE BOTH RIGHT.
IN OUR OWN WAY.
WHAT DO YOU THINK MAGIC IS FOR, NIGHTINGALE?
"POWER TO CHANGE THE WORLD, SIR."
THE END

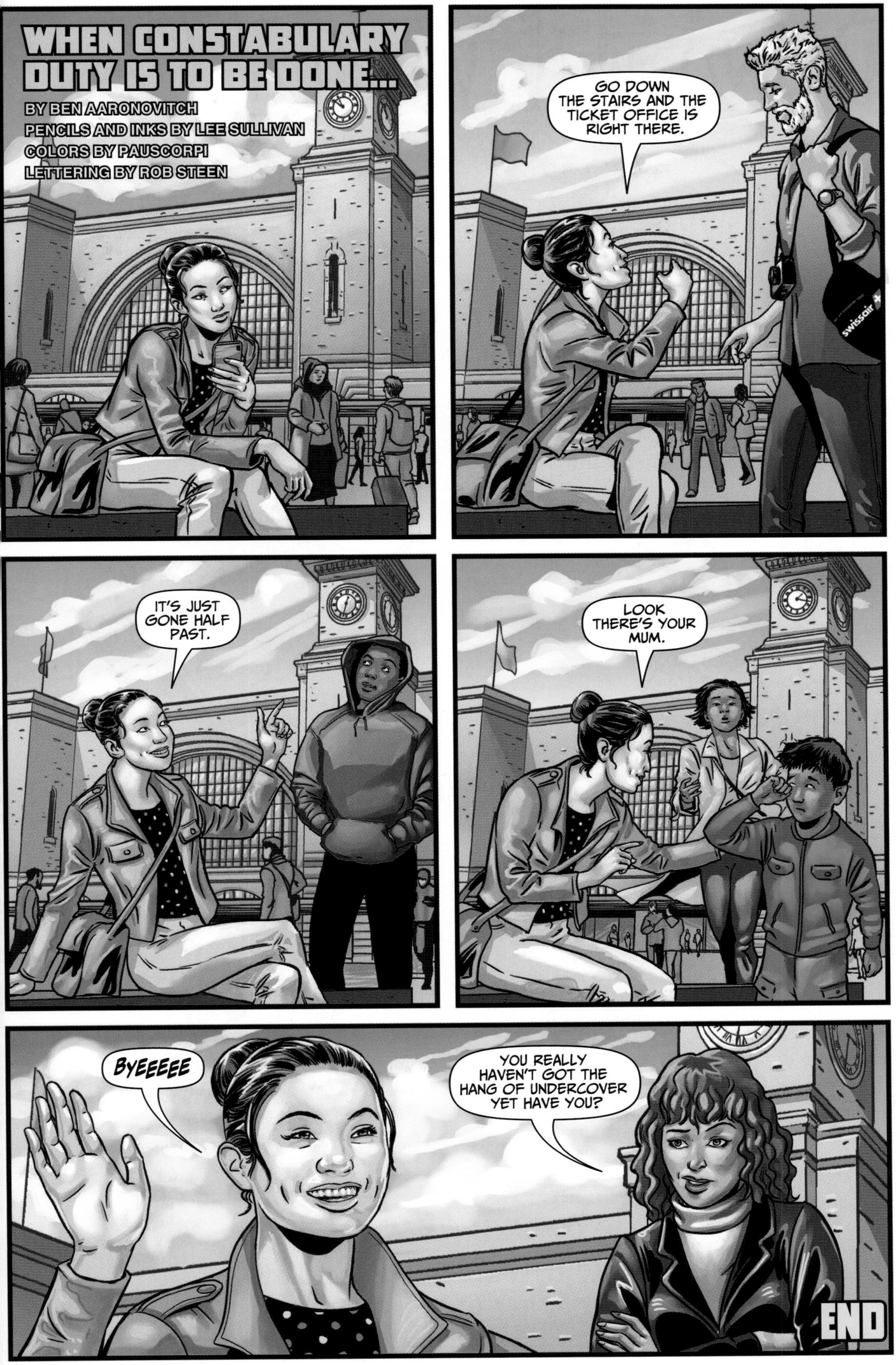
WHEN CONSTABULARY DUTY IS TO BE DONE...
BY BEN AARONOVITCH
PENCILS AND INKS BY LEE SULLIVAN
COLORS BY PAUSCORPI
LETTERING BY ROB STEEN
GO DOWN THE STAIRS AND THE TICKET OFFICE IS RIGHT THERE.
swissair
IT'S JUST GONE HALF PAST.
LOOK THERE'S YOUR MUM.
BYEEEEE
YOU REALLY HAVEN'T GOT THE HANG OF UNDERCOVER YET HAVE YOU?
END

Down with Wizzard Skool!

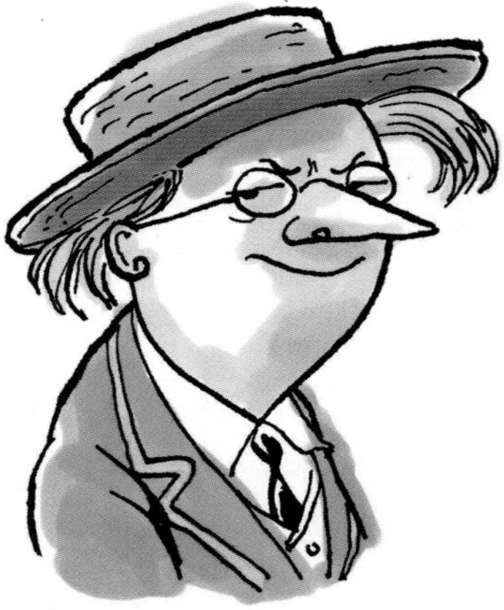

'N. Taupwert Esq. – our hero'

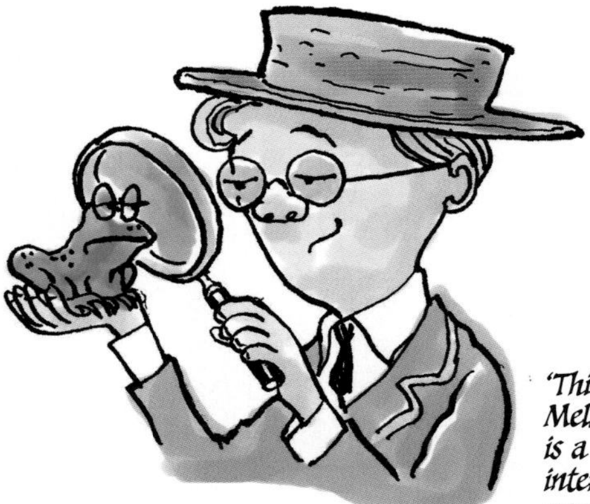

'This is David Mellenby who is a swot and interested in everything.'

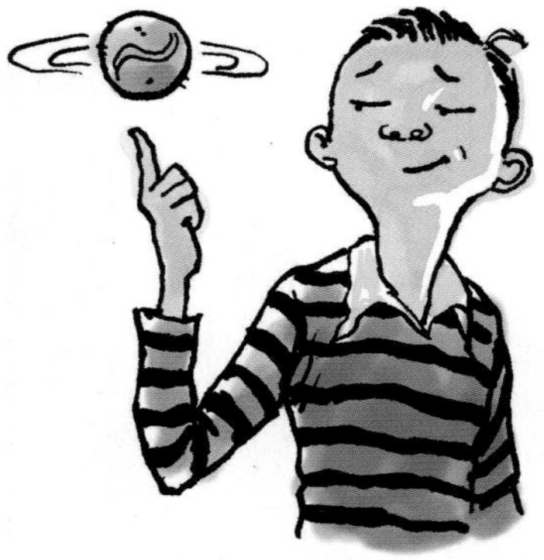

'This is T. Nightingale who is a prefect and tops at everything.'

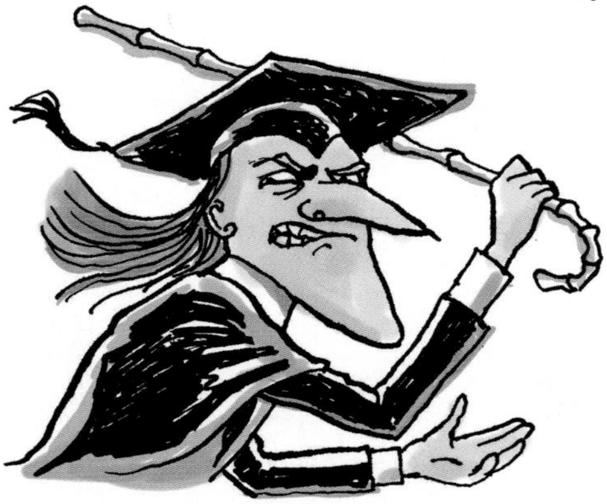

'This is the headmaster who also teaches spells.'

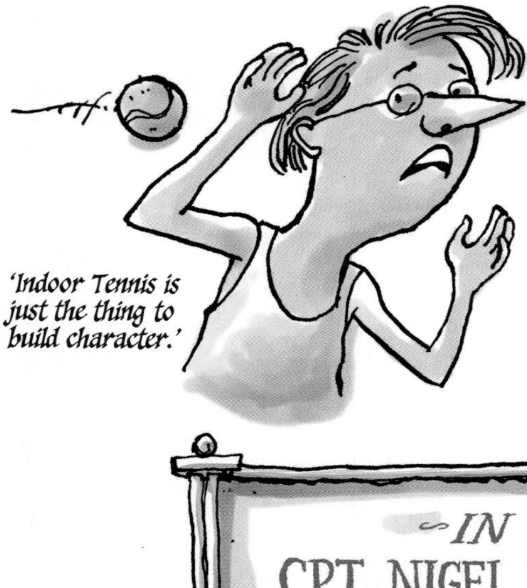

'Indoor Tennis is just the thing to build character.'

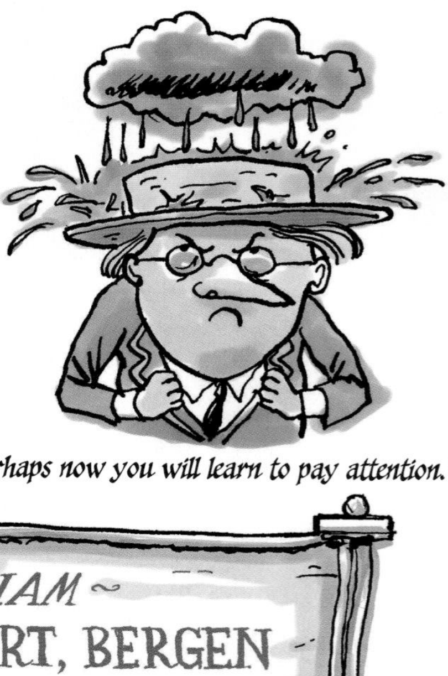

'Perhaps now you will learn to pay attention.'

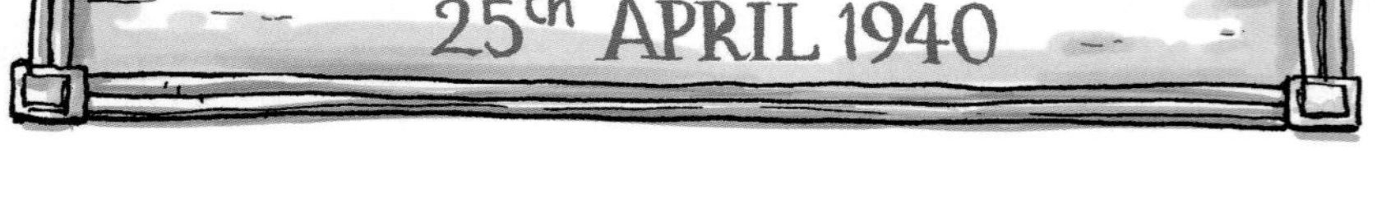
IN MEMORIAM
CPT. NIGEL TAUPWERT, BERGEN
25th APRIL 1940

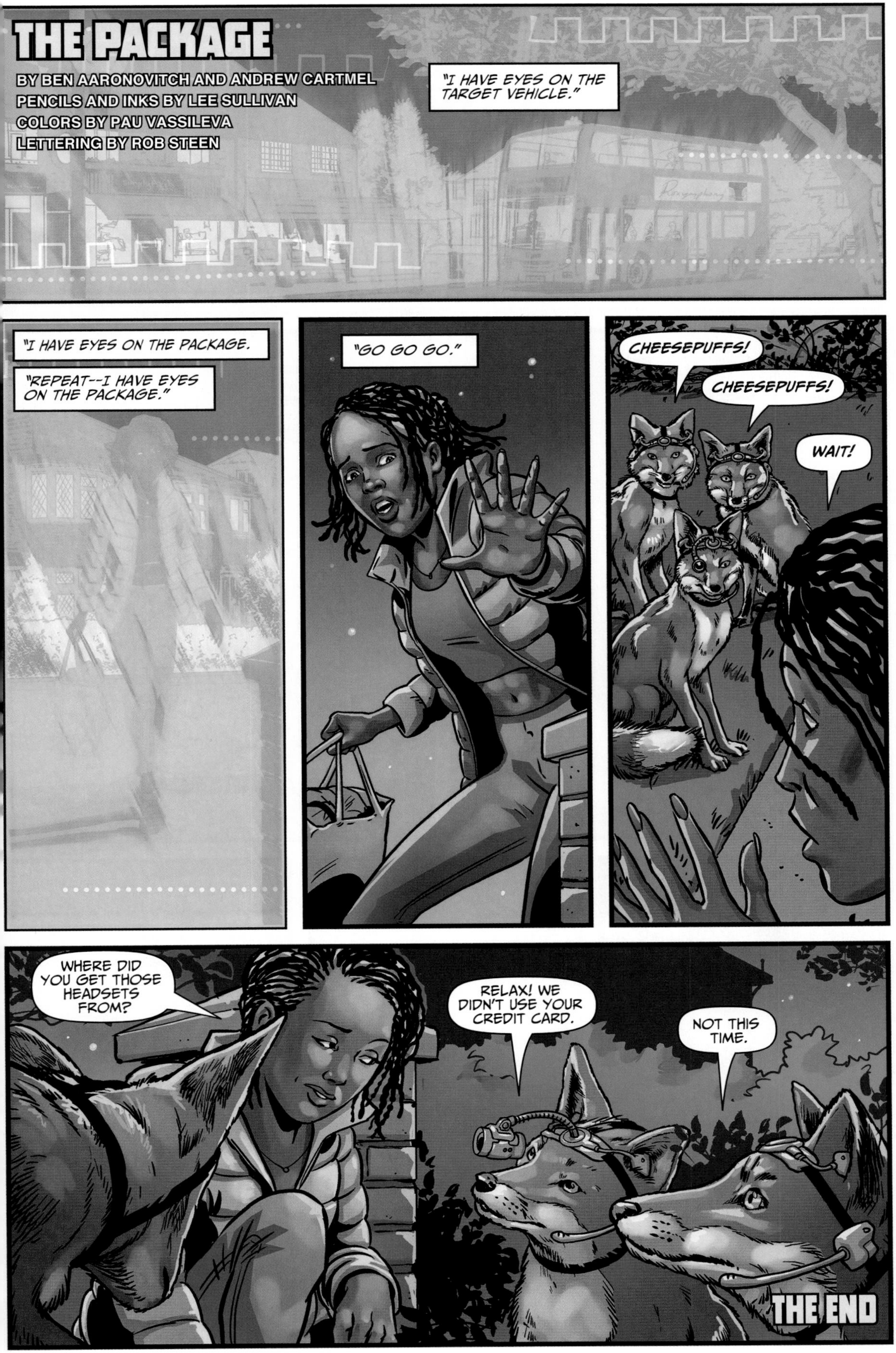
THE PACKAGE
BY BEN AARONOVITCH AND ANDREW CARTMEL
PENCILS AND INKS BY LEE SULLIVAN
COLORS BY PAU VASSILEVA
LETTERING BY ROB STEEN
"I HAVE EYES ON THE TARGET VEHICLE."
"I HAVE EYES ON THE PACKAGE.
"REPEAT--I HAVE EYES ON THE PACKAGE."
"GO GO GO."
CHEESEPUFFS!
CHEESEPUFFS!
WAIT!
WHERE DID YOU GET THOSE HEADSETS FROM?
RELAX! WE DIDN'T USE YOUR CREDIT CARD.
NOT THIS TIME.
THE END

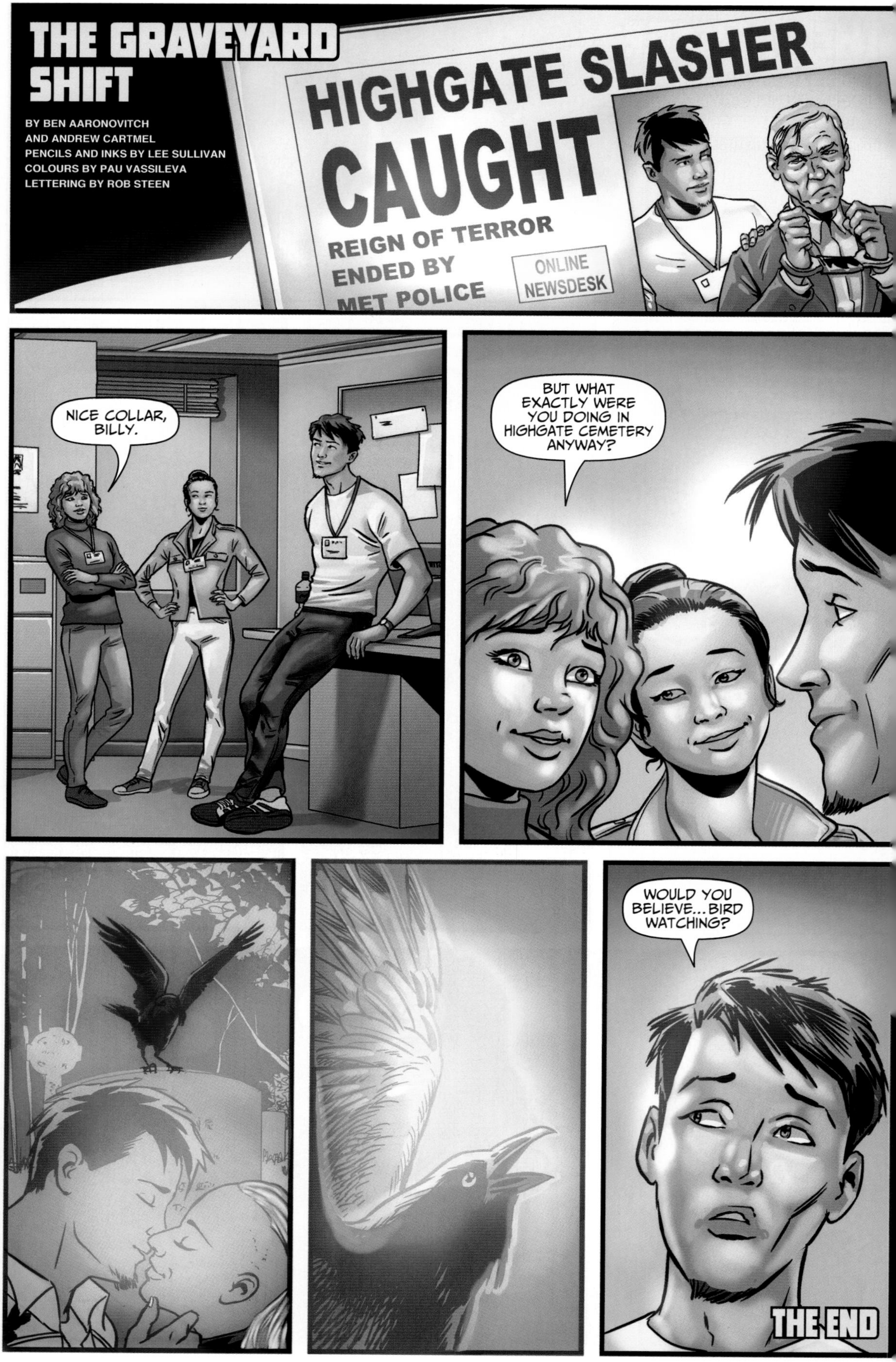
THE GRAVEYARD SHIFT
BY BEN AARONOVITCH
AND ANDREW CARTMEL
PENCILS AND INKS BY LEE SULLIVAN
COLOURS BY PAU VASSILEVA
LETTERING BY ROB STEEN
HIGHGATE SLASHER
CAUGHT
REIGN OF TERROR ENDED BY MET POLICE
ONLINE NEWSDESK
NICE COLLAR, BILLY.
BUT WHAT EXACTLY WERE YOU DOING IN HIGHGATE CEMETERY ANYWAY?
WOULD YOU BELIEVE... BIRD WATCHING?
THE END

BONUS SECTION

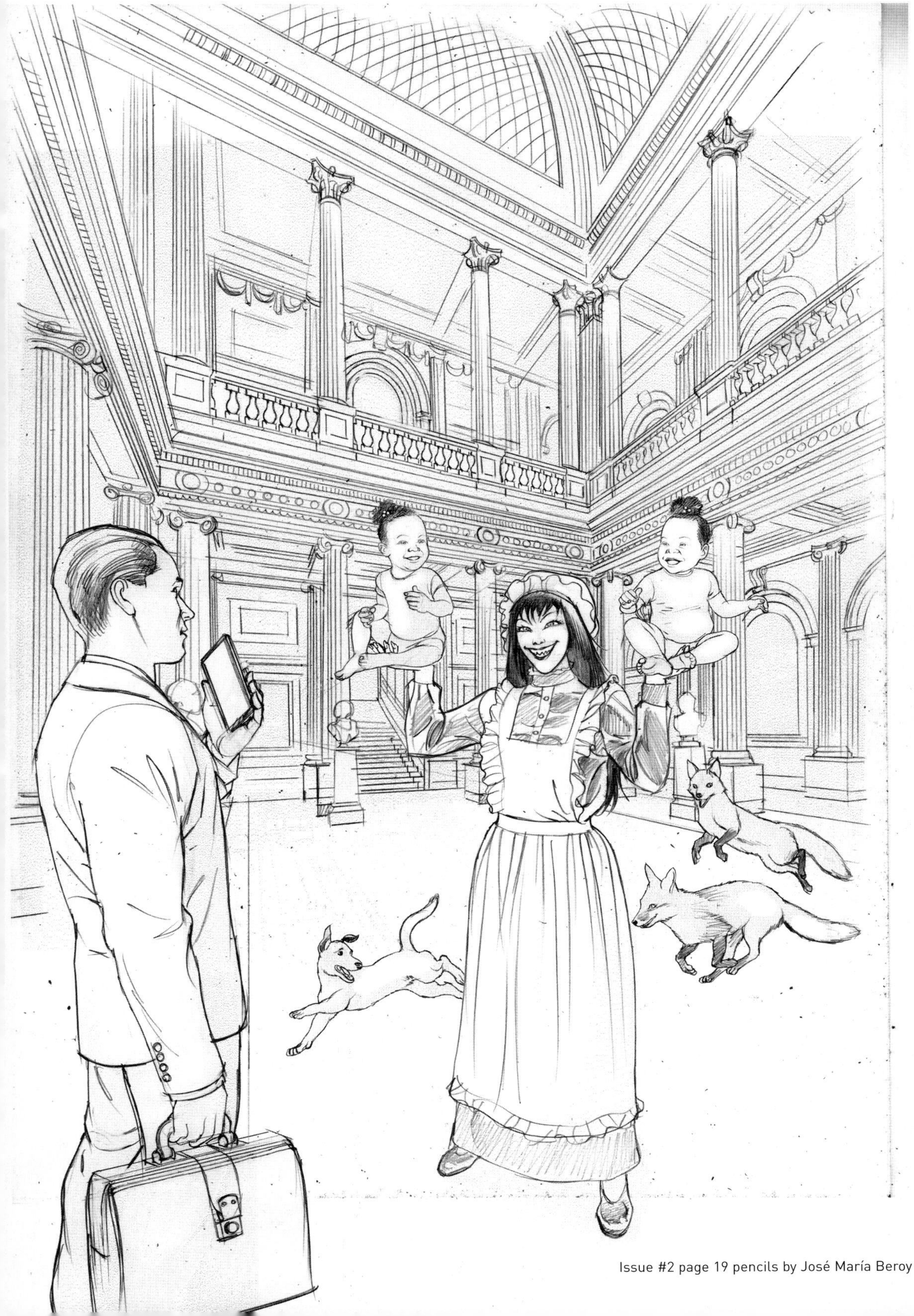

Issue #2 page 19 pencils by José María Beroy

COVER GALLERY ISSUE 1

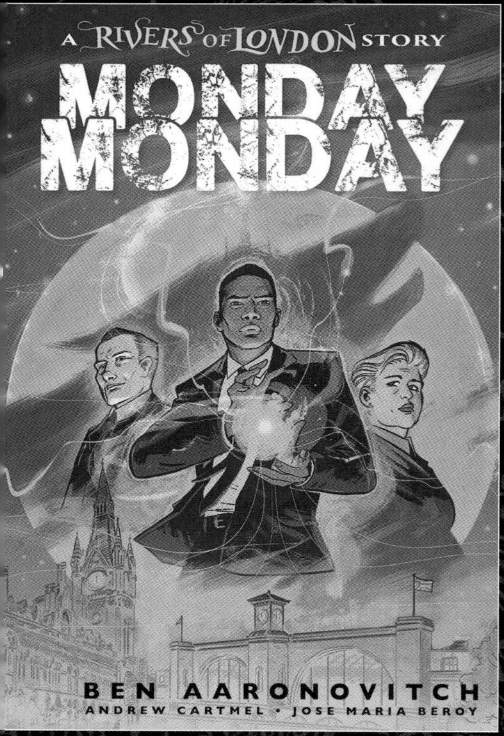
A RIVERS OF LONDON STORY
MONDAY MONDAY
BEN AARONOVITCH
ANDREW CARTMEL • JOSE MARIA BEROY

COVER A: **VERONICA FISH**

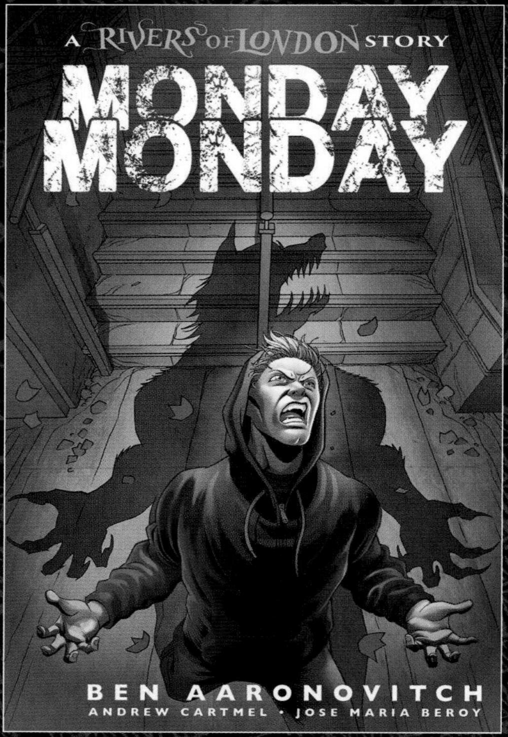
A RIVERS OF LONDON STORY
MONDAY MONDAY
BEN AARONOVITCH
ANDREW CARTMEL • JOSE MARIA BEROY

COVER B: **JOSÉ MARÍA BEROY / JORDI ESCUIN LLORACH**

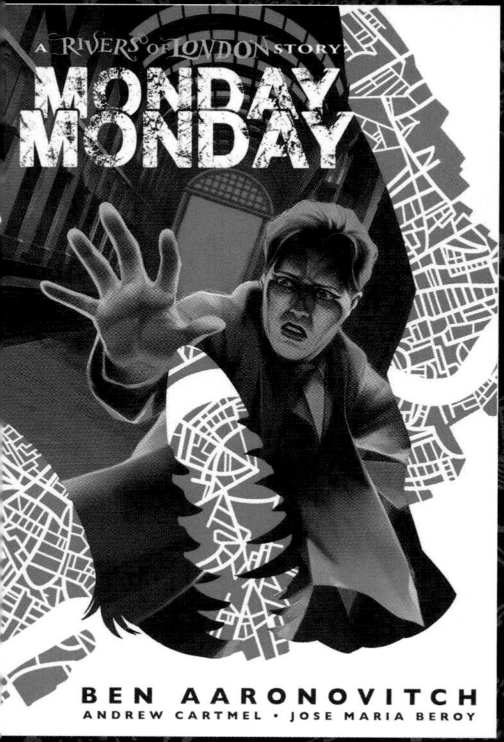
A RIVERS OF LONDON STORY
MONDAY MONDAY
BEN AARONOVITCH
ANDREW CARTMEL • JOSE MARIA BEROY

COVER C: **V.V. GLASS**

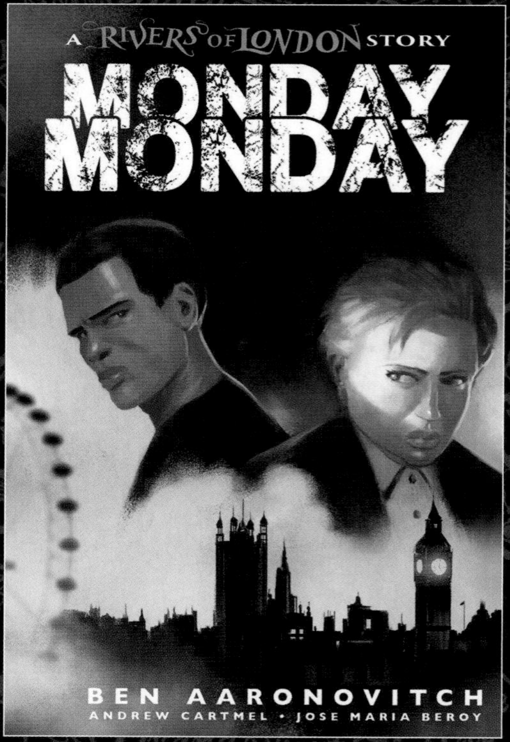
A RIVERS OF LONDON STORY
MONDAY MONDAY
BEN AARONOVITCH
ANDREW CARTMEL • JOSE MARIA BEROY

COVER D: **GYULA NEMETH**

COVER GALLERY ISSUE 2

COVER A: **SANYA ANWAR**

COVER B: **V.V. GLASS**

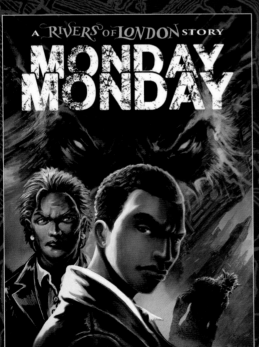

COVER C: **PATRICIO CLAREY**

COVER D: **JEN HICKMAN**, PRIDE VARIANT

COVER GALLERY ISSUE 3

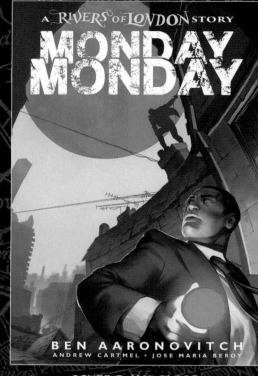

COVER A: **RIAN HUGHES**

COVER B: **V.V. GLASS**

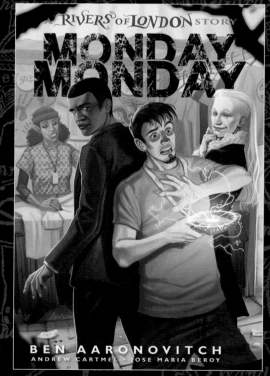

COVER C: **CLAUDIA IANNICIELLO**

COVER A: **ABIGAIL HARDING**

COVER B: **V.V. GLASS**

COVER D: **DAVID M. BUISAN**

RIVERS OF LONDON: MONDAY MONDAY
ISSUE BREAKDOWN

Before the script is written, writers Ben Aaronovitch and Andrew Cartmel wrote a document breaking down each issue of the mini-series, detailing the key plot points and main characters of each issue. Presented here, for the first time, is that issue breakdown..

Rivers of London: Monday, Monday is the latest instalment in the bestselling series by Ben Aaronovitch. After a series of petty thefts and muggings land a fellow police officer in the hospital for shock after seeing a "Dog Boy", Peter Grant and Thomas Nightingale are called in to hunt down this delinquent werewolf. Meanwhile, magical "junior apprentice" Abigail Kamara and Foxglove – the newest addition to the Folly – seek mischief and find it in the form of a wayward Swedish wolf-man.

ISSUE BREAKDOWN

ISSUE ONE: Setting the scene for the series. After a failed arrest of two suspected muggers leaves a police officer in the hospital, DI Miriam Stephanopoulos is enlisted to help find the criminals. After setting up a sting to catch the thieves at King's Cross Station, one of the teenagers (Kyle) is brought into custody, but the other – somewhat magically – escapes. But when Stephanopoulos discovers that her juvenile suspect may

be working with a werewolf, she calls in Peter Grant.

NOTABLE CHARACTERS
Peter Grant
DI Miriam Stephanopoulos
Kyle Hanslaw

ISSUE TWO: Thomas Nightingale, current and only master in the Folly, looks back on his youth and remembers what magic means to him. Whilst teaching new members of the Met Police about "Falcon" (aka, magical) cases, Nightingale is called in to consult on the muggings, and has flashbacks to his last encounter with a werewolf during the second world war.

NOTABLE CHARACTERS
Thomas Nightingale

ISSUE THREE: Peter Grant must struggle being a new father (to twins, nonetheless) with his duties as a member of the Folly (the unofficial name for magical Special Assessment Unit of the police). His investigation into the muggings lead him to a Goblin Market underneath Camden Lock, and then to

a rooftop den, where the classic East End villain climbs from the woodwork. However, before Peter has the chance to celebrate the victory, a call from the emergency room turns his world upside down...

NOTABLE CHARACTERS
Peter Grant
DC Billy Costas
The twins (Taiwo and Kehinde) and their talking-fox guardians (Sugar Niner and Able Baker)
Beverly Brook

ISSUE FOUR: Abigail and Foxglove get sucked into mischief as they witness the police sting at King's Cross station and see Dog Boy in action. The pair realise that Dog Boy is no hardened criminal, just a lost tourist caught up in a bad situation. So, to avoid the world of trouble that would come if Peter and the police caught up with the teen wolf, Abigail makes it her personal mission to help Dog Boy back to his family in Sweden.

NOTABLE CHARACTERS
Abigail Kamara
Foxglove
Dog Boy

CHARACTER DESCRIPTIONS

Presented here are a selection of character designs by artist José Marie Beroy, based on Ben and Andrew's character descipitions

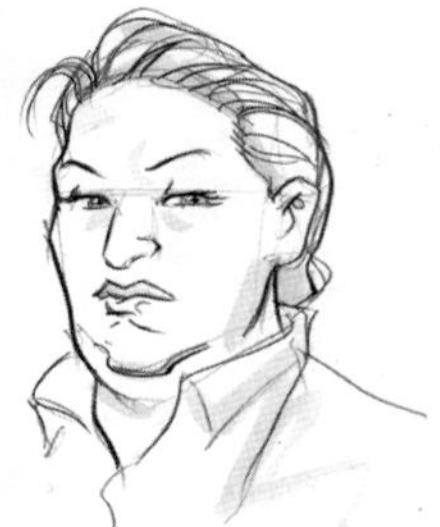

▲DI MIRIAM STEPHANOPOULOS
Stephanopoulos is a large, heavy set white woman. Trademark outfit is a black suit with white shirt.

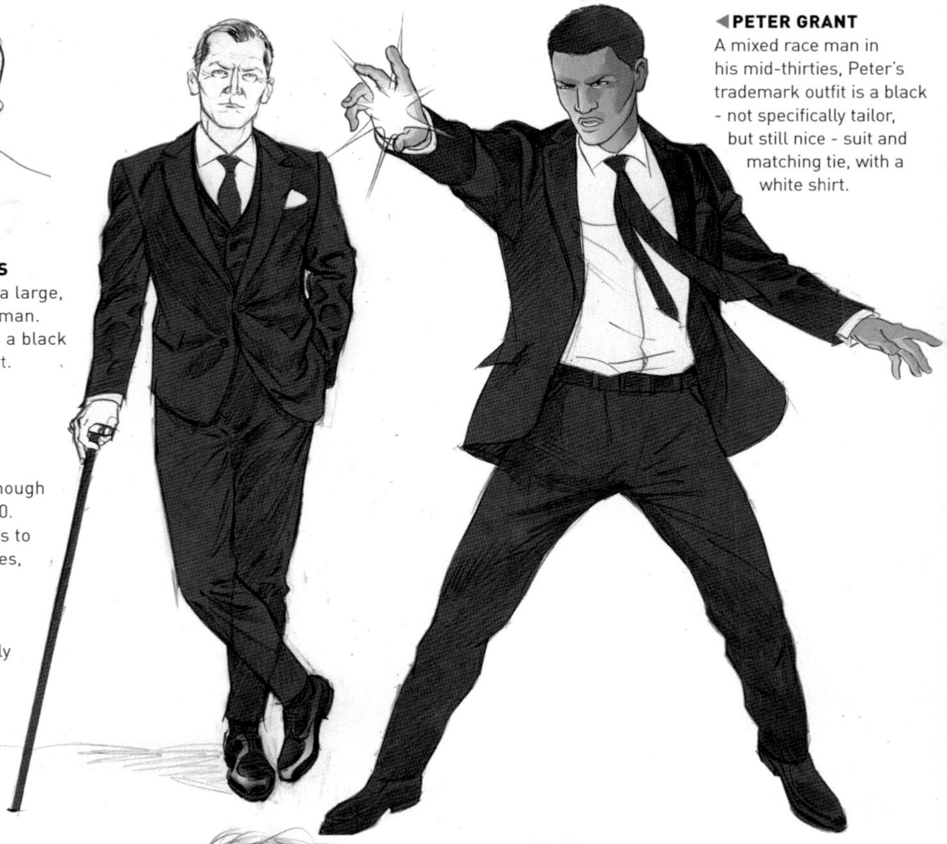

▶THOMAS NIGHTINGALE
A master wizard, though he was born in 1900. Nightingale appears to be in his early forties, with finely boned features, grey eyes and short brown hair. But he typically wears slightly old-fashioned suits.

◀PETER GRANT
A mixed race man in his mid-thirties, Peter's trademark outfit is a black - not specifically tailor, but still nice - suit and matching tie, with a white shirt.

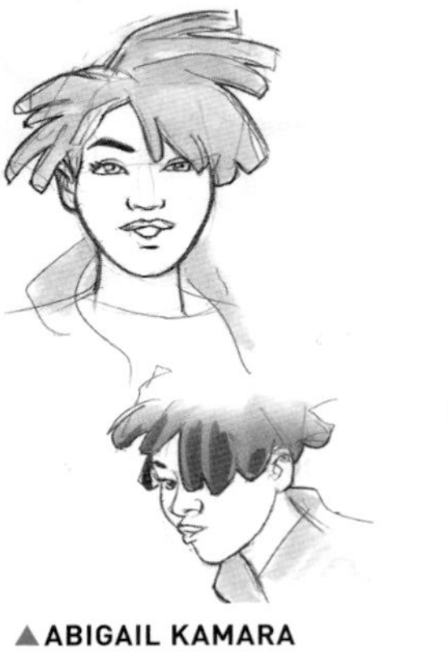

▲ABIGAIL KAMARA
Abigail is a skinny mixed race young woman – It's been a couple of years since we saw her last, but she hasn't really changed that much - except for her hairstyle.

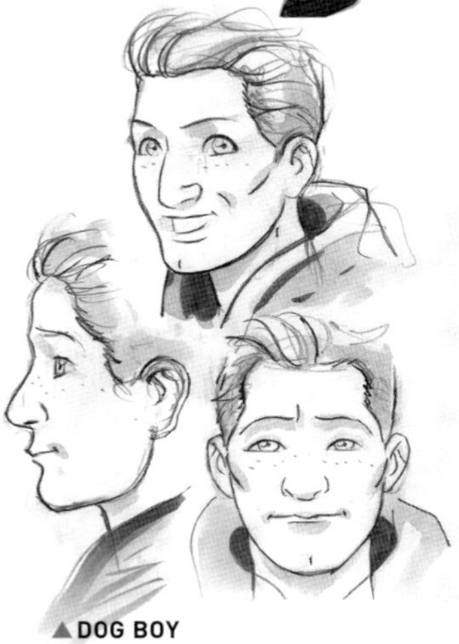

▲DOG BOY
Dog Boy is an adolescent werewolf just on the cusp of starting his physical transition to full wolf (this will take 10-20 years). When we get a look at him in close-up, he has the classic chiselled Nordic looks only with amber eyes and blond hair the colour and texture of a golden retriever.

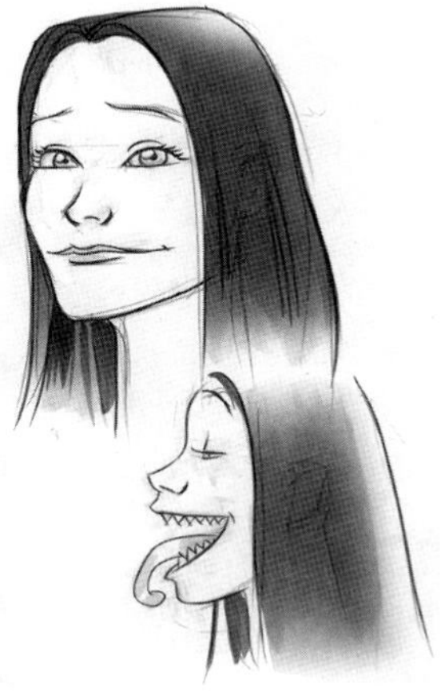

◀FOXGLOVE
She was impossibly tall and slender, with elongated arms that emerged from a loose brown sleeveless smock and ended in long-fingered hands. She had supermodel legs in black leggings that ended at the ankles to expose dainty pink feet. Her face was long and oval, with a small mouth and chin, prominent cheekbones and big hazel eyes. Her hair was a cascade of gleaming black down her back.

Rivers of London: Monday, Monday
Issue #1

I Know Why The Detective Inspector Sings

Written by **Ben Aaronovitch** and **Andrew Cartmel**
Pencils and inks by **José María Beroy**
Colours by **Jordi Escuin Llorach**
Lettering by **Rob Steen**

(Page 1 – 'Starting the day with a bang')

EXT: GARDEN, CHEZ STEPHANOPOULOS - MORNING
The large back garden of a large suburban 1930s semi-detached house in the outer London Boroughs. The garden is about half standard lawn and flower bed and half Good Life tribute band with vegetable patches and a well defended chicken coop.

A large sundial marks the demarcation between the two gardens.

The back of the house has a conservatory (attached to the kitchen) and neat modern PVC windows. It is trim, well-kept but not obsessively so.

Panel 1
Dawn light slants over the back fence and paints the rear wall of the semi with golden light, flashing off the conservatory and back windows. It is going to be a crisp, bright October Day.

A magnificent COCKEREL is making its journey from the coop to the sundial.

Panel 2
The cockerel has jumped onto the sundial and has thrown back his head and puffed out his chest ready for the morning crow. He should be framed so that he seems dominant, the master of the henhouse, the garden and all he surveys.

The first floor rear bedroom window should be visible in order for the approaching joke to work.

Panel 3
Same framing as Panel 2

The cockerel has been startled by a loud noise and his crowing has explosively aborted. Feel free to be a little cartoony here with bug eyes, protruding tongue and a bit of spontaneous moulting.

FROM BEDROOM WINDOW: (Huge) YES!

FROM BEDROOM WINDOW: (Large) YesYesOhGodYesyesyesyes

CAPTION: Unlike some people, Pam and I like to start off Monday with a bang.

Panel 4
A large suburban kitchen with sturdy high-end fittings that have undergone a few years of moderately hard use. It has mustard yellow walls, and add layers of fridge notes, cookbook piles and favourite mugs, etc.

DI MIRIAM STEPHANOPOULOS is sitting at the kitchen table tucking into a proper English breakfast while PAM, her wife, is standing on the cusp of leaving for work, coffee in one hand and toast in the other.

Stephanopoulos is a large, heavy set white woman. She is dressed in a baggy sweatshirt and tracksuit bottoms and looks happy and relaxed as she eats.

Pam is also white but shorter and slimmer than her wife, wears her hair shoulder length but tied back for work. She is dressed in a smart skirt suit and is obviously relating an anecdote or telling a joke.

CAPTION: ...and a full English breakfast.

CAPTION: Start the week as we mean to go on.

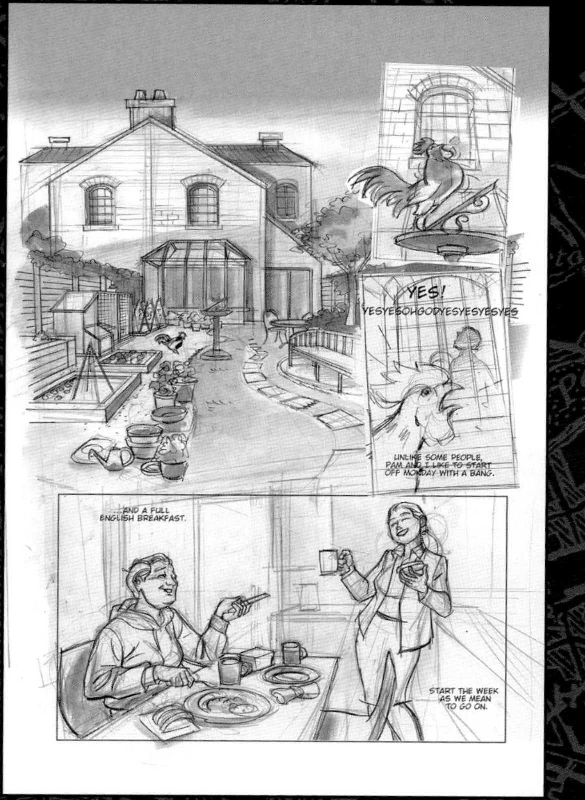
YES!
YESYESOHGODYESYESYESYES
UNLIKE SOME PEOPLE, PAM AND I LIKE TO START OFF MONDAY WITH A BANG.
...AND A FULL ENGLISH BREAKFAST.
START THE WEEK AS WE MEAN TO GO ON.

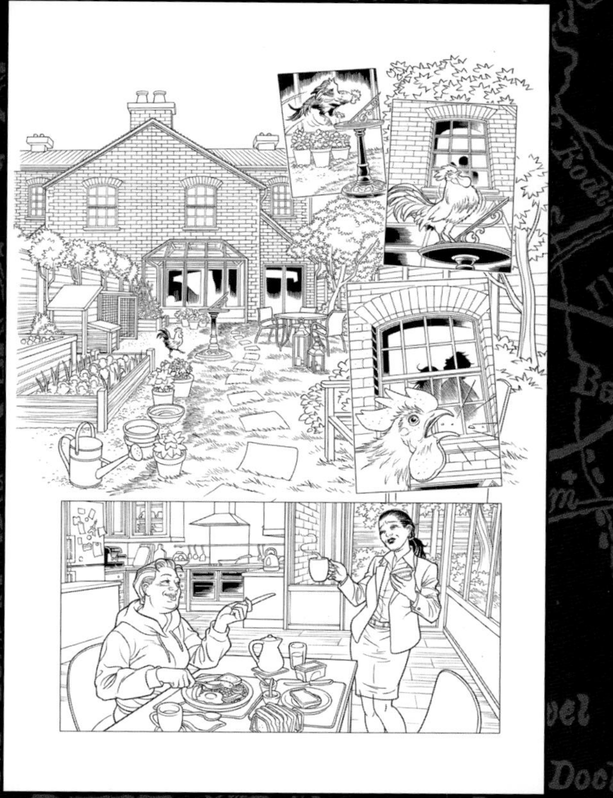

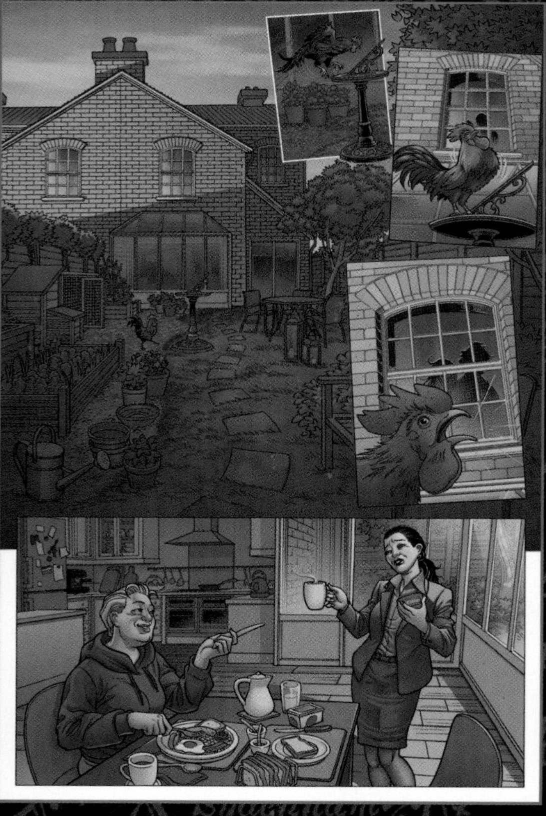

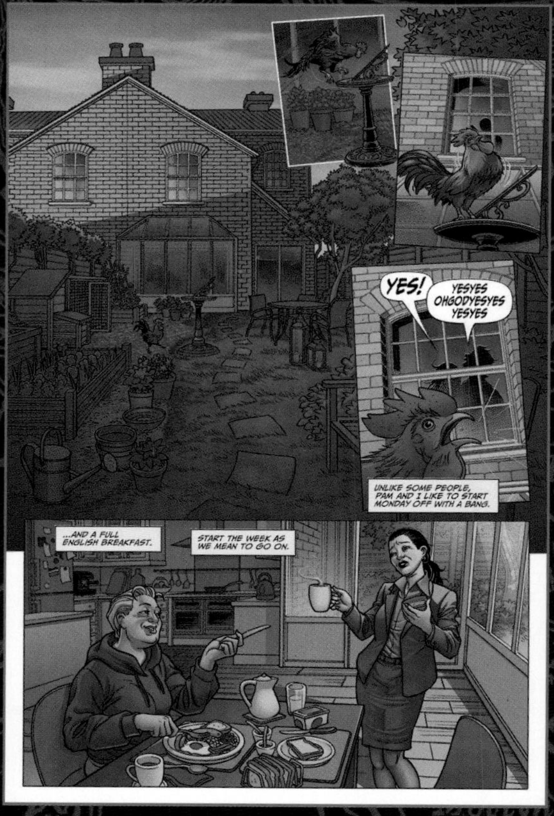
YES!
YESYES OHGODYESYES YESYES
UNLIKE SOME PEOPLE, PAM AND I LIKE TO START MONDAY OFF WITH A BANG.
...AND A FULL ENGLISH BREAKFAST.
START THE WEEK AS WE MEAN TO GO ON.

Rivers of London: Monday, Monday
Issue #3

Cause and Effect

Written by **Ben Aaronovitch** and **Andrew Cartmel**
Pencils by **José María Beroy** Inks by **Sandra María Perea** Colours by **Jordi Escuin Llorach** Lettering by **Rob Steen**

(Page 10 – The Goblin Market)

EXT. CAMDEN LOCK – DAY
Panel 1
CAMDEN LOCK – establishing shot.
Half page establishing shot of the entrance to Camden Market. We've provided an alternative angle in case the artist wants to get the bridge in as well, but we prefer the main entrance angle with its combination of red brick, plate glass and cobbles.
It's Monday lunchtime so the crowd will not be huge (on Sunday it's packed tight).

CAPTION: Camden Lock.

CAPTION: What happens when a 1970s flea market is exposed to a massive burst of gamma radiation.

CAPTION   And occasional home to London's peripatetic Goblin Market.

INT. STAIRS DOWN, CAMDEN LOCK – DAY
This is an entirely fictional location. The walls should match the red brick from the rest of Camden Market and the staircase should be ornamented in the Victorian style.
　　The canal water is dark with an oily sheen and in shadow (it's actually an old loading dock from when the canals freighted timber down from the Midlands).
　　The only lit part are the steps which go down below the water level. The steps are wrought iron with ornamented handrails. Globe lights are set into the walls – lighting the way.

Panel 2
From behind as Peter and Billy walk down the Victorian-era cast iron staircase.

BILLY　　Peri-what?

PETER　　It means it doesn't stay in one place.

BILLY　　And "Goblin Market"?

EXT. THE GOBLIN MARKET – DAY
A long, vaulted cellar with arches running along each side, like railway arches they have depth and the various stalls/shps are installed in there. The stalls/shops superficially look much the same as the ones in Camden Market (see reference pics) but they should be shadowy and mysterious.
　　In addition to the stalls/shops mentioned in the script, the following are available to fill in backgrounds as needed. All the stalls are temporary and often jury rigged so signs, hangers and shelves are attached to scaffolding poles or directly to the walls etc.
　　The demi-monde exists only a finger's width away from our own world, so on one level this looks like a mundane trendy London market. Only when you look closer and get into the detail is the strangeness revealed.
　　Basically – don't try and make it too weird – we don't want to oversell it...

　　A Bookseller – selling second-hand books, ranging from used paperbacks to obviously rare vintage hardbacks.
　　At least two arches are taken up by a café/bar with wrought iron Edwardian garden tables and chairs for the customers. The waitresses are young women in their late teens (family members of the owner) and are dressed for a 70s disco and tooling around on roller skates, Everything from pots of tea, cakes, sandwiches, bottled beer and wine are being served.
　　A small sign that says Enter at your Own Risk.
　　Another is a stall named WINDYMS WONDERFUL MASKS. The masks on display are translucent death masks, each one carefully suspended in front of a candle so that the light glows eerily out of the dead faces.

Panel 3
Establish – Goblin market with Peter and Billy walking down the central space. Billy is looking around in amazement but Peter is heading purposefully for a T-shirt and clothes stall halfway down.
The T-shirt/Clothes store looks much like its mundane counterparts above. From a distance we can't see the nature of the designs but the sign above the arch reads THOSE THAT WALK IN THE TWILIGHT.

CAPTION: Where the demi-monde goes to do business.

PETER:　　Hang back a bit.

PETER:　　They get nervous around the filth.

Panel 4
Focus on Billy hanging back as Peter approaches the T-shirt stall.

BILLY:　　That makes a change.

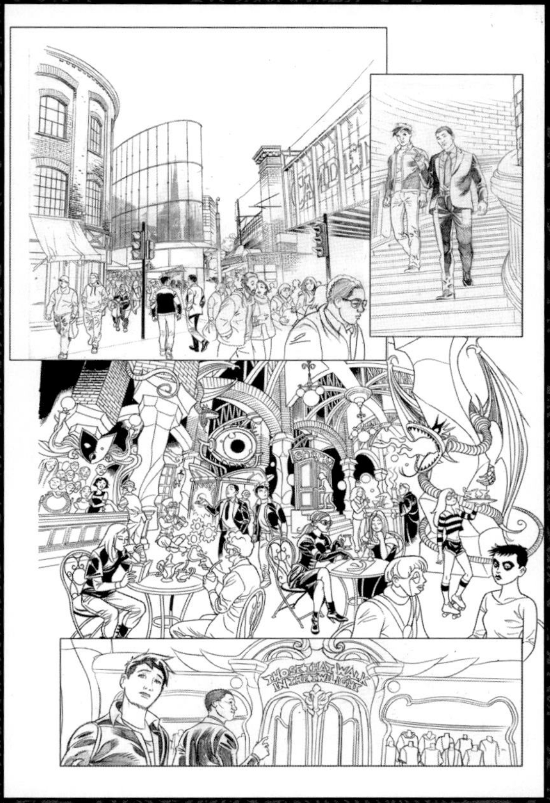

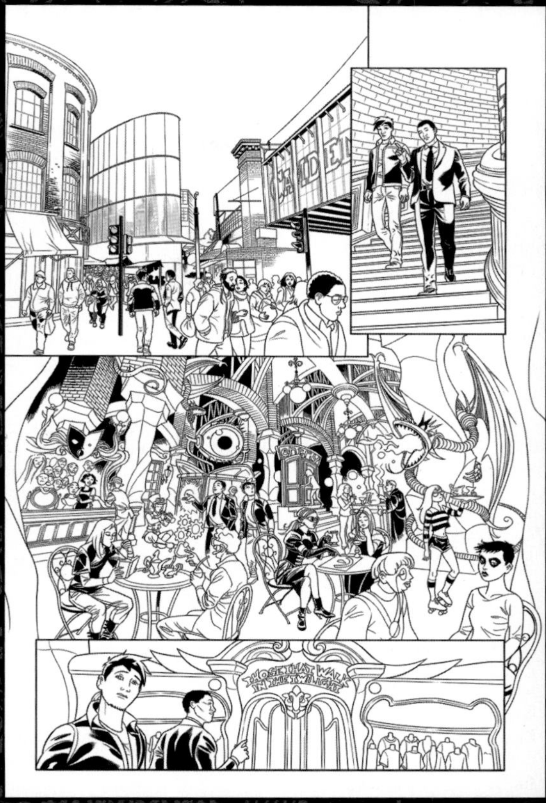

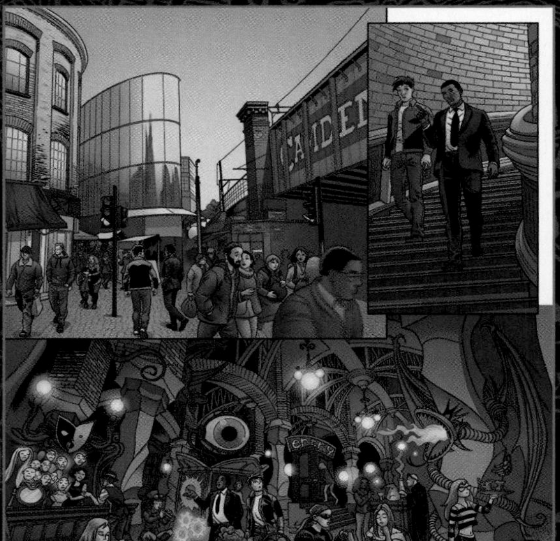

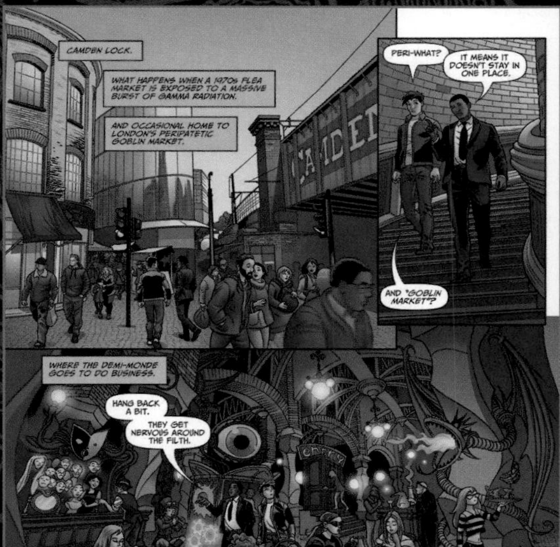
CAMDEN LOCK.
WHAT HAPPENS WHEN A 1970s FLEA MARKET IS EXPOSED TO A MASSIVE BURST OF GAMMA RADIATION.
AND OCCASIONAL HOME TO LONDON'S PERIPATETIC GOBLIN MARKET.
PERI-WHAT?
IT MEANS IT DOESN'T STAY IN ONE PLACE.
AND "GOBLIN MARKET"?
WHERE THE DEMI-MONDE GOES TO DO BUSINESS.
HANG BACK A BIT.
THEY GET NERVOUS AROUND THE FILTH.
THAT MAKES A CHANGE.
THOSE THAT WALK IN THE TWILIGHT

CREATOR BIOGRAPHIES

ANDREW CARTMEL

Andrew Cartmel began his career in TV and publishing as script editor on *Doctor Who*. His legendary three-year run on the show ('the Cartmel Masterplan') remains widely admired and influential today. Besides the *Rivers of London* comics, he is busy writing plays for the London stage (most recently *Dug Out* and *Suffragette Suite*, a double bill about World War One and its aftermath) and the successful *Vinyl Detective* series of crime novels, the sixth of which, *Attack and Decay* has just been completed. He lives in London with too many LPs and just enough cats.

BEN AARONOVITCH

Ben Aaronovitch is perhaps best known for his series of Peter Grant novels, which began with 2011's *Rivers of London*. Mixing police procedural with urban fantasy and London history, these novels have now sold a million copies worldwide. The latest instalment, *False Value*, was released in February 2020.

Ben is also known for his TV writing, penning fan-favourite episodes of *Doctor Who*; *Remembrance of the Daleks* and *Battlefield*. He wrote an episode of BBC hospital drama, *Casualty*, and contributed to cult SF show, *Jupiter Moon*.

Ben was born, raised and lives in London, and says he will leave the city when they prise it out of his cold, dead fingers.

JOSÉ MARÍA BEROY

Artist José María Beroy has produced hundreds of comic book pages over his lengthy career, from early fanzines to work in *Heavy Metal*, *Totem*, *Creepy*, *Zona 84*, *Cairo* and *Cimoc*. His latest works range from stories about World War II to pencils for a book on the French Revolution. Previous credits include *Dr. Horrible*, *Doctor Who* and *Star Trek*, *The Big Book of Grimm* and *The Big Book of Hoaxes* and a 4-issue *Deadman* miniseries. In 2020 José drew the critically acclaimed *Phantom of the Opera* graphic novel.

He lives in Barcelona with his life-long partner and his work studio is filled with the wonderful sounds of his son's violin.

JORDI ESCUIN LLORACH

Born in Catalonia (Spain) and trained at the Llotja Art School (Barcelona), Jordi Escuin Llorach is a comic book colourist, who has worked on books as diverse as *Dan Dare*, *MASK*, *Strawberry Shortcake*, *The Seven-Per-Cent Solution*, *Lion King* and *Aladdin*. He recently finished working on the smash-hit series *ExtraOrdinary* for Titan Comics. He lives in a small town where he spends the hours with one of his major passions, comic books.